佛教

兩千六百年入門

INTRODUCTION:
2600 YEARS OF BUDDHISM

淨因 著
Jing Yin

中華書局

前 言

「文殊師利，導師何故，眉間白毫，大光普照。

雨曼陀羅，曼殊沙華，栴檀香風，悦可眾心。

以是因緣，地皆嚴淨，而此世界，六種震動。

時四部眾，咸皆歡喜，身意快然，得未曾有。」

　　佛陀宣講《法華經》前所現之種種瑞相，預示着佛陀將要宣説妙義無窮的大法。然而「會中有比丘、比丘尼、優婆塞、優婆夷、五千人等，即從座起，禮佛而退」。佛陀借此機會開導大眾説，大乘佛法，過於深奧，晦澀難明，我們必須依據眾生之根性，「以無數方便，種種因緣，譬喻言辭，演説諸法」。歷代祖師大德，效佛所行，以佛經故事、禪宗公案啟發社會大眾領悟佛陀菩提樹下悟證的心法。這些故事被雕刻於公元前一世紀前後的巴呼特（Bharhut）與桑奇（Sanchi）佛舍利塔周圍的石欄楯上。到了公元五世紀，佛陀本生故事畫更成為敦煌石窟早期壁畫中最常見的題材，成為大眾了解一乘佛法的方便之門。

　　寶蓮禪寺智慧老和尚、健釗長老自 2000 年起，一直致力於興建功能齊全的萬佛寶殿，與天壇大佛相互呼應，使得寶蓮禪寺成為一個集佛教文化、園林景觀、雕塑藝術、傳統與現代化於一體的綜合性佛教聖地，透過藝術、文化、建築，「無言説法」，引導大眾領悟佛教文化之精髓。2004 年 10 月，五層高的「萬佛寶殿」正式啓用，其建築面積為 6000 多平方米，內設萬佛殿、藏經閣、方丈室、法堂、永久戒壇以及多功能廳。這標誌着寶蓮禪寺硬件建設基本完成，為寶蓮禪寺文化教育的發展打下堅實的基礎。

　　「萬佛寶殿」一樓為萬佛殿，整個殿內供奉 10307 尊佛，包括五尊五方佛、35 尊大佛、53 尊中佛、108 尊中小佛及 10106 尊小佛，以「像教」引導人們體悟佛陀圓融無碍的境界。在萬佛牆下方安置了八十八個須彌座，每個須彌座上均有一幅佛教故事，八十八幅佛教故事分為成六個板塊：覺悟之路（18 幅）、正法久住（18 幅）、無盡燈（18 幅）、十六觀（18 幅）、牧牛圖（10 幅）和參透因果（6幅），構成精簡版佛教兩千六百年佛教發展史。

　　法不孤起，仗緣方生。期盼書中佛陀善巧說法的遺風、古代大德為法忘軀的情懷、無數禪師隨緣度化眾生的風采和知恩報恩的中華文化核心元素，啟發讀者承擔起中華文化化世導俗的重任。

淨因

南京大學中華文化研究院

2021 年 8 月

Preface

O Mañjuśrī!

Why has the Leader

Emitted this great ray of light far and wide

From the tuft of white hair

Between his eyebrows,

Raining down māndārava and mañjūṣaka flowers,

And gladdening the people

With the fragrant winds of sandalwood?

For this reason

The earth is completely adorned,

And this world quakes in six ways.

And the fourfold assembly

Is completely enraptured,

Delighted in body and mind at the experience of

Such an unprecedented marvel.[1]

The various auspicious signs prior to the Buddha's expounding of the *Lotus Sutra* foretold that the Buddha was going to explain a great teaching of infinite wonderful meanings. However, "There were around five thousand people among the assembly, including bhikṣus, bhikṣuṇīs, upāsakas, and upāsikās, who rose from their seats, bowed to the Buddha, and withdrew."

---

1 *The Lotus Sutra*. Translated from the Chinese of Kumārajiva by Tsugunari Kubo and Akira Yuyama. Numata Center for Buddhist Translation and Research. 2007.

The Buddha took this opportunity to explain to the assembly that the Mahayana teachings were too profound and obscure for understanding, and that we must "give the teachings with innumerable skillful means, various conditions, explanations and analogies" according to the capacities of sentient beings. The patriarchs and eminent masters of the past followed the example of the Buddha and inspired people with stories from Buddhist scriptures and Chan koans, helping them understand the citta-dharma realized by the Buddha under the bodhi tree. These stories were carved on the stone railings of the stupas at Bharhut and Sanchi around the first century B.C. By the fifth century AD, the paintings about the stories of the Buddha's previous lives became the most common subject in the early murals at Dunhuang Grottoes, serving as a convenient way for people to understand the One Vehicle teachings.

Since 2000, Venerable Chi-wai and Venerable Kin Chiu of Po Lin Monastery had worked to build a fully functional Ten Thousand Buddha Hall that would echo the Tian Tan Buddha, aiming to make Po Lin Monastery a comprehensive Buddhist sanctuary that would integrate Buddhist culture, landscape, sculptural art, tradition and modernity, so as to guide the public to understand the essence of Buddhist culture through art, culture, and architecture, hence "teaching the Dharma without words." In October 2004, the five-story Ten Thousand Buddha Hall was officially opened, with a building area of more than 6,000 square meters, including Ten Thousand Buddha Hall, Sutra Repository, Abbot Quarters, Dharma Hall, Permanent Ordination Platform, and a multi-purpose hall. This marked the basic completion of the physical construction of Po Lin Monastery and laid a solid foundation for the development of cultural education at Po Lin Monastery.

The first floor of the Ten Thousand Buddha Hall is the Hall of Ten Thousand Buddhas. 10,307 Buddha statues are enshrined in the hall, including five statues of Buddhas of the Five Directions, 35 big-sized Buddha statues, 53 medium-sized Buddha statues, 108 small-and-medium-sized Buddha statues, and 10,106 small-sized Buddha statues, guiding people to understand and realize the completely interpenetrated and unobstructed realm of the Buddha through the Buddha images. Below the wall where these Buddha statues are enshrined are 88 Sumeru thrones, and in each of the thrones a Buddhist story is depicted. These are divided into six sections, including The Path to Enlightenment (18), The Long Abiding of the True Dharma (18), Inexhaustible Lamps (18), Sixteen Visualizations (18), The Ten Oxherding Pictures, and The Penetrating Cause and Effect (6), which constitute a concise version of the 2,600-year history of Buddhist development.

The skilful means of the Buddha's preaching, the ancient masters' selfless dedication to the transmission of the Dharma, the mien of Chan masters when delivering sentient beings according to conditions, as well as emphasis on the importance of recognizing and repaying kindness which are core elements of Chinese culture will inspire the reader to take on the vital task of guiding and transforming people in this world of the mundane.

Jing Yin

The Institute for Chinese Culture Studies, Nanjing University

August 2021

目

録

Contents

覺悟之路

Part One:
The Path to Enlightenment

正法久住

Part Two:

The Right Dharma Abides Permanently

三 無盡燈

Part Three:
Everlasting Lamp

（四）十六觀

Part Four:
The Sixteen Visualizations

⑤ 牧牛圖

Part Five:
Ten Ox-herding Pictures

六 参透因果

Part Six:
Understanding Cause and Effect

Part One:

The Path to Enlightenment

兜率下降

三十三天天外天，九霄雲外有神仙。

神仙本是凡人做，只怕凡人心不堅。

—— 古德

　　宇宙之大，豈止我們熟悉的這個世界？所謂天外有天、天有多重，我們所說的天界，通常是指比這個世界優越的境界，而能夠升遷到天界的，就必然是修得天福、天德的大善眾生。

　　釋迦牟尼佛成佛之前，生在兜率天 (Tuṣita)，成為一生補處的護明菩薩，為諸天說法，待因緣成熟時，就從兜率天降生人間，度化眾生。

- ## 為何佛教徒特別重視兜率天

　　根據佛教理論，每當佛陀降生人世之前，都要先在兜率天上為諸天講說佛法。兜率天宮分為內外兩院，外院為天人所居，內院為補處菩薩（即將成佛者）的住處，補處菩薩常由此天下生而成佛。釋迦牟尼佛為一生補處菩薩時，也曾在此天修行，然後由此處下生人間，現為補處菩薩的彌勒今也在此處說法教化。所以兜率天在一切天中，受到了特別的重視。

Descent from Tuṣita Heaven

Above the Thirty Three Heavens is yet one higher,

Over the loftiest clouds celestial deities reside;

Since these deities were originally humans,

Could it be that the ordinary minds are uncertain?

— An ancient sage

　　The universe is so vast that it is beyond the world we know. As the saying goes, there are many worlds and these worlds are multi-dimentional. The celestial realms we normally talk about refer to those that are superior to our own world. And those who are able to ascend to those realms are surely beings who have cultivated great virtues and are worthy of the joys and merits of the heavens.

Before he attained Buddhahood, Śākyamuni had been born in Tuṣita Heaven. as the Light-protecting Bodhisattva, in the Stage of One Life to Replacement. He preached the Dharma to the heavenly beings. When karmic conditions are mature, he will be born in the human world from the heavens and save all sentient beings.

✲ Basics of Buddhism:

- **Why do Buddhists attach so much importance to Tuṣita Heaven?**

According to the Buddhist doctrines, Tuṣita Heaven is where a Buddha teaches the Dharma before he descends to the human realm. It is divided into the inner court and the outer court. Celestial beings dwell in the outer court, while the inner court is the residence of a bodhisattva who will be born as a Buddha in the next life (a Buddha-to-be). The bodhisattva normally descends from this heaven to the human world and will then attain Buddhahood. When Śākyamuni Buddha was at the position of One Life to Accomplishment of Buddhahood, he had also practiced in Tuṣita Heaven, from where he then descended to the human world. Maitreya, the next Buddha, is living in Tuṣita Heaven, teaching the Dharma and guiding the celestial beings. As such, Tuṣita Heaven is given special attention among all the heavenly realms.

菩薩入胎

> 諸佛世尊，唯以一大事因緣故，出現於世，
> 欲令眾生開、示、悟、入佛之知見。

——《法華經》

　　兩千六百多年前，古印度境內諸國林立，其東北部恆河邊有個迦毗羅衛國，國王叫淨飯，王后叫摩耶，淨飯王和王后摩耶夫人結婚多年，卻一直膝下無子。

　　住在天國兜率宮的護明菩薩，決定投生人間，成佛度化眾生。於是選擇了仁慈的淨飯王夫婦作為父母。

　　一天晚上，摩耶夫人於夢中清晰地見到菩薩騎着一頭六牙白象，從空中而來，從她的右肋進入胎腹。當時她的身心，均感到無比的清涼、爽快和愉悅。

　　摩耶王后醒來後，就去見淨飯王，告訴他夢中之事。淨飯王也很驚異，立即召集大臣們詢問王后之夢是何預兆，一名婆羅門占卜者回答說：「此夢甚佳！王后已懷孕，必生王子，這王子是千古聖人，定能光顯釋迦族！」淨飯王聽後不勝歡喜。

- 摩耶夫人以何功德成為佛陀生母？

　　一生補處位的護明菩薩觀機緣成熟，將要降生人間時，兜率天內院諸神、大菩薩一起討論過佛母應有的素質。大家一致認為，佛母必須具有三十二種功德相，例如：正德而生，肢體具足，上下相稱，容貌端正，從未生育。所生之處尊貴，德行無缺，種族清淨，心常隨順一切善事，無有邪心，身、口、意三業自然調柔。要多聞，極工巧，心無所畏、無諂曲、無誑詐、無瞋恚，無嫉妒、無慳吝，能忍辱、有慚愧，薄淫、怒、癡，無有女人過失，孝順父母，心向丈夫，能生一切諸功德等。最後大家一致認定，天臂城中善覺長者的女兒摩耶完全符合條件，堪為佛母。

Bodhisattva Entering the Womb

The greatest purpose of the Buddhas' appearance in the world is that they want living beings to open a way to the Buddhas' insight, they want to demonstrate the buddhas' insight to living beings, they want living beings to apprehend things with the buddhas' insight, they want living beings to enter into the way of the buddhas' insight.

— The Lotus Sutra

　　More than 2,600 years ago, there were many countries in Ancient India. Lying to the Northeast by the Ganges was the kingdom of Kapilavastu. The king was Śuddhodana and the queen Mahāmāyā. They had been married for

many years without any child.

When Light-protecting Bodhisattva, who was living in Tuṣita Heaven, decided to descend to the human world for attainment of Buddhahood to deliver sentient beings, he chose King Śuddhodana and Queen Mahāmāyā as his parents.

One night, Queen Mahāmāyā had a dream, in which she saw the bodhisattva riding on a white elephant with six tusks and coming to her from the sky, finally entering her womb through her right side. At that moment, she felt pleasant and joyful, just like drinking nectar.

Once she woke up, the queen told the king about her dream, and the king became inexpressibly astonished. Immediately, he called on the ministers for inquiry about the significance of the queen's dream. A Brahman diviner said to the king, "It is an auspicious dream! The queen is pregnant now; she will surely give birth to a prince, who will be a sage through all ages and bring great honor to the Śākya clan!" Hearing this, the king was overwhelmed with joy.

☷ Basics of Buddhism:

- **Why would Queen Mahāmāyā deserve to be the biological mother of the Buddha?**

  When Light-protecting Bodhisattva was ready to descend to the human world, the gods and bodhisattvas of the inner court of Tuṣita Heaven gathered together to discuss about the qualities of the future Buddha's mother. They agreed that the Buddha's mother should possess thirty-two merits, which were as follows: born with true merits; body complete with limbs; well-proportioned figure; decent facial features; having not given birth; born of noble family; perfect moral character; pure ethnic line; according with virtuous deeds; purity in mind; pliancy in bodily actions, speech, and thoughts; erudition in art and craft; fearlessness; no flattery; no deception; no hatred; no jealousy; no stinginess; patience; sense of conscience; little sexual desire, sense of anger, and doubt; no typical faults of women; filial piety towards parents; love and loyalty to husband; capacity to breed all good qualities; and so forth. At last, they reached a conclusion that Mahāmāyā, daughter of Elder Suprabuddha from Devadarsita, met all the criteria and was thus qualified to be the mother of Buddha.

太子降生

> 天上天下，唯我獨尊；
> 三界皆苦，吾當安之。
>
> —— 悉達多太子

　　古時候印度有一個習俗，婦人頭胎生孩子的時候，要回到娘家待產。摩耶王后亦不例外，臨近孩子出生之時，她就與侍婢、僕從一起回娘家去。就在途中，經過藍毗尼園稍作憩息時，摩耶王后伸手攀扶一株無憂樹枝，驚動了胎氣，就在樹下生下了太子。據佛經上說，太子是從摩耶王后的右肋出生的，摩耶王后夜夢的白象，也是從右肋進入體內而懷孕的。

　　這時，天上出現九龍吐水，為小太子沐浴，花園裏清香四溢，人天共慶。太子剛生下來，就能自己行走七步，每走一步，他的腳下就湧出一朵蓮花，太子右手指天，左手指地，大聲宣稱「天上天下，唯我獨尊；三界皆苦，吾當安之」。這是公元前五百多年的四月初八日。

　　迦毗羅衛國舉國歡騰，淨飯王為兒子取名喬達摩・悉達多，意思為「成就大志者」，而這位悉達多太子，就是日後為我們示範圓滿覺行的人天大導師——佛陀釋迦牟尼。

　　悉達多太子出生後七天，摩耶王后便與世長辭，幸好太子得到姨母的悉心照顧和愛護，轉眼間便進入了童年。

- 佛陀是一生下來就偉大嗎？

《西遊記》中孫悟空無法無天，大鬧天宮，惹出滔天大禍，十萬天兵天將無法降服他，結果他還是逃不出如來佛祖的手掌心。這則神話故事説明，在一般人心目中，佛陀是至高無上的神，無論怎麼説，他都應該是偉大的。

然而，德國著名佛教學者奧登堡（Oldenberg）教授以大量的證據證明，佛陀是一位真實的歷史人物。考古學家在鹿野苑，發現了公元前三世紀印度古代最偉大的國王，阿育王雕刻的「法敕」，進一步説明佛陀是真實的歷史人物。悉達多太子降生後七日，親生母親摩耶夫人便不幸去世，他由姨母摩訶波闍波提夫人撫養成人。年幼時，悉達多太子和我們普通人一樣擁有原始的本能，飢餓時需要喝奶、吃飯，天冷時需要穿衣。由此可知，佛陀並非一生下來就偉大。

Birth of Prince Siddhārtha

Above and below the heavens, I alone am the honored one.

Beings in the Three Realms are in suffering, and I will save them all.

— Prince Siddhārtha

In ancient India, the tradition was that a woman conceiving her first baby should return to her parents' home to await the baby's birth. So did Queen Mahāmāyā. Days before the birth of the prince, she set off with her maids and servants for her parents' home. While taking a rest on the way at

Lumbini Park, the queen reached for a branch of an asoka tree. This action of hers stimulated the infant and induced the birth of the prince beneath the tree. According to Buddhist scriptures, the prince was born from the right side of the queen. In her dream, the white elephant had also entered her body through the right side.

At that moment, nine dragons appeared in the sky spouting water to give the prince a shower, and the park was floral-scented. Both humans and gods were extremely happy. The newly born prince walked seven steps, and after each step he took, a lotus flower appeared below his foot. With his right hand pointing to the sky and the left towards the earth, he proclaimed, "Above and below the heavens, I alone am the honored one. Beings in the Three Realms are in suffering, and I will save them all." This day was the eighth day of the fourth lunar month more than 500 years before the Common Era.

The whole kingdom of Kapilavastu celebrated the birth of the prince with great joy. King Śuddhodana named the prince Siddhārtha Gautama, which means "the one who can accomplish a great goal." Prince Siddhārtha Gautama later became the great teacher of both humans and Devas— Śākyamuni Buddha, an example of perfect enlightenment and practice.

Seven days after Prince Siddhārtha was born, Queen Mahāmāyā passed away. Fortunately, his aunt Mahāpajāpatī took very good care of him till he grew up.

Basics of Buddhism:

• Was the Buddha born a great being?

As recorded in A Journey to the West, Sun Wukong, the monkey king, was ungovernable and wreaked great havoc in the Heavenly Palace. Even one hundred thousand celestial troops and generals could not subdue him. But at last, he still could not escape from the palm of Śākyamuni Buddha. This mythical story shows that in people's eyes, the Buddha is a god with supreme power, so he must be great.

However, a great deal of research data made by Oldenberg, a famous German Buddhist scholar, shows that the Buddha was a real person in human history. Further evidence was found in saranga- nāthá, where archaeologists discovered the 'imperial edict' carved by the order of Aśoka, one of the greatest kings in India in the third century BC. Seven days after Prince Siddhārtha was born, his mother passed away. He was raised up by his aunt Mahāpajāpatī. The young prince had the same instincts as we have, that is, the need to eat when hungry and wear more clothes when it is cold. As such, the Buddha was not born a great being.

王耕靜思

此身實不久，當睡於地下，
被棄無意識，無用如木屑。

——《法句經》

　　每年春天，迦毗羅衛國都舉行「王耕節」，淨飯王很重視這個節日，並且會親臨主禮。這年，太子初次參與這個春耕活動，本來非常興奮，對所有的活動和儀式都很有期待，但當他目睹：烈日如火，農夫裸身曝曬於烈日之下；老牛受鞭，皮開肉綻，血流成行；犁出之蚯蚓，為雀鳥所啄食；雀鳥復為蛇鷹所捕，死於非命。太子見此慘狀，心生不忍，初次見到生命中的苦相。他獨自來到一棵蕃櫻桃樹下盤腿而坐，靜思這天所見所聞。

[佛教小知識]

- 解脫從了知苦開始

　　扁鵲進見蔡桓公，在蔡桓公面前站了一會兒，扁鵲說：「您在肌膚紋理間有些小病，不醫治恐怕會加重。」蔡桓公說：「我沒有病。」扁鵲離開後，蔡桓公說：「醫生習慣給沒病的人治『病』，以此來顯示自己的本領。」過了十天，扁鵲再次進見蔡桓公，說：「您的病在肌肉裏，不及時醫治將會更加嚴重。」蔡桓公不理睬。扁鵲離開後，蔡桓公又不高興。

又過了十天，扁鵲再一次進見蔡桓公，說：「您的病在腸胃裏了，不及時治療將要更加嚴重。」蔡桓公又沒有理睬。扁鵲離開後，蔡桓公又不高興。

又過了十天，扁鵲遠遠地看見桓侯，掉頭就跑。蔡桓公特意派人問他。扁鵲說：「小病在皮膚紋理之間，湯熨的力量可以達到；病在肌肉和皮膚裏面，用針灸可以治好；病在腸胃裏，用火劑湯可以治好；病在骨髓裏，那是司命神管轄的事情了，醫生是沒有辦法醫治的。現在病在骨髓裏面，我因此不再請求為他治病了。」

過了五天，蔡桓公身體疼痛，派人尋找扁鵲，扁鵲已經逃到秦國了。蔡桓公於是病死了。

這則故事告訴人們，只有病人因痛苦而感覺到自己生病，才會找醫生去診斷病情，是哪裏出了問題。醫生給他開藥，他服用以後，病可痊癒。同樣，普通人只有覺知生命的無常之苦，才會反思生命；出家人只有知道六道輪迴之苦，才會修道；菩薩只有了知眾生之苦，才會生起救度眾生的菩提心。從這種意義上講，解脫從了知苦開始。

Meditation at the Royal Ploughing Festival

Before long will this body lay upon the ground, rejected, devoid of consciousness, like a worthless log.

— The Dhammapada

In the kingdom of Kapilavastu, the Royal Ploughing Festival was held every spring. King Śuddhodana took this festival very seriously and would personally come to preside over the ceremony. When the prince attended this festival for the first time, he was excited at the beginning with high expectations on the activities and rituals. But then he saw that farmers were topless working under the burning sun; that old oxen were whipped with their skin cut open, flesh torn, and blood dripping; that earthworms were eaten by birds; and that birds were then eaten by snakes or eagles. These pitiful sights saddened the prince, who got to know, for the first time, the miserable things in life. He then went to a sweet cherry tree alone, sitting cross-legged and meditating on what he had seen and heard during the day.

- **Understanding suffering is the beginning towards liberation**

Bian Que came to see the Marquis Huan of Cai and stood in front of him for a while before saying, "You seem to have some minor ailment in the texture of your skin, which will get worse without medical treatment." "I am fine without any disease," said the Marquis Huan of Cai. After Bian Que had left, the Marquis Huan of Cai continued, "Doctors like to give medication to those who actually don't have any disease to show off their so-called superb medical skill." Ten days later, when he saw the Marquis Huan of Cai again, Bian Que said, "Now your disease is already in your muscle, and it will get worse if you don't get it cured." The Marquis Huan of Cai gave no reply, for he felt disgruntled.

After another ten days, the moment he saw the Marquis Huan of Cai, Bian Que said, "Now your disease has come into the intestines and stomach, and it will get worse if you fail to have timely medical treatment." The Marquis Huan of Cai still did not answer to that. After Bian Que left, he was very much displeased.

Another ten days passed. And when he caught sight of the Marquis Huan of Cai in the distance, Bian Que immediately sheered off in the opposite direction. The Marquis Huan of Cai sent an official to ask Bian Que why he turned away in such a hurry. Bian Que replied, "The disease in the skin can be driven away with some herbal medicine; when in the muscle, it can be cured with acupuncture; and when in the intestines and stomach, it can be removed with fire medicine soup. Once the disease gets into the marrow, the patient is under the charge of the Lord of Death, and no doctor can do anything for him. Now the disease has already gone into the marrow of the Marquis Huan of Cai. It's beyond my reach to save his life."

Five days passed by. The Marquis Huan of Cai felt pain in his body, so he sent his men to search for Bian Que, who had already escaped to the Kingdom of Qin. Finally, the Marquis Huan of Cai died of his disease (that could have been cured long before).

The story tells us that a patient would go to see a doctor to check what's wrong only when he or she feels the pain of disease. Then, after he or she takes the medicine prescribed by the doctor, the disease can be completely cured. Similarly, the worldlings will start reflecting upon their life only when they feel the pain of impermanence in life; the monastics will practice the Way only when they understand the pain of cyclic existence within the six realms; the bodhisattvas will develop Bodhicitta to save all sentient beings only when they understand their sufferings. In this sense, understanding suffering is the beginning towards liberation.

人間生活

常在燃燒中，何喜何可笑？
幽暗之所蔽，何不求光明？

——《法句經》

　　作為一國之君，淨飯王期望太子日後繼承王位，做個能幹的國君，他悉心栽培太子，讓悉達多從小就習文練武，並請來最優秀的老師，教太子多方面的學識。

　　青少年的悉達多，在每一方面的學習都非常出色，他的表現令所有王族成員都引以為傲。在一次比武大會中，太子出色的表現輕取冠軍，但卻謙遜不驕，贏得了佳人耶輸陀羅的芳心，彼此結為夫婦。至此，淨飯王老懷安慰，決定為太子建瑰麗堂皇、冬暖夏涼的三時王宮，好讓他們能安享宮廷的豪華生活。後來，耶輸陀羅更為太子生了一個兒子，名叫羅睺羅。有了美滿的家庭之後，一切都顯得那麼圓滿美好，但對悉達多而言，這種羨煞旁人的奢華生活、權貴人生，又有何真正意義？

- 自我的人格 —— 成家立業

　　據說，佛陀在人間的世俗生活延續了二十九年。

　　年輕時，他和我們一樣練文習武，為實現自我而奮鬥。

　　他跟隨名師學習印度古代的各種哲學流派，在比武大會上獲得冠軍，贏得美若天仙的少女耶輸陀羅的芳心，並結為夫妻，生有一子。

　　他成家立業後，住在瑰麗堂皇的三時宮殿，時刻有醇酒、音樂、美人相伴，享盡人間榮華富貴，人世間苦苦追求的財富、名譽、地位乃至學問、武功，無不成就，自我得到最大的滿足。

Life in the Secular World

What laughter? Why joy? When is everything constantly burning? Covered by darkness, you do not seek light?

— The Dhammapada

As head of state, King Śuddhodana expected the prince to inherit the throne and become a capable monarch in the future. He devoted all his attention to educating the prince. When the prince was still a child, the king arranged for him to study liberal arts and practice martial arts. The king also found the best tutors to teach him knowledge in various fields.

As a teenager, Siddhārtha excelled in all areas, and all the royal family was very proud of him. Once in a martial arts competition, the prince won the championship but remained humble. Princess Yaśodharā was there watching the competition, and from that moment she had a crush on Siddhārtha. They soon got married, and the king was so happy that he decided to construct a splendid palace for the new couple to enjoy the luxuries of a royal life. After their son Rahula was born, it seemed that the prince would live a wonderful and perfect life. However, Siddhārtha was skeptical about the meaning of such a luxurious royal life that most people would envy.

- **Personal character—starting a family and building a career**

According to legend, the Buddha lived his secular life for twenty-nine years.

When he was young, he studied liberal arts, practiced martial arts, and fought for self-realization as we do.

He followed famous teachers to study classical philosophies of ancient India. He once won the championship in a martial arts competition and married a beautiful girl named Yaśodharā, who gave birth to a son for him.

After getting married Prince Siddhārtha lived in a magnificent Three-season Palace, enjoying all kinds of worldly splendor and wealth, always surrounded with fine wines, music, and beautiful girls. He accomplished almost everything strived for by worldly people, such as wealth, fame, status, martial arts, and so on. He seemed to have achieved the highest satisfaction of himself.

太子出家

人天長夜，宇宙黯闇，誰啟以光明？
三界火宅，眾苦煎迫，誰濟以安寧？

—— 三寶歌

深居宮中的悉達多太子，甚少與外界接觸，他的生活圈子離不開皇親貴冑，他日常的所見所聞，並不廣泛。

這天，太子興之所至，突然想到宮外走走，於是讓侍從車匿，陪他到城裏的四門巡遊。主僕倆駕着馬車，首先在東門見到一個白髮曲背、盡露衰相的老叟；繼而在南門見到一個在路旁痛苦呻吟的垂危病者；接着又於西門遇上送葬儀隊，見到死屍躺在木架上，四周圍繞着痛哭的親人。面對這些從未見過的景象，太子心中立時生起了疑問：如果人人都免不了老、病、死之苦，那目前的快樂豈非短暫徒然？

滿懷惆悵，太子最終來到了北門，卻見到一位神態安詳、面目慈和的修道者，太子直覺這位沙門選擇的道路才是人生的意義所在。為了幫自己、親人，以及所有的眾生解除生命中的痛苦，悉達多太子決定出家修道，去尋找解脫生、老、病、死的終究方法！

- 超我的人格 —— 出家求道

　　經過二十多年的忙碌、奮鬥，想得到的都能如願以償，悉達多太子的內心反而感到寂寞與空虛起來。

　　生活在醉生夢死的皇宮，他不斷反問自己，「生命如此短暫，生老病死時刻威脅。每一個人，卻沒有人有危機感，反而把全部精力用於爭奪名利等身外之物上。爭到手的東西遲早會失去，根本無法永遠佔有，這種爭奪又有何意義？人生的意義何在？」

　　既然皇宮裏博古通今的老師無法提供答案，悉達多太子只有一種選擇，走出皇宮，為芸芸眾生尋找離苦得樂的答案。

　　這個決定使悉達多太子超越了自己的本性，成就了超我的人格，使得悉達多太子超越常人。

　　正如俄國哲學家車爾尼雪夫斯基（1828—1889）云：「要是一個人的全部人格、全部生活都奉獻給一種道德追求，要是他擁有這樣的力量，一切其他的人在這方面和這個人相比起來都顯得渺小的時候，那我們在這個人的身上就看到崇高的善。」

Renouncing the Secular Life

In the long dark night of the human and heavenly realms,

In the universe with complete darkness,

Who will illuminate us?

In the burning house of the Three Realms,

Where we are tormented by various sufferings,

Who will bring us serenity and peace?

— Song of the Three Jewels

　　Living in the palace, Prince Siddhārtha was rarely in touch with the outside world. He was surrounded by royal relatives and the nobles. He did not see much of the world and knew little about the ordinary life.

　　One day, the prince had an idea to go outside of the palace to have a look, so he asked his attendant Chandaka to accompany him to visit the four gates of the city. At the eastern gate, they saw an old man with grey hair and a humpback. At the southern gate, they came across a sick, dying man groaning painfully at the roadside. At the western gate, they met a funeral procession and saw a dead body lying on a wooden rack surrounded by his bitterly crying family. After the prince saw such miserable scenes which he had never seen before, doubts arose in his mind: If everyone has to experience the sufferings of aging, sickness, and death, isn't the present happiness temporary and in vain?

Full of melancholy, the prince arrived at the northern gate, where he met a kind and peaceful meditator. The prince had an instinct that the real meaning of life lies in the path of the meditator. In order to help himself, his relatives, and all sentient beings to liberate from the sufferings of life, Prince Siddhārtha decided to leave the court and his family for spiritual cultivation in search of the ultimate way to liberate himself from birth, aging, sickness, and death!

Basics of Buddhism:

• **Transcendence of personality—becoming a monk and seeking the way to liberation**

After more than twenty years of hard work, Prince Siddhārtha achieved all that he had wished for, but he began to feel lonely and empty.

Living in the palace where everyone led a befuddled and meaningless life, he kept asking himself, "Life is so short; it is threatened by birth, aging, sickness, and death at every moment. But people have no sense of crisis; they devote all their energy to fighting for fame, wealth, and other extraneous things. Sooner or later, everything that they have won will be lost, for what they possess will not last forever. What's the point of such a fight? What is the meaning of life?"

Since the learned teachers in the palace could not provide answers to his questions, Prince Siddhārtha had only one choice, and that is to leave the palace in search of a way to liberate all sentient beings.

In making this decision, Prince Siddhārtha went beyond himself and achieved transcendence of his own personality. Because of this, Prince Siddhārtha is distinguished from the ordinary man.

Russian philosopher Nicholas Chernyshevsky (1828–1889) said, "If a man's whole personality and life are devoted to moral pursuit, and if he has the power to do so, then all other people would seem small compared with this man, and we can see the noble goodness in him."

六年苦修

除滅一切諸心毒，思惟修習最上智，
不為自己求安樂，但願眾生得離苦。

—— 《華嚴經》

悉達多太子決意出家的心願獲得了賢妻耶輸陀羅的諒解和支持，但淨飯王對兒子的決定，卻始終反對。太子反覆思量，知道自己並不是為了逃避國家社稷、家庭的責任而遁世隱修，他很清楚自己是真心想為眾生得離苦而出家，他更承諾一朝得道，必定與大眾分享。

一天晚上，太子靜悄悄地離開了王宮，踏上了出家修行之途。他最初追隨幾位有名的精神導師修行，但即使達到了導師認可的最高境界，仍未找到徹底消除苦惱的方法，於是他轉向自己尋找出路，嘗試以苦修的方式進行身心的磨練，希望從中悟道。悉達多走進了苦行林獨自修行，過着極刻苦的生活，每日只吃一麻一麥來維持生命。就這樣，太子持續了六年的苦行生涯，以致身體變得十分虛弱，但始終沒有尋到脫苦之道。

極端的苦行，是否正確的修行途徑？太子對此作出了反思。

- 人格的磨練 —— 六年苦修

　　古希臘雅典著名的哲學家、教育家蘇格拉底説過，「患難與困苦是磨練人格的最高學府。」為了真理，悉達多太子先到苦行林參訪苦行仙人，然後又到雪山去苦修，每日只吃一麻一麥維持生命。苦修雖然沒有使太子找到解脱的答案，卻磨練出他偉大的人格：勇於承認錯誤 —— 苦修無法使人獲得解脱。

Ascetic Practice for Six Years

To get rid of all of the klesas,

To contemplate and practice the highest wisdom,

I do not seek peace and happiness for my own,

But wish emancipation from sufferings for all beings.

— The Avataṃsaka Sūtra

Prince Siddhārtha was determined to renounce the secular life. His decision was understood and supported by his good wife Yaśodharā but persistently opposed by his father, King Śuddhodana. The prince thought it over. He knew very well that it was not for escaping his responsibility for the country and family that he chose to renounce the secular life and be an ascetic; it was to find a way of freeing all beings from sufferings. He promised himself that he would share the wisdom with all beings upon his enlightenment.

One night, the prince left the palace quietly and embarked on a spiritual journey. He first followed a few famous teachers, but even after reaching the highest level recognized by them, he still could not find a way to completely end suffering. So, he turned to find a way out by himself. He adopted extreme ascetic practice to train his body and mind, hoping to attain enlightenment this way. Siddhārtha walked into the ascetic forest to practice alone. He led a life of extreme austerity, eating only a grain of wheat and one sesame seed a day to stay alive. The prince continued his ascetic practice this way for six years and became very weak. Yet, he still could not find a way to end sufferings.

"Is extreme ascetic practice the right way?" The prince asked himself.

- **Honing the personality—ascetic practice for six years**

Socrates, the famous philosopher and educator in Athens of ancient Greece, once said, "Adversity and suffering is the highest institution to hone one's personality." To seek truth, Prince Siddhārtha first went to the forest to learn from accomplished ascetics and practiced asceticism in the snow mountains, eating only a grain of wheat and one sesame seed a day to keep alive. Although he did not find the answer to liberation, he cultivated a great personality with the courage to admit his mistake—ascetic practice does not lead to liberation.

聽琴覺醒

> 牟尼入村落,譬如蜂採華,
> 不壞色與香,但取其蜜去。

—— 《法句經》

這天,瘦骨嶙峋的悉達多感到四肢乏力,正於林中躺下小憩時,一陣美妙的琴聲自遠處傳來,打破了四周的沉寂。

聽着聽着……這些琴音似乎將太子的思緒喚醒過來,令他感到一陣清新。他頓然想到,一隻琴要發出悅耳的聲音,有賴調弦的藝術 —— 琴弦調得太鬆,根本就發不出聲音來,琴弦調得過緊,則弦線更易斷掉;最理想的琴音,是來自不鬆不緊的琴弦!

他此刻聯想到自己往昔在宮中奢華的享受,對比目前的極端苦行,就如琴弦的過鬆過緊一樣,永遠難以發出理想的效果,縱情欲樂固然難以成就修行,但折磨自己體膚的鍛練,亦不能達至開悟。太子覺悟到他往後不應偏離中道、傾向任何一邊,這樣才能保持身心平穩安定,專注於用功修行。

• 人格的發展 ── 降伏心魔

　　通過三十五年的苦苦探索，悉達多太子終於明白一個道理，苦難來自我們一顆有所執着的心。固執地追求人世間「五欲」之樂，固然無法使人獲得長久的快樂，頑固地執着於某一種修行形式（如極度的苦行），也不是修行的正途。因為這只會使人在修行形式上打轉，到了一定的境界，便無法突破。「不識本心，學法無益」。只有將生命之弦調到不鬆不緊的狀態，才能彈出美妙的音樂。同樣，修行人應超越對任何修行形式的執着，從心入手，「無所住而生其心」，修行道路上才能進入一個新的天地。如此思維，悉達多太子降伏了有所住的心魔，走出自我束縛，使自己的人格得到自由表現。

Awakening on Hearing the Lute

A holy man should behave in the village like a bee which takes its food from a flower without hurting its appearance or its scent.

— The Dhammapada

　　One day, the skinny Siddhārtha felt very tired. When he was lying down in the forest, beautiful sounds of the lute (a musical instrument in ancient India) from afar broke the silence around him.

　　Listening and listening... the lute seemed to have awakened the prince from his deep thoughts, giving him a sense of refreshment. He suddenly realized that the pleasant sound of the lute came from strings that were

properly tuned—if the strings were too loose, there would be no sound at all; if too tight, the strings would likely break. So the ideal sound must have come from strings neither too loose nor too tight!

At that moment, he recalled the luxurious pleasures he used to enjoy in the palace and compared that with the extreme ascetic practice he had adopted—like the strings, they were either too loose or too tight to produce desirable music. In a similar way, indulging in pleasure could hardly bring about achievement in his practice, but tormenting his body would not help attain enlightenment either. The prince realized that he should not deviate from the middle path or lean on either side in the future. Only then could he maintain the stability of his body and mind and stay focused on his practice.

✸ Basics of Buddhism:

- **Development of personality—Conquering the Demon of the Mind**

Through thirty-five years of painstaking exploration, Prince Siddhārtha finally understood that sufferings came from one's own clinging mind. Stubbornly pursuing the happiness of the five cord of sensual pleasure in the human world, of course, cannot make people long-lasting happiness, and persistent attachment to a certain form of practice (such as extreme asceticism) is not the right way either. Merely focusing on the form of practice, practitioners cannot break through after reaching a certain level, because "If one does not recognize the fundamental mind, studying the Dharma is of no benefit." Only when the string of life is properly tuned, neither too loose nor too tight, can it produce beautiful music. Likewise, attachments of all sorts need to be transcended. Focus on the mind, and have "the mind function free from any ties." Only in this way can they enter into a new stage on the path of cultivation. Realizing this, Prince Siddhārtha subdued the demon within him, and freed himself from past self-inflicted bondages to become who he truly was.

降魔成道

奇哉！奇哉！大地眾生皆有如來智慧德相，
但以妄想執着不能證得。

—— 佛陀

　　得到了新的啟悟，悉達多拖着骨瘦如柴的身軀，離開了苦行林，前往尼連禪河畔的樹林中，在中途又獲得牧女供養乳糜，得以恢復體力。進入樹林之後，悉達多在一棵很大的樹下設座修行，時而到附近的村莊行乞化緣，時而接受牧童給他送來的供食。

　　這個晚上，悉達多知道自己的修行已到了一個關鍵時刻，他到大樹下的草墊上結跏趺坐，立誓要在那兒靜坐不起，直至悟道。整個夜晚，悉達多在定中悟到很多宇宙運行的秩序法則 —— 各各世界的成住壞空、萬法的生住異滅、眾生在業力驅動下的生死輪轉等等。

　　此時，邪惡的魔王，當然不願見到悉達多成道，整個晚上用盡各種方法擾亂他的定力，以期破壞他的正覺，但悉達多一點也沒有被動搖，以堅定的意志降服了一切魔境。

　　在晨星出現之際，悉達多證得了圓滿的覺悟，為眾生找到了脫苦之道。

• 人格的昇華 —— 大徹大悟

　　悉達多太子來到菩提樹下，從心入手，靜坐反思，終於明白，人生的苦難淵源於因我執而產生的貪瞋癡等不健康的思維，由此而引發不健康的行為和語言，成為未來苦難的動力，這就是佛教業力緣起的理論。因此自淨此意是離苦得樂的法寶。對於已經深陷苦海的人們，佛陀又悟出離苦得樂的方法，共有四個步驟：勇敢地面對困境（苦諦）、客觀地分析陷入困境的原因（集諦）、建立起脫離困境的信心和勇氣（滅諦），並以實際行動走出困境（道諦），這就是四聖諦。了知佛陀大徹大悟的內容 —— 緣起法和四聖諦，就能使一個人的思維得到重整，人格得到昇華。

Subduing the Demon King and Becoming Enlightened

How wonderful! How wonderful! All living beings, without exception, possess the wisdom of the Tathāgata. It is because of their erroneous and distorted views and attachments that they fail to realize it.

— The Buddha

Inspired by the new insight, Siddhārtha, dragging along his scrawny body, left the ascetic forest and headed towards the woods on the banks of Nairañjanā River (the present-day Lilaja River). On the way there, he was offered a bowl of milk porridge by a shepherdess and thus renewed his physical strength. After entering the woods, Siddhārtha set up a seat for meditation under a large tree. Sometimes he went to the nearby villages for alms round, and sometimes he received food offered by the shepherds.

One evening, Siddhārtha knew that he had reached a critical stage in his practice, so sitting with crossed legs on the straw mat under a big tree, he vowed not to rise from the seat until he reached enlightenment. Throughout the night, Siddhārtha realized many universal laws through meditation—the formation, existence, decay, and disappearance of the worlds; the arising, abiding, changing, and extinction of all dharmas; sentient beings' transmigration through birth and death driven by the power of karma; and more.

At this time, the evil demon, of course, did not want to see Siddhartha attain enlightenment. He tried all kinds of methods to disturb his concentration throughout the night in order to destroy his enlightenment, but Siddhartha did not waver at all; he triumphed over all the Demon King's disturbances with his willpower.

When the morning star rose, Siddhārtha attained perfect enlightenment and found the way to end the sufferings for all beings.

Basics of Buddhism:

• **Perfection of personality—supreme enlightenment**

Prince Siddhārtha came to the Bodhi tree, sitting in meditation to reflect within and contemplate. He finally realized that all sufferings in life originate from unhealthy thoughts such as greed, hatred, and delusion rooted in self-grasping. Such thoughts would then lead to unwholesome actions and words that become the causes of future suffering. This is the theory of karmic causation in Buddhism. Therefore, purification of one's own mind is the best means to end sufferings and attain happiness. For those who have already fallen into the deep sea of suffering, the Buddha teaches a four-step method: bravely face the difficulties (the truth of suffering), objectively analyze the causes (the truth of the arising of suffering), establish the confidence and courage to get out of the difficulties (the truth of the cessation of suffering), and take actual action to get out of the difficulties (the truth of the path to the cessation of suffering). This four-step teaching that leads one to liberation is also called the Four Noble Truths. Having the knowledge of what the Buddha was enlightened to—Dependent Origination and the Four Noble Truths, one can transform the mind and further develop the personality.

梵天勸請

供養供應者，脫離於虛妄，超越諸憂患，佛及佛弟子。
若供養如是，寂靜無畏者，其所得功德，無能測量者。

——《法句經》

　　昔日的悉達多太子，現在已是大徹大悟的大覺者，人們稱他為佛
陀，而他證悟時在樹下禪坐，因此這棵樹被稱為菩提樹。佛陀證悟後曾
歎謂：「一切眾生皆有如來智慧德相，惟因妄想執着而不可證得！」佛
陀慶倖眾生都有開悟的種子 —— 佛性，但他亦同時知道，要破除眾生
久遠累積的迷執，讓他們本有的智光重明，並不容易。

　　佛陀自己的所證所覺，是他親身的體悟，當中法理甚深、妙義
無窮，要用語言來表達其內容，讓眾生起信修行、悟入佛見，這有可
能嗎？

　　當帝釋、梵天等天界之首，知道佛陀意欲默然，不為世間說法之
時，他們便再三懇請佛陀要弘揚大法、廣利眾生，出於慈悲的本懷，佛
陀答應了他們，並決定日後會隨着眾生的根機，權將語言作為善巧方便
的工具，為眾生說法。

✖✖✖ [佛教小知識] ⸻⸻⸻⸻⸻⸻⸻⸻⸻⸻

- 方便度眾

　　在現實生活中，人活得並不容易，不僅要辛勤勞動，創造物質財富，以保障最基本的生存空間，而且還要經受各種情緒的困擾、心靈的折磨。處於這種雙重考驗下的大多數世人，難以靜心深入思考佛法中深奧的人生哲理，也是情理中的事。佛陀慈悲，不捨任何一個可度眾生，常以深入淺出的故事啟發大眾，使人們了知佛法的精要。這些故事在佛經中隨處可見，並佔有很大的比重。歷代的祖師大德們，效佛所行，大力推動通俗弘化事業。早在公元二、三世紀，活躍於印度北部罽賓一帶的譬喻師們，在重視內修禪觀的同時，時常引用「本生」故事來教化眾生。中國的禪師們，更是發揚光大了先聖們的光輝事跡，以禪宗公案啟發學人，建立起通俗弘化的機制，為後人留下近三萬個禪宗公案故事，成為人類珍貴的文化遺產。

　　今天，人類的精神健康指數並未隨着科技的進步和經濟的發展而有所增加，與此相反，越來越多的人覺得，人積累的身外之物越多，活得越累。人生苦難多，如何以佛陀方便度眾的智慧來幫助現代人減壓，找回失去的精神樂園，是我們今後弘法時值得探索的問題。

Brahmā's Request

He who reveres those worthy of reverence, the Buddhas and their disciples, who have transcended all obstacles and passed beyond the reach of sorrow and lamentation - he who revers such peaceful and fearless ones, his merit none can compute by any measure.

— The Dhammapada

The former Prince Siddhārtha is now the great enlightened one, who is called Buddha. He realized enlightenment when sitting under a tree, which is called the Bodhi tree.

After achieving enlightenment, the Buddha exclaimed, "All sentient beings have the wisdom and virtue of the Tathāgata, but they fail to realize it due to their delusion and attachments!" He rejoiced that all beings have the seed of enlightenment—the Buddha nature; yet, he also knew that it was not easy to help them let go of their long accumulated delusions and attachments to regain their original light of wisdom.

What the Buddha was awakened to was his personal realization of wisdom and insight into profound principles that have infinite wonderful meanings. Is it possible to employ language to arouse faith in sentient beings, so that they would practice accordingly and be enlightened on the Buddha's view?

When Deva kings such as Indra and Brahmā knew the Buddha's intention to remain silent and not to preach the Dharma for the world, they repeatedly beseeched him to disseminate the Dharma to benefit all living beings. Out of compassion, the Buddha agreed to them and decided that in the future, following the roots of sentient beings, provionally use language as a skillful and convenient tool to preach dharma for the sentient beings.

• **Save living beings with skillful means**

In the reality of daily life, people normally have a tough time. They not only need to work hard to create material wealth in order to maintain a minimum level of living, but also have to suffer from all kinds of emotional troubles and mental torments. It is understandable that most people under such trials would find it difficult to calmly explore the profound philosophy within the Buddhadharma. The Buddha, out of his kindness and compassion, was unwilling to give up any living being that might be saved, so he often inspired people with simple yet meaningful stories to let them understand the essence of the Dharma. These stories can be found everywhere in sutras and account for a large proportion of Buddhist texts. Patriarchs and eminent monastics of past generations followed the Buddha's example and greatly facilitated and promoted the cause of Dharma dissemination. As early as the second and third century AD, Dārṣṭāntikas who were active in Kashmir in northern India often cited stories from the Garland of Birth Stories to teach people apart from their emphasis on practicing meditative introspection. Chinese Chan masters continued to further these glorious deeds of the ancestral sages by inspiring learners with koans. This approach established a popular way to spread the Dharma and left future generations with nearly 30,000 koans, which have become a precious cultural heritage of mankind.

Today, the mental health index of human beings has failed to grow with the advancement of science and technology and economic development. On the contrary, more and more people feel that the more external things they possess, the more exhausted they become. Life is full of suffering. It is worth exploring how the expedient means employed in Buddhist Dharma dissemination to deliver living beings could help modern people reduce their daily pressures and rediscover their lost spiritual paradise.

無上甚深微妙法，百千萬劫難遭遇，
我今見聞得受持，願解如來真實義。

—— 開經偈

　　佛陀離開了菩提樹、走出了尼連禪河畔的樹林，踏上了說法之途，開始與大眾分享他所證得的解脫之道。

　　佛陀初轉法輪是在鹿野苑，他為昔日的五個同修朋友說四聖諦——「苦」，在世間存在的普遍性、客觀分析；「集」，苦的原因；「滅」，除苦惱是可能的；實踐滅苦之「道」的核心為八正道——正見、正思惟、正語、正業、正命、正精進、正念、正定。

　　之後，佛陀應機說法四十九年，講經三百餘會，當中所開示的教化，包括了緣起法、因果業力等基礎道理。佛陀入滅後，僧團裏的弟子將他所說過的法理都結集起來，成為了日後三藏十二部經教的內容，為佛法的長遠流傳奠定了基礎。

- 人格的感化 —— 説法利生

　　德國詩人歌德（1749－1832）曾經説過，「只有偉大的人格，才有偉大的風格」。大徹大悟的佛陀，以度化眾生為己任，四十九年間足跡遍及全印度，以其崇高的人格，感化無數苦難眾生，為人類留下極其珍貴的精神資糧，直至今日，我們仍沐浴在佛陀的慈光下。

Turning the Wonderful Dharma Wheel

The unsurpassed, profound, and wonderful Dharma,

Is difficult to encounter in hundreds of millions of eons,

I now see and hear it, receive and uphold it,

And I vow to fathom the Tathagata's true meaning.

— Verse for Opening a Sutra

The Buddha left the bodhi tree, stepped out of the forest by the Nairañjanā River, and set forth on the journey to preach his teachings and share with people the path to liberation that he had realized.

The Buddha first turned the Dharma wheel in the Deer Park. He taught five ascetics who had been his former companions the Four Noble the truth of suffering, universality and objective analysis of existence in the world; the causes of the arising of suffering; the possibility of the cessation of suffering; and the core of practicing the path to the cessation of suffering being the Eightfold Path: right view, right thought, right speech, right action, right livelihood, right effort, right mindfulness, and right concentration.

During the following forty-nine years, the Buddha taught sentient beings the Dharma according to their capacities and gave Dharma talks for more than three hundred times. The teachings he instructed include the fundamental principles such as Dependent Origination, cause and effect, and karma. After the Buddha entered Nirvana, the disciples in the Sangha compiled all his teachings, which later became the content of the Tripitaka in 12 Divisions, thus having laid a foundation for the long-term dissemination of the Dharma.

- **Influence of the personality—teaching the Dharma to benefit living beings**

German poet Goethe (1749–1832) said, "Great style comes only with great personalities." The enlightened Buddha took it upon himself to help and save all sentient beings. He travelled all over India during a period of forty-five years and transformed innumerable beings who were in distress with his noble personality, leaving extremely precious spiritual resources for mankind. Till this day, we are still bathed in the light of the Buddha's loving-kindness.

調教頑童

正信而具戒，得譽及財者，

彼至於何處，處處受尊敬。

———《法句經》

　　佛陀說法的對象普及所有階層，無論男女老幼、出家在家、皇孫公子、又或當時社會上最卑微的賤民，都接受過佛陀的教化。佛陀智慧任運、應機說法，不僅用比喻法來教化眾生，還對已出家為小沙彌的兒子 —— 羅睺羅，以一盆洗腳水作比喻，給他作出有效的訓導。

　　話說羅睺羅很愛說謊，常捉弄別人。這天，佛陀囑他給自己打水洗腳，之後便作出比喻：髒了的洗腳水被倒掉，就如同變壞了的孩子，再沒人會珍惜他；而盛載過洗腳水的盆，我們也不會用來盛載食物，這就如同說謊的孩子，行為上有了污點，再不會被人信任和重用。

　　就這樣，佛陀不用嚴責呵斥，羅睺羅便已領會到比喻所帶出的道理，明白到良好品格及誠信的重要，自此再不說謊。

❈❈ ［佛教小知識］────────────────────────────

• 應病與藥、應機說法

　　目犍連有兩位弟子，無論目犍連如何努力，兩位弟子進步都不大。

佛陀得知此後問目犍連，「你教給他們甚麼方法？」

目犍連説：「打鐵出生的弟子修不淨觀，洗衣出生的弟子修數息觀。可是倆弟子心智愚滯，總不得要領。」

佛陀聽後微笑説，「是方法不對，而不是他倆愚笨。現在你只需要將他們的修禪方法調換一下，就可以了。」

目犍連恍然大悟。原來，打鐵出生的弟子熟悉呼吸，修數息觀比較容易進入禪定狀態，而洗衣出生的弟子熟悉污穢不淨之物，修不淨觀容易找到感覺。目犍連調換了兩個弟子的修習方法後，兩位弟子進步很快，最終修得了羅漢果。

在《涅槃經》中，佛陀被人們稱為大醫王。如同世間良醫治病一樣應病與藥，佛陀針對聽眾的教育背景和根機，應機説法，從而達到最佳效果。

Guiding the Naughty Child

With trust, possessed of virtue, endowed with fame and wealth - to whatever region does he resort, he is respected everywhere.

— The Dhammapada

The Buddha taught the Dharma to people from all the castes, regardless of whether they were men or women, old or young, monastics or laities, sons of emperors and high officials or the untouchables in society. All of them had received the teachings from the Buddha. He was effortless in using both his wisdom and compassion to expound the Dharma for his audience according to their capacities. He liked to use metaphors to guide living beings. He even gave his son Rāhula, a little śrāmaṇera, an effective lesson through the analogy of a basin of water for washing his feet.

It was said that Rāhula liked to tell lies to play tricks on others. One day, the Buddha asked Rāhula to fetch him water to wash his feet. He then told a parable: Just as the basin of water will be poured away after the feet have been washed, a child who has turned bad will never be cherished again. As for the basin that held the water, it will not be used to hold food; similarly, a child who lied will never be trusted and put in an important position again since his actions are stained.

In this way, without any harsh rebuke, the Buddha helped Rāhula understand the truth behind the parable and the importance of good conduct and integrity. He never lied again.

⁂ Basics of Buddhism: ───────────────────────────

- **Prescribing medicine according to one's illness; teaching the Dharma according to individual capacities.**

    Maudgalyāyana had two disciples who made little progress no matter how hard he tried to teach them. On hearing this, the Buddha asked Maudgalyāyana, "How did you teach them?"

    Maudgalyāyana said, "I taught the disciple who had been a blacksmith to practice meditation on impurity (the meditation on the uncleanness of the human body), and the disciple who had been a launderer to practice the breath counting meditation. Yet the two of them are dull and failed to grasp the main point."

    The Buddha said with a smile, "It is not because they are dull, but because they. Now all you need to do is to swap their meditation methods."

    Maudgalyāyana suddenly realized that the blacksmith disciple was familiar with breath counting, so it would be easier for him to enter meditative concentration through counting the breath. And the launderer disciple was familiar with dirty clothes, so it would be easier for him to get the feel through meditation on impurity. After Maudgalyāyana swapped their ways of practice, they made rapid progress and finally realized the state of an arhat.

In the Mahaparinirvana Sutra, the Buddha is known as the Great Healing King. Like the doctors prescribe medication according to the patient's specific conditions, the Buddha preached dharma according to the audience's educational background and capacities to achieve the best results.

訓誠悍婦

不慢不自大，知足念反覆，
以時誦習經，是為最吉祥。

——《法句經》

　　對於一些桀傲驕橫的人，不論是男是女，佛陀會毫不含糊地直斥其非。佛陀就曾遇過一個悍婦，最終亦被他感化過來。

　　根據《玉耶女經》記載，玉耶女出生於富裕家庭，自幼驕生慣養，又自恃生得貌美聰明，故嫁與須達長者的小兒子後，不但輕慢丈夫，對家婆家公也不恭不敬、漠不關心、諸事忤逆，又與妯娌不和，令夫家雞犬不寧、糾紛頻生。

　　為此，須達長者十分懊惱，於是，請佛陀到他家中訓誠玉耶女，而佛陀直接給玉耶女講解了婦人之道，讓她明白身為人婦的家庭責任、與丈夫相處應有的態度、與家人親友和諧相處的重要性等等。佛陀又給玉耶女說了不同類別的妻子，當中有好有壞，繼而請她好好反省自己屬於哪一種，令玉耶女自覺羞愧，不但甘願悔改，更請佛陀收她為在家弟子，從此虔心學佛。

• 《玉耶女經》

《玉耶女經》講述的是，佛陀因須達長者（用黃金鋪地建立祇園精舍的長者）的請求，對須達長者的媳婦玉耶女進行教化。玉耶女因出身名門貴族，容貌姣好而不信佛法，出嫁到大長者家為人妻後，驕慢無理，不守婦道。佛陀因機施教，使玉耶女深知自己的罪過，決心洗心革面，痛改前非，並就此在佛前請受十戒為優婆夷，皈依三寶，並甘願做個婢婦。

Taming of a Shrew

Put down arrogance and ego,

Bear in mind to be content,

And recite and learn sutras regularly,

Such deeds are the most auspicious.

— The Dhammapada

For some unruly and arrogant people, whether male or female, the Buddha would not hesitate to point out their faults. He once met a shrewish woman, who was eventually transformed by him.

According to the Sujata Sutra, Sujata, born in a rich family, had been pampered since childhood. And considering herself beautiful and smart, she not only slighted her husband after marriage but also treated her parents-in-law with disrespect, indifference, and disobedience. Besides, she was on bad terms with her sisters-in-law. The husband's family was stirred into a tempest with a lot of disputes.

Sudatta was very annoyed about it. He invited the Buddha home to give Sujata some advice. The Buddha directly explained to Sujata the proper conduct of wives, so that she could understand her responsibilities as a woman in the family, her proper attitude towards her husband, the importance of living in harmony with her family and friends, and so forth. The Buddha also told Sujata the different kinds of wives, some being good and some being bad, and then asked her to reflect on which kind she belonged to. This made Sujata consciously ashamed. She was not only willing to repent and mend her ways but also asked the Buddha to accept her as a lay disciple. She then learned Buddhism with devoutness.

Basics of Buddhism:

• The Sujata Sutra

The Sujata Sutra tells the story of how the Buddha, at the request of Sudatta (an elder who floored Jetavanavihāra with gold), guided and transformed Sudatta's daughter-in-law Sujata. Sujata was born in a noble family with good looks, but she did not believe in Buddhism. After marrying to Sudatta's son, she was arrogant and unreasonable, not observing the proper conduct of wives. The Buddha taught her accordingly, which made her realize her faults and determine to completely reform and rectify her errors. She took the opportunity to ask the Buddha to let her receive the ten precepts and become an upāsikā. She also took refuge in the Three Jewels and willingly vowed to be an obedient wife.

點化愚癡

返本還源便到家，亦無玄妙可稱誇；
湛然一片真如性，迷失皆因一念差。

—— 明・浮峰普恩

　　佛陀的足跡遍佈恆河流域，他所度化的人亦不計其數，其中不乏一些惡漢狂徒，包括當時被人視為最危險的人物無惱指鬘。

　　無惱指鬘本來是個才貌雙全的優秀青年，他追隨了一位師父學習，卻因拒絕師母的色誘而遭到誣陷，其師聽信妻子之言，怒火中燒，暗中設計陷害無惱指鬘，對他說：「你若能在七日之內殺一千人，將每人的一隻手指割下，串成手指花環，便可升天。」礙於愚癡，無惱指鬘信以為真，喪失常性，成了見人便殺的狂魔，七日內殺了九百九十九人之後，更因生母前來勸阻，欲殺死自己的母親以補足一千隻手指。

　　幸好佛陀及時出現，引導他恢復理性，阻止了他弒母的衝動，並為他開示，讓他懂得自省悔改，最終皈依佛法，成為了佛陀最精進修行的弟子之一，不久更證得了阿羅漢的果位。

　　對於無惱指鬘的改邪歸正，當時聽聞的人都不大相信，直至事實被確認後，他們都深深被佛陀的大智威德所感動。

- 放下屠刀，真的能立地成佛嗎？

　　「放下屠刀，立地成佛」一語的源頭可以追溯到北涼譯出的《涅槃經·梵行品》：「波羅㮈國有屠兒名曰廣額，於日日中殺無量羊。見舍利弗，即受八戒，經一日一夜。以是因緣，命終得為北方天王毗沙門之子。」

　　「八戒」中的第一戒為「不殺生」。佛教認為殺生屬於應受地獄報應的最大惡業之一。放下屠刀就是不殺生，亦泛指不造一切惡業。不造一切惡業，就能得到種種福報，進而擺脫輪迴，直至成佛。從這種意義上講，從自願放下屠刀那一刻起，善念生起，一路修行，定能成佛。

Enlightening an Ignorant Man

Just return to the original state and that will be home;

There is nothing mysterious to boast about in all this.

Clearly in one whole piece is the nature of Tathata;

Delusions are all due to one thought going astray.

— Pu'en of the Ming dynasty

　　The Buddha enlightened countless people all over the Ganges River area, including some brutes such as the most dangerous person Aṅgulimālīya.

　　Aṅgulimālīya was once an outstanding young man, smart and handsome. He learned from a master but was framed by his master's wife because he refused her seduction. The master was inflamed by his wife's words and secretly designed a trap, telling him, "If you can kill a thousand people within seven days, cut one finger from each of the dead and string them into a finger garland, then you can ascend to heaven." Out of ignorance, Aṅgulimālīya believed his master. He lost his senses and became a frenzied killer. After killing 999 people in seven days, his mother came to dissuade him, but he even wanted to kill his mother to get the final finger for the garland.

Fortunately, the Buddha appeared in time. He guided Aṅgulimālīya to recover his senses, thus preventing him from killing his mother. The Buddha also taught him how to repent and atone for his past misdeeds. Finally, Aṅgulimālīya took refuge in the Dharma and became one of the most diligent disciples of the Buddha. Soon after that, he attained the state of an arhat.

Most of the people at that time did not believe the story of Aṅgulimālīya, who had given up vice and returned to virtue. But when it was confirmed, they all became deeply touched by the Buddha's great wisdom and inspiring virtue.

Basics of Buddhism:

- **Can a butcher become a Buddha at the moment he drops his cleaver?**

  The origin of the phrase "a butcher becomes a Buddha the moment he drops his cleaver" can be traced back to the Chapter of Pure Conducts of the Mahaparinirvana Sutra translated in the Northern Liang Dynasty, it says that "In the state of Varanasi, there was a butcher called 'Broad-Forehead', who every day killed an innumerable number of sheep. Having encountered Sariputra, he received the eight precepts and practiced them for a day and a night. Because of this, he was reborn after his death as the son of Vaisravana, the king of the northern heaven."

The first of the Eight Precepts is "no killing." Buddhism believes that killing is one of the gravest transgressions with the retribution of being reborn in the hells. Dropping the cleaver means no more killing and generally implies no creating of unwholesome karma. If you stop creating unwholesome karma, you will get all kinds of blessings and be liberated from the cycle of rebirths (samsara) until finally you become a Buddha. In this sense, good thoughts arise the moment you voluntarily drop the cleaver. Progressing on the way of practicing Buddhism, you will finally attain Buddhahood.

釋迦孝親

哀哀父母，生我劬勞；十月三年，懷胎乳哺；
推乾去濕，嚥苦吐甘，才得成人。

——《勸發菩提心文》

當初佛陀身為太子，淨飯王希望他能繼自己之後，成為釋迦族之首、迦毗羅衛國之王，故而一直反對太子出家修道，以致太子悄悄離宮，才達成自己的出家心願。

即使太子離開了父王、姨母及妻兒，但他從未忘記他們，更沒有因為父王與自己志向有所分歧，而對父親心存隔膜。佛陀成道後不久，他便履行了起初的承諾，回到迦毗羅衛國為家人、釋迦族及國民分享他所證悟到的真諦。這時，淨飯王不但完全接受了佛陀，而且對他能夠成就道業、從此可以為眾生弘揚正法，感到十分的光榮和安慰。

淨飯王病重之時，已是人天大導師的佛陀，帶領着弟子回去見父親最後一面、守侍在側，之後又親抬父棺送往火葬。佛陀在世間親情上的表現，難道不是為我們提供了父子互諒、父慈子孝的最佳典範嗎？

• 孝名為戒

中國有句古語：「百善孝為先。」在各種美德中，孝敬父母佔第一位。一個人如果連有養育之恩的父母都不孝敬，就很難想像他會善待苦難眾生。所以佛家特別重視孝道，甚至將之看成是眾戒之首，正如《梵網經》云：「孝順父母師僧三寶，孝順至道之法，孝名為戒，亦名制止。」

Śākyamuni's Filial piety

Our compassionate parents have indeed suffered to labor hard for our care, carrying us to term for ten lunar months and through three years of nursing, and endless diaper changes to bring us up. They swallow the bitter and give us sweetness.

— An Exhortation to Resolve Upon Bodhi

When the Buddha was a prince, King Śuddhodana hoped that he would be the leader of the Śākya clan and the king of Kapilavastu. Thus, he was always against the prince's wish for spiritual cultivation. The prince had to secretly leave the palace to achieve his wish of renouncing the secular life.

Even though the prince left his father, his aunt, his wife, and his son, he never forgot them. And he never became estranged from his father because of their differences in thoughts. Shortly after the Buddha's enlightenment, he fulfilled his initial promise and returned to Kapilavastu to share the supreme truths he had realized with his family, the Śākya clan, and the nationals. At this time, the king not only fully accepted the Buddha but also felt proud of him and comforted to see him achieve enlightenment and spread the right Dharma to all sentient beings.

When the king was seriously ill, the Buddha was already the great teacher of all living things. Yet, he returned with his disciples to meet his father for the last time. He waited upon his father till his death before carrying his coffin to the cremation ground. Is this not an excellent example the Buddha had set for us on how to treat our family members, a demonstration on the mutual understanding between a benevolent father and a filial son?

Basics of Buddhism:

• Filial piety as a precept

There is an old saying in China which goes, "Of all virtues, filial piety is the most important." In all kinds of virtues, being filial to one's parents stands in the first place. If a person is not even filial to his parents, it is hard to imagine that he will treat the suffering living beings well. Therefore, Buddhism pays special attention to filial piety and even regards it as the first of all rules of discipline. As the Bodhisattva Precepts of the Brahmājala Sutra states, "The Buddha set forth the Bodhisattva prātimokṣa out official compliance towards his parents, his masters among the Sangha, and the Triple Jewels. Filial compliance is a Dharma of this ultimate way. Piety is known as Precepts. It is also called restraint and stopping."

以怨止怨，終無止息；
以慈止怨，古仙人道。

——《法句經》

佛陀在菩提樹下證得的圓滿覺悟，體現在他見地上的大智慧與心地上的大慈悲。佛陀以他的大智慧開示人天眾生，而眾生亦同時被佛陀的大慈悲所感懾。

提婆達多是佛陀的堂兄，亦是他的弟子。因為妒忌佛陀的成就，提婆達多曾三番設計謀害佛陀，好讓自己成為僧團之首。

他遣殺手到山上刺殺佛陀，只是殺手倒被佛陀感化，慚愧而逃；他第二次又於佛陀慣常行走的山路，安排人推下巨石，以期壓死佛陀，但佛陀有神助，閃身躲開，只傷了一隻腳趾；第三次佛陀在鬧市中的行走，被灌醉了的狂象來踐踏佛陀，但是醉象反被他慈悲的目光感懾，千鈞一髮之際，在佛陀跟前跪下，令圍觀的人莫不驚歎。

提婆達多知道自己敵不過佛陀的慈悲，後來請求佛陀寬恕，而佛陀則再次展現他的慈悲，不但沒有責怪提婆達多，更讓他知道他亦終有一天成佛。

- 佛陀已成就圓滿佛果，是否還會受報？有些經典記載佛陀頭痛、身體不舒服，也有些經典說，佛陀不受業果。究竟怎麼理解這些問題呢？

  在《大智度論》中，記載着佛陀一生中所受十難之因緣，比如佛陀頭疼、木槍刺腳等。而《妙法蓮華經》則說佛陀感受業果之說是不了義的，這只是佛陀在眾生面前的一種示現，是為了告訴我們因果不虛。

  事實上，佛陀在無量劫中，已圓滿福慧二種資糧，摧毀了一切煩惱習氣。如同種子被燒死，不會再發芽。佛陀已超離輪迴、超離因果，超越一切自然規律的束縛。我們凡夫的思維，無法想像和理解佛陀的境界。

Unrivalled Compassion

Hatred is never appeased by hatred in this world.

By compassion alone is hatred appeased. This is the path of ancient Buddhas.

— The Dhammapada

The perfect enlightenment the Buddha attained under the Bodhi tree is best manifested in his great wisdom and compassion. The Buddha used his great wisdom to guide sentient beings in the human and heavenly realms, and sentient beings were also moved by his great compassion.

Devadatta is a cousin and a disciple of the Buddha. Because of his jealousy of the Buddha's achievements, Devadatta planned three times to murder the Buddha, in order that he himself could become the head of the Sangha.

For the first time, he sent a killer to the mountain to assassinate the Buddha, but the killer was moved by the Buddha and fled out of shame.

For the second time, he arranged for a killer to push a huge rock down to the mountain road often used by the Buddha, hoping to crush the Buddha to his death, but the Buddha escaped providentially with only one toe hurt. For the third time, when the Buddha was walking downtown, a drunken elephant was released to charge at him. However, moved by the compassionate eyes of the Buddha, the elephant suddenly stopped at the moment of imminent peril and knelt down before him. Everyone at the scene was very surprised.

Devadatta knew that he could not rival the Buddha's compassion, so he asked for the Buddha's forgiveness. The Buddha once again showed his compassion. He did not blame Devadatta. Instead, he told Devadatta that one day he would also achieve Buddhahood.

Basics of Buddhism:

- **Having attained perfect Buddhahood, would the Buddha still suffer retributions? Some scriptures record that the Buddha had experienced headaches or physical discomforts, and some state that the Buddha would not experience the effect of karma. How should these instances be understood?**

The Treatise on the Perfection of Great Wisdom records the ten sufferings the Buddha experienced in his life, such as headaches, the injury to his foot from a wooden spear, and so on. However, the Lotus Sutra asserts that the explanation of the sufferings experienced by the Buddha being his karmic retributions is not the complete truth; for the Buddha was just demonstrating in front of sentient beings to show them the existence of the law of cause and effect.

In fact, in immeasurable kalpas, the Buddha had already accumulated the two resources of merit and wisdom through annihilation of all afflictions and habitual tendencies. For the Buddha, the afflictions and habitual tendencies were like seeds that had been burned and will never germinate. The Buddha was already freed from samsara, cause and effect, and all the bondages of the natural laws. With our ordinary human mind, it is impossible for us to imagine and understand the state of the Buddha.

境隨心轉

若能轉物即如來，春至山花處處開；
自有一雙慈悲手，抹得人心一樣平。

—— 白雲守端

　　據《佛說四十二章經》記載，佛陀在世時，曾遇到一個對他十分
妒忌的人。有一天，此人見到佛陀，即以惡言穢語辱罵佛陀，但佛陀卻
沒有動氣，更沒有用同樣的惡言穢語跟此人相罵。

　　佛陀只淡然說道：「請問當你給別人送禮物時，如果對方不願接納，
你會如何？」那人即回答說：「我當然會收回禮物。」佛陀便微笑着說道：
「剛才你給我送的那份厚禮，我是不會接受的，請你帶回自用吧！」

　　佛陀這樣的回答，不但避免了一場對罵，自己心裏不惱，更讓對方大
感沒趣，好使他反思自己惡言謾罵的意義何在。面對本應惱人的情況時，
只要換個心態看待、轉個角度應對，或許我們的日子也會過得快活一些！

❀ ［佛教小知識］

• 降伏其心

　　曾經有一位哲人做過一個實驗：他問兩個男人，如果有人出一百元
買你們的愛妻，你們是否願意，兩人都搖頭，他又問道：如果出一百萬

呢？其中一個點點頭，他繼續問道，一百億呢？結果另一個人也點了頭。

一百元的價格上，兩個男人都是道德的，面對一百萬時一個男人走向了不道德，而面對一百億時另一個也下了水。是不是接受一百億的男人比接受一百萬的男人更道德些？我不敢肯定，但有一點可以肯定，前者比後者經得起誘惑一些，他抗誘惑的臨界點更高。正如英國大哲學家羅素說：「人之所以有道德，是因為受的誘惑太少。」

我不敢苟同羅大哲人的觀點，因為在如今這個五光十色的人類社會中，權力，金錢，美色等等如同一把把利劍高懸於我們的頭上，自始至終伴隨着我們走完人生的路程。面對如此眾多的誘惑，《金剛經》教導我們如何降伏其心，「是故，須菩提！諸菩薩、摩訶薩應如是生清淨心，不應住色生心，不應住聲、香、味、觸、法生心，應無所住而生其心。」

至此，我們終於有了答案：當心與色、聲、香、味、觸、法六相接觸時，應無所住而生其心，心則不會被外境所污染，清淨心自然生起，當下就是莊嚴的淨土，不必他求。

Transforming Circumstances through Transformation of Mind

If capable of turning matters around, then Tathagata is attained;

As spring arrives mountain flowers are blooming everywhere,

Naturally having a pair of compassionate hands

To smooth out all human minds to the same evenness.

— Shou Duan of Baiyun Monastery

As the Sutra of Forty-Two Chapters records, when the Buddha was in this secular world, he met a man who was very jealous of him. One day, when the person saw the Buddha, he cursed him with evil words, but the Buddha did not get angry, nor did he use similar words to retort.

The Buddha just said calmly, "When you give someone a gift, but he is unwilling to accept it, what would you do?" The man replied, "Of course I will take it back." The Buddha continued with a smile, "You just brought me a gift that I will not accept. Please take it back!"

The Buddha's answer not only avoided a confrontation without feeling annoyed, but also made the other person feel snubbed. This would make that person reflect upon himself and realize that there was no point in cursing others. When facing annoying situations, a change in our attitude and perspective may make us less unhappy!

Basics of Buddhism:

• **Taming the mind**

There was once a philosopher who did an experiment. He

asked two men if they would accept an offer of one hundred yuan to buy their beloved wives. Both of them shook their heads. He asked them again with an offer of one million, and one of them nodded. He continued to ask until the offer reached ten billion, at which point the other person nodded too.

At the temptation of one hundred yuan, the two men remained moral. When the price was one million, one of them went into immorality. When offered ten billion, the other one also fell. Is the man succumbing to ten billion more moral than the man to one million? I am not sure, but one thing is certain. The former can resist a greater temptation than the other, and he had a higher threshold of falling into immorality. The great British philosopher Russell said, "The reason why people have morality is because they are rarely tempted."

I cannot agree with Russell. In today's dazzling human society, power, money, beauties, and so on are like swords hanging above our heads, accompanying us in the journey of life from beginning to end. The Diamond Sutra teaches us how to tame our minds: "Therefore, Subhuti, fearless bodhisattvas should thus give birth to a thought that is not attached and not give birth to a thought attached to anything. They should not give birth to a thought attached to a sight. Nor should they give birth to a thought attached to a sound, a smell, a taste, a touch, or a dharma."

At this point, we finally have the answer: When the mind gets in contact with a sound, an odor, a taste, a touch, or a dharma, we should not give birth to a thought attached to anything. When the mind is not polluted by the external environment, a thought that is not attached will naturally arise. Accordingly, the here and now becomes the pure land; we don't need to seek from the outside.

得大自在

> 大海之水可飲盡，剎那心念可數知，
> 虛空可量風可繫，無能說盡佛境界。

—— 《華嚴經》

出生於印度迦毗羅衛國的悉達多太子，因為發願為眾生尋找脫苦之道，毅然出家，經過六年苦修，終在菩提樹下證得圓滿覺悟，成為了佛陀，其後說法四十九年，遍地弘揚正法、度化眾生。在他八十歲那年的二月十五日，於拘尸那迦城娑羅雙樹間寂然入滅，得大自在。

他不僅為人天眾生開示了萬法的實相、解脫生命種種苦惱的法門，還為我們帶來了甚麼啟示？悉達多對眾生滿懷悲憫，繼而生起了無私的抱負，甘願舍去太子王位、榮華富貴，再下來又為了成就眾生悟道，不惜過着奔波勞頓、刻苦清淡的遊化生涯，直到生命的最後一刻為止。或許要達到真正的自在，我們此生也要像佛陀為法忘軀一般，首先放下個人的私利，發心終此一生，為大眾的利益奉獻！

[佛教小知識]

• 人格的圓滿 —— 得大自在

　　人們常常把「涅槃」看成是死亡的代名詞，其實涅槃的本意不是生命的終結，而是貪瞋癡等不健康思維的「死亡」，帶來的是清淨、自在的人生，所以稱為得大自在，標誌着人格修養的最高境界 —— 人格的圓滿。

Attaining the State of Being Totally Carefree and at Ease

Water in a great ocean can still be exhausted by drinking,

Thoughts within a split second can still be counted,

Empty sky can still be measured, and winds tied down,

And yet it is impossible to describe exhaustively the spheres of Buddhas.

— The Avataṃsaka Sutra

Prince Siddhārtha was born in Kapilavastu, India. Because he aspired to find a way out of suffering for all living beings, he left the royal court and his family. After six years of ascetic practice, he was finally enlightened under the Bodhi tree and became a Buddha. After that, he expounded the Dharma for forty-nine years to promote the True Dharma and to enlighten all living beings. On the Fifteenth day of the Second Month in his eightieth year, he entered into Nirvana and obtained great freedom in the twin Sala trees in Kuśinagara city.

The Buddha revealed the true reality of all phenomena for sentient beings of the human and heavenly realms and taught various Dharma gates to help release all kinds of distress in life. What other insights did he bring us? Out of compassion for all sentient beings, Prince Siddhārtha developed the selfless ambitions to give up the royal throne, glory, and wealth. Then,

for helping sentient beings get enlightened to the Way, he willingly lived the hard and simple life of a mendicant, teaching people until the last moment of his life. From this we know that in order to achieve real freedom, we should first let go of our personal interests and then resolve to serve for the interests of all living beings for the rest of our life, as the Buddha did.

Basics of Buddhism:

• The perfection of personality is to obtain great freedom

People often consider "Nirvana" as a synonym of "death." In fact, the original meaning of "Nirvana" is not the end of life, but the "death" of unhealthy thinking such as craving, aversion, and ignorance, which would bring about a pure and free life. That is why we call it the attainment of great freedom. It marks the highest state of personality cultivation—the perfection of personality.

正法久住

Part two:

The Right Dharma Abides Permanently

此佛大威德，離欲得寂靜；

釋迦牟尼佛，皆悉供養來。

—— 佛陀

在上古時期，有一位古佛誕生，身體被吉祥的光芒籠罩着，就好像夜晚帶給人光明的燃燈一樣，於是就被稱作燃燈太子。成年的燃燈太子離開了享樂的宮廷生活，出家修行，證得佛果，號燃燈如來。

一天，燃燈佛被燈照大王請到他的都城說法。有一個叫善慧的隱士聽說此事，歡喜不已，立刻跑去想用鮮花去供養燃燈佛，可是這天全城的花都被大王買去供佛了。這時，他遠遠望到一個青衣的王室女子提着一隻隱約露出一瓣蓮花的花瓶。善慧忙追上去並願意用身上所有的五百文錢向這位青衣女子買她的七支蓮花。

燃燈如來經過此處，善慧將七支蓮花散於佛前，這些花卻止於空中並不落地，諸天龍等都來圍繞讚歎。燃燈佛走到善慧前，說：「善哉！善哉！善男子，你在未來一定會成為佛陀的！那時你的名號就是釋迦牟尼佛！」

• 授記

　　授記即預言成佛。被授記者，無論中間經歷怎樣輪迴，終能在一段不長的時間裏成佛。

　　一般來説只有佛有資格預言別人成佛。釋迦牟尼佛是受燃燈佛授記的，當時燃燈佛説：「汝於來世當得作佛，號釋迦牟尼。」釋迦牟尼也為許多人授記過，比如地藏菩薩。授記有四種：

1. 未發心授記。佛推察眾生素質，為了使未發菩提心者發心，而為他授記。

2. 共發心授記。有菩薩與大眾一起發心學佛，佛推察後，為這一群人一起授記。

3. 祕密授記。有人修行精進，佛欲為他授記，但怕授記後彼人驕傲懈怠，怕不授記時，他周圍的人對他起懷疑心，於是祕密授記，使周圍的人知道，他自己不知道。

4. 標準授記。因緣成熟時，佛在大眾面前公開為菩薩授記，預言其成佛（如釋迦牟尼為彌勒、地藏等授記）。

Ancient Buddha Dīpaṃkara

This Buddha is of awe-inspiring virtue,

In the state of stillness and free from desires;

Śākyamuni Buddha offered all he had to him.

— The Buddha

In ancient times, one of the Buddhas of the Past was born. His body was surrounded by auspicious light, like lamps that lightened up the night. Therefore, he was called the "Crown Prince of Dīpaṃkara" ("Maker of Light"). When he grew up, the Crown Prince of Dīpaṃkara left his palace life of pleasure and practiced austerities. When he attained Buddhahood, he was called Tathāgata of Dīpaṃkara.

One day, Dīpaṃkara Buddha was invited by a king to preach the Dharma in his royal capital. Upon hearing the news, an ascetic called Sumedha was overjoyed. In the hope of venerating Dīpaṃkara Buddha with fresh flowers, he immediately ran out, only to find all the flowers around the city had been bought by the king as his own offerings to the Buddha. At that time, Sumedha saw a royal lady in green in a distance. She was carrying a vase, from which a petal of lotus flowers was revealed. Sumedha rushed to her and expressed his willingness to purchase from her seven lotus flowers with all the five hundred coins he had.

When Dīpaṃkara Buddha was passing by, Sumedha tossed the seven lotus flowers before the Buddha. However, the flowers did not fall on the ground but floated in air. All the devas appeared surrounding and praising the scene. Dīpaṃkara Buddha walked up to Sumedha and said, "Good! Good! Good man, you will definitely become a Buddha in the future, and you will be called Śākyamuni Buddha!"

❋ Basics of Buddhism:

• Vyākaraṇa

Vyākaraṇa refers to the prediction of Buddhahood. Those who have received a vyākaraṇa will eventually realize Buddhahood in the near future, no matter what kind of samsara they have experienced.

Generally speaking, only a Buddha is entitled to make such predictions. Śākyamuni Buddha received vyākaraṇa from Dīpaṃkara Buddha, who had stated, "You will achieve Buddhahood in the next life, and your name shall be Śākyamuni." Śākyamuni Buddha also granted vyākaraṇa for many others, and one example was for Bodhisattva Kṣitigarbha. There are four types of vyākaraṇa:

Vyākaraṇa for those who have not yet initiated Bodhicitta. Buddhas observe the qualities of all sentient beings and grant assurances of Buddhahood in order to encourage those who have not initiated Bodhicitta to do so.

Vyākaraṇa for collective initiation of Bodhicitta. When Buddhas observe that bodhisattvas and people initiate Bodhicitta and study the Dharma together, Buddhas would grant vyākaraṇa for the whole assembly.

Secret vyākaraṇa. Suppose someone practices diligently, and a Buddha intends to predict his enlightenment. However, the Buddha worries that if he did, this person would become arrogant and lazy; if he did not, people around this person would doubt this person. Therefore, the Buddha assures people around this person of his eventual Buddhahood without this person himself knowing it.

Standard vyākaraṇa. When the causes and conditions are ripe, Buddhas would predict the attainment of Buddhahood of bodhisattvas in public, as in the case of Śākyamuni Buddha granting vyākaraṇa for Maitreya and Kṣitigarbha.

釋迦應化

> 汝當自努力！如來唯說者。
> 隨禪定行者，解脫魔繫縛。
>
> ——《法句經》

釋迦牟尼佛是娑婆世界的教主，經歷了無數阿僧祇劫勤苦不懈的修行而於此世證得了無上正等正覺，功德圓滿，得大自在。釋迦牟尼佛的重要事跡一般被概括為八相成道：兜率降世、白象入胎、住胎說法、右脅誕生、逾城出家、樹下成道、初轉法輪、雙林入滅。

事實上，佛陀的法身清淨不滅，然而世尊大慈大悲，為了度化無量眾生而示現生滅、隨機權教，也就是應化身的釋迦牟尼佛。也就是說，佛陀感於眾生的苦惱，憐憫輪迴中的群迷，故而應現於世，化為釋迦剎帝利種，以法身垂跡八相，以八相顯明法身，二者相融無礙，俱皆不可思議。

釋迦的應化教導人們：「沒有天生的釋迦，也沒有自然的彌勒。」欲成賢作聖，需仰賴行者精進不懈、循序積累的修行。

❀ ［佛教小知識］

• **以法為師**

在佛陀即將入滅之前，阿難陀非常難過，並請問佛陀在世尊入滅後誰

來領導僧團，僧團應當依誰來作為歸依，並請示佛陀給與最後的開示。佛陀充滿了慈悲與人情，他講的一段話非常動人。佛陀對阿難陀講道：

「阿難啊！僧團對我還有甚麼希求呢？我已經將法（真理）不分顯密地全都教給了你們，關於真理，如來無隱祕。當然，如果有人認為他應當領導僧團，僧團應當依靠他，他自應留下遺教。可是如來並沒有這種想法，為甚麼他應當留下教誨呢？

我現在已經年邁，阿難！我已八旬，像用舊的車子，須經修理方能繼續使用，同樣地，如來色身須經修理才能繼續存活下去。

阿難啊！你們應當依自己而作島嶼，要依靠自己，不依靠他人而作歸依，依法為島嶼，依法為歸依。」（南傳《大般涅槃經》）

這段話的意思很清楚，佛陀教導阿難陀以法為師，依自己為歸依，不要向外求助他人或任何神祇，因為只依靠自力，我們才能達到最終的解脫。

Nirmāṇakāya as Śākyamuni Buddha

It is for you to strive ardently!

Tathāgatas simply point out the way.

Those who practice, absorbed in dhyāna,

From Mara's bonds they'll be freed.

— The Dhammapada

Śākyamuni Buddha is the founder of Buddhism in the Sahā World. After diligent and tireless practice for innumerable asaṃkhyeya-kalpas, he attained supreme perfect enlightenment, achieved all virtues, and realized absolute liberation. Major life events of Śākyamuni Buddha are generally summarized as the "Eight Stages of Buddha's Progress": Birth from Tuṣita Heaven, Dream of the White Elephant, Teaching the Dharma in Womb, Born from the right side of the queen. Renunciation of Palace Life, Enlightenment under the Bodhi Tree, First Turning of the Dharmacakra, and Parinirvāṇa between Two Trees.

In fact, the Dharmakāya (Dharma-body) of the Buddha is pure and never extinguishes. However, out of great compassion, the World-Honored One manifested in the Nirmāṇakāya (body of transformation) of Śākyamuni Buddha, who experienced life and death and used expedient means according to the situation. That is to say that the Buddha manifested himself in our world, born into the Śākya clan of kṣatriya caste, because he responded to the sufferings of all sentient beings and sympathized the deluded ones in the cycle of samsara. The Buddha is manifested through his Dharmakāya in the "Eight Stages of Buddha's Progress," while the "Eight Stages of Buddha's Progress" revealed Dharmakāya. The two are in harmony and mutually unimpeded, which is beyond thought or description.

The manifestation of Śākyamuni teaches us that "there is no Śākyamuni by birth, and there is no Maitreya by default." If one wishes to become a sage, one can only rely on untiring perseverance and cumulative practice in proper order.

❄ Basics of Buddhism:

• Regarding the Dharma as the Teacher

Before the Buddha entered Nirvana, Ānanda, extremely saddened, asked the Buddha who would lead the Sangha when the World-Honored One entered Nirvana and in whom the Sangha should take refuge. He also asked the Buddha to give his last teachings. The Buddha, full of compassion and emotion, expressed something very touching. The Buddha told Ānanda:

"Ānanda, what more does the Sangha expect from me? I have taught you the Dharma completely, exoteric or esoteric. Regarding the truth, the Tathāgata has nothing to hide. If anyone thinks that he should lead the Sangha and the Sangha should rely on him, he should certainly leave some teachings. However, the Tathāgata has no such idea, why should he leave behind his teachings?"

"Now I am old, Ānanda! I am in my eighties. My body is like an old cart, and its use can only be continued after repair. Likewise, the physical body of the Tathāgata can only survive after repair."

"Ānanda! You should be islands for yourselves, take refuge in yourselves, and seek refuge in no one else; with the Dharma as your island, take the Dharma as your refuge." (Mahāparinibbāna Sutta in Pāli Canon)

It is clear from his words above that the Buddha instructed Ānanda to take the Dharma as the teacher and to take refuge in himself, seeking no help from anyone else or any divinities, as only by relying on ourselves can we achieve final liberation.

結集三藏

長行重頌並授記，孤起無問而自說，因緣譬喻及本事，
本生方廣未曾有，論議共成十二部。

—— 十二分教偈

　　世尊入滅之後，個別弟子以為，世尊既然涅槃了，就可以為所欲
為；另外，有些弟子無法準確領會世尊的聖教，把一些不符合正法的知
見說成是佛法，大迦葉有感於此，召集上座比丘聚在一起，把這些年來
聽聞的佛法誦出並確定下來。雨季將至，他們就在王舍城外的七葉窟中
結夏安居。

　　阿難認為自己在佛陀身邊侍奉了這麼久，佛陀的教法聽得最多，
記得最准，準備結集經典。大迦葉卻說：「你還尚未證悟菩提，所以你
不能參加。」阿難十分傷心，決心證道，果然在一夜之間，得阿羅漢
果，回到七葉窟內參與結集。

　　佛法的第一次結集，由大迦葉主持，持戒第一的優波離尊者誦出
律藏，多聞第一的阿難尊者誦出經藏。由此，佛陀聖教妙法得以常住
世間。

• 雨安居

安居又作夏安居、雨安居、坐夏、夏坐、結夏、九旬禁足、結制安居。

在印度，夏季的雨季長達三個月，佛陀乃訂定四月十六日至七月十五日為安居之期，在此期間，出家人禁止外出，聚居一處精進修行，稱為安居。這是雨季期間草木、蟲蟻繁殖最多，恐外出時誤蹈，傷害生靈，而遭世人譏嫌，因此禁止外出。

安居一般在夏季舉行，也有於十月十六日至次年元月十五日舉行者，稱為結冬安居。安居的地點不一定，小屋、樹下、山窟、聚落等處皆可，不過，不可在危險、沒有救護的地方安居。

安居的首日，稱為結夏，圓滿結束之日稱為解夏、過夏。安居旨在嚴禁無故外出，以防離心散亂，因此是一種自修自度的觀照功夫，是養深積厚，自我沉潛的修行。

Compilation of the Tripiṭaka

Sūtra, geya, and vyākaraṇa; gāthā, udāna; nidāna, avadāna, itivṛttaka; jātaka, vaipulya, and adbhuta-dharma; along with upadeśa, there are altogether twelve.

— The Gāthā of Twelve Divisions of Sūtras

After the Buddha's passing into Parinirvāṇa, some disciples thought that since the Buddha had entered Nirvana, they could do as they pleased; others were unable to understand accurately the Buddha's teachings, mistaking heretic views as the Dharma. Thus, Mahākāśyapa convened elderly bhikṣus to recite and codify the Dharma they had received over the years. As the monsoon season was approaching, they stayed in Saptaparni Cave outside the city of Rājagṛha for rains retreat.

Having been a longtime personal attendant of the Buddha, Ānanda thought that he was the one who heard most of the discourses of the Buddha and remembered them most accurately. When he was getting ready for the council, Mahākāśyapa said, "You are not entitled to participate, because you have not attained enlightenment." Ānanda was very disappointed but determined to reach realization of the Way. Fortuitously, he attained the state of an arhat and returned to the council in Saptaparni Cave.

The first Buddhist Council was presided over by Mahākāśyapa. Senior monk Upāli recited Vinaya Piṭaka, while the most-informed Ānanda recited Sūtra Piṭaka. This is how the sacred teachings and wonderful Dharma of the Buddha were perpetuated in this world.

- **Raining Retreat**

Varṣa refers to Summer Retreat (xia anju), Raining Retreat (yu anju), and is also called zuoxia, xiazuo, jiexia, jiuxun jinzu, jiezhi anju in Chinese.

In India, the monsoon season in summer lasts for three months. The Buddha established the varṣa between the sixteenth day of the fourth month and the fifteenth day of the seventh month. During this period, monastics are not allowed to travel but remain in one place for practice, because with particularly lush vegetation and flourishing insects during this period, they can avoid unintentionally harming living beings and suffer from people's contempt.

Varṣa is normally organized in the summer. Sometimes, it is organized during the winter. Called Winter Retreat, it lasts from the sixteenth day of the tenth month to the fifteenth day of the first month in the following year. Locations of varṣa vary, such as huts, under the trees, caves, and villages. Nevertheless, places of danger and with no shelter should be prohibited.

The first day of the varṣa is called jiexia ("forming the summer") in Chinese; the last day of completion is called jiexia ("releasing the summer") or guoxia ("passing the summer"). Varṣa prohibits travel without a purpose, so as to help monastics to focus on self-cultivation and inner reflection.

雞足入定

覺樹枯榮幾度更，靈山寂寂待重興；
此來不用傷遲暮，佛法弘揚本在僧。

—— 太虛法師

　　三藏結集結束，眾比丘從七葉窟中出來，大迦葉心想：「三藏結集
終於結束，佛、法、僧可以憑此久住於世，眾生也可依此而得解脫。我
的使命已經完成，如今可以追隨如來善逝，入於涅槃了！」

　　於是，大迦葉一手持缽一手執杖，騰飛於空中，放大光明。接着
從一個身體突然化成九個身體，各個身體用金光連成一個法輪，快速旋
轉，顏色變化。最後合併成一個迦葉，下降到地面。眾人也同時趕來，
阿難代表大眾請求迦葉尊者留住人間：「摩訶迦葉尊者，請你為眾生利
益，不要入無餘涅槃！」大迦葉合十言：「那麼，願我肉身不壞！待彌
勒成佛之時，我將憑此身骨返回世間度化眾生！」雙手合十，隱入石壁
之內，石壁就像水面波動了一下。然後有些弟子繞過阿難衝上去摸，石
壁已經堅硬。阿難便說：「善哉！善哉！」

• **頭陀第一摩訶迦葉尊者**

　　摩訶迦葉人格清廉，深受佛陀信賴，於佛弟子中曾受佛陀分與半座。佛陀入滅後，成為教團之統率者，於王舍城召集第一次經典結集。直至阿難為法之繼承者，始入雞足山入定，以待彌勒出世，方行涅槃。禪宗以其為佛弟子中修無執着行之第一人，特尊為頭陀第一，又以「拈花微笑」之故事，成為禪宗初祖，傳承不絕。此外，過去七佛之第六佛亦稱迦葉佛。佛弟子中，優樓頻羅迦葉、伽耶迦葉等皆有迦葉之稱。佛陀入滅後三百年之小乘飲光部之祖亦與迦葉同名。

Mahākāśyapa Entering Samadhi at Mount Jizu

The Bodhi Tree withers and flourishes again and again,
The Vulture Peak remains silent waiting to be revived;
One should never be saddened by the end of prime,
As propagation of the Dharma relies on the Sangha.

— Tai Xu

After the Council of Tripiṭaka, all bhikṣus came out of Saptaparni Cave. Mahākāśyapa thought to himself, "The Council of Tripiṭaka has finally concluded. The Buddha, the Dharma, and the Sangha will abide permanently, so that all sentient beings can be liberated. Since my mission has been completed, I shall follow Tathāgata and depart well by entering Nirvana."

Therefore, holding an alms bowl in one hand and a staff in the other hand, Mahākāśyapa flew up swiftly and radiated abundant light. His body immediately transformed into nine bodies, forming a dharmachakra of golden light. It turned quickly and changed colors. Eventually, they merged into Kāśyapa and descended onto the ground. Meanwhile, the congregation arrived in a hurry. As their representative, Ānanda pled with Venerable Kāśyapa to stay in this world, "Venerable Mahākāśyapa, for the benefit of all sentient beings, please do not enter Nirvana without remainder." Mahākāśyapa joined palms, saying, "May my physical body never decay! When Maitreya achieves Buddhahood, I will return to this world in this body and save all sentient beings." Then he disappeared into the cliff, the surface of which moved for a while like rippled water. However, when some disciples went around Ānanda and touched the cliff, it felt solid. Ānanda said, "Good! Good!"

Basics of Buddhism:

- **Foremost in ascetic practices: the revered Mahākāśyapa**

Mahākāśyapa is honest and upright, deeply trusted by the Buddha. Among all the disciples, the Buddha once shared his seat with him. After the Buddha entered Nirvana, Mahākāśyapa became the leader of the Sangha and convened the First Buddhist Council in Rājagṛha. He did not enter Nirvana until Ānanda became his Dharma successor. After that he meditated at Mount Jizu waiting for the birth of Maitreya. In Chan Buddhism, being the most accomplished one in the practice of non-attachment, Mahākāśyapa was venerated as the foremost disciple in ascetic practices. According to the allusion where he held up a flower and smiled, Mahākāśyapa became the first patriarch of Chan Buddhism, which has lasted up to this day. Among the Seven Buddhas of the Past, the sixth is Kāśyapa Buddha. Moreover, Buddha's disciples Uruvilvā-kāśyapa and Gayā-kāśyapa both bear the Kāśyapa name. Three hundred years after Buddha's Parinirvāṇa, Kāśyapīya School emerged within the Hinayana traditions, and their patriarch also bore the same name.

育王造塔

大聖孔雀王，知法大饒益；

處處廣起塔，莊嚴閻浮提。

——《阿育王經》

公元前三世紀，孔雀王朝在阿育王的統治下迅速擴張了自己的疆域。但是，戰亂頻繁，生靈塗炭，阿育王感到自己罪孽深重。他深表懺悔，願造八萬四千寶塔，將佛舍利置之於內，分於四方，令人民廣為供養，正法久住，饒益有情。

阿育王所造的八萬四千佛塔，有十九座在中國。在阿育王的支持下，長老目犍連子帝須派遣高僧遠播佛法：東至金地（緬甸），南入錫蘭（斯里蘭卡），西赴臾那（波斯大夏），北越雪山（巴基斯坦），促進了佛教進一步發展為世界性的宗教。

- **阿育王**

　　阿育王（Asoka），（公元前 273－前 232 年在位）佛教護法明王。古代印度摩揭陀國孔雀王朝的第三代國王，早年好戰殺戮，統一了除南亞次大陸的整個印度，晚年篤信佛教，放下屠刀，又被稱為「無憂王」。阿育王在全國各地興建佛教建築，據説總共興建了八萬四千座奉祀佛骨的佛舍利塔。為了消除佛教不同教派的爭議，為佛教在印度的發展做出了巨大的貢獻。阿育王邀請著名高僧目犍連子帝須長老召集一千比丘，在華氏城舉行大結集（此為佛教史上第三次大結集），驅除了外道，整理了經典，並編撰了《論事》。阿育王的知名度在印度帝王中是無與倫比的，他對歷史的影響同樣也可居印度帝王之首。

Emperor Aśoka Building Stupas

Great Sage of Maurya understood the Dharma and benefitted the masses;

He erected stupas everywhere to adorn Jambudvīpa (the terrestrial world).

— Tales of the King Aśoka

　　In the 3rd century BCE, under the rule of King Aśoka, the Mauryan dynasty rapidly expanded its territories. However, due to frequent warfare, people were plunging into the abyss of misery, which moved King Aśoka into great remorse. To repent of his grave wrongdoings, King Aśoka vowed to construct 84,000 stupas, each containing the relics of the Buddha. They were distributed to the four directions for people to worship, so that the Right Dharma abode permanently and benefitted all sentient beings.

Among the 84,000 stupas, nineteen of them are in China. Under the patronage of King Aśoka, senior monk Moggaliputta-Tissa sent eminent monks to spread the Dharma. They reached Suvarṇabhūmi (present-day Myanmar) in the east, Ceylon (present-day Sri Lanka) in the south, Yona (Persian Bactria) in the west, beyond snowy mountains (Pakistan) in the north, making Buddhism further develop into an international religion.

Basics of Buddhism:

• King Aśoka

King Aśoka was the third-generation emperor of the Mauryan dynasty in Magadha. In his earlier years, he waged many destructive wars and conquered almost the whole Indian subcontinent. In his later years, he found deep faith in Buddhism and put down his weapons. Praised as "the King with No Grief," King Aśoka constructed Buddhist architecture around the country, which included 84,000 stupas holding the Buddha's relics. He also helped to resolve disputes among different sects, making great contributions to the development of Buddhism in India. He invited eminent monk Moggaliputta-Tissa and 1000 bhikṣus to organize a great assembly at Pāṭaliputra, known as the "Third Buddhist Council" in Buddhist history. They expelled the heretics, arranged the scriptures, and compiled the Kathāvatthu. The fame of Aśoka is incomparable among all the emperors of India; he is also foremost in terms of his influence on history.

龍樹造論

密富禪貧方便淨，唯識耐煩嘉祥空，
傳統華嚴修身律，義理組織天台宗。

—— 八宗偈

公元二世紀，龍樹已經閱盡三藏，聽說在雪山有世間不共的佛經，特地前去求取，這就是般若波羅蜜多大乘經。但若想究竟通利這一甚深的大乘法門，還需要進一步的修行體證。後來，在龍王的幫助下，龍樹又去龍宮看了眾多的大乘經，修行更加勇猛精進。

自此，龍樹大弘佛法、摧伏外道。為宣明大乘勝義，他撰寫了十萬頌的《大智度論》以及《十住毗婆沙論》，使得大乘佛教大行於天竺；他還寫作有《中論》五百偈及其注釋《無畏論》十萬偈，同時總結《中論》要義而著《十二門論》，從而成為大乘中觀學派的創始人，亦被尊為東土八宗之共祖。後人為了讚揚龍樹推廣大乘佛教的功德，尊稱他為龍樹菩薩。龍樹之後，他的學生提婆又繼承了龍樹的學風，撰寫了《百論》、《百字論》等中觀論著。

• **中觀**

　　中觀派發揮了大乘初期《大般若經》中空的思想。認為世界上的一切事物以及人們的認識甚至包括佛法在內都是一種相對的、依存的關係（因緣、緣會），一種假借的概念或名相（假名），它們本身沒有不變的實體或自性（無自性）。所謂「眾因緣生法，我說即是空，亦為是假名，亦是中道義」，在他們看來，只有排除了各種因緣關係，破除了執着名相的邊見，才能證悟最高的真理——空或中道。中觀派在破除人們執着空有的兩邊中提出了「八不」的學說。所謂八不，即不生不滅（從實體方面看）、不常不斷（從運動方面看）、不一不異（從空間方面看）、不來不去（從時間方面看）。在他們看來，生滅、常斷、來去、一異是一切存在的基本範疇，也是人們認識之所以成立的根據。如果否定了這四對範疇，否定了主觀認識和客觀世界，從而就顯示了空性真理。他們還提出兩種真理說（二諦），認為在最高真理（真諦）空之外，還應承認相對真理（俗諦），對修持佛法的人應該說真諦，說空性真理，對覆蓋無明（無知）的凡夫，應該說俗諦，即承認世界和眾生的存在。

Nāgārjuna Composing Śāstras

Esoteric School of Wealth, Chan of Impoverishment, and Pure Land of Convenience; Yogācāra of Patience and Madhyamaka of Emptiness; Huayan of Tradition and Vinaya of Discipline; Tiantai of Doctrines and Organization.

— The Gāthā of the Eight Schools

In the 2nd century, having read through the Tripiṭaka, Nāgārjuna went on a search for extremely rare Buddhist sutras in the Himalayas, which were Prajñāpāramitā sutras of Mahayana Buddhism. However, to completely understand the teaching of Mahayana, it requires further practice. With the help of the king of nāgas, Nāgārjuna was able to read more Mahayana sutras at the palace and made bold progress in his practice.

Since then, Nāgārjuna was dedicated to propagating the Dharma and subduing heresies. To promote and illuminate the superlative teachings of Mahayana, he compiled Mahāprajñāpāramitā-śāstra (Great Treatise on the Perfection of Wisdom) that consists of 100,000 gāthās, and Daśabhūmika-vibhāṣā-śāstra (The Commentary to the Ten Stages Sutra), popularising Mahayana Buddhism in ancient India. He also wrote Mūlamādhyamikakārikā (Fundamental Verses on the Middle Way) with 500 gāthās, annotated Akutobhayā with 100,000 gāthās, and summarised Mūlamādhyamikakārikā into Dvādaśanikāya Śāstra. Therefore, he is regarded as the founder of the Madhyamaka School of Mahayana Buddhism as well as a patriarch of all the eight Schools of East Asian Buddhism. To praise him for his merit of spreading Mahayana Buddhism, he is venerated as Bodhisattva Nāgārjuna by later generations. After Nāgārjuna, his disciple Āryadeva assumed his mantle and compiled Madhyamaka classics such as Śataśāstra and Aksarasataka.

Basics of Buddhism:

• The Madhyamaka School

The Madhyamaka School is built on the idea of emptiness (śūnyatā) in the Mahāprajñāpāramitā Sūtra that emerged in the early stage of Mahayana tradition. According to Madhyamaka thought, all things and human perceptions, even including the Dharma, are in a relation of relativity and dependent origination (causes and conditions or conjunction of conditions). As borrowed concepts as well as names and appearances (or nominal designations), they do not have substantial essence or intrinsic nature (niḥsvabhāva), as Nāgārjuna said, "We state that all the dependently-arisen phenomena are emptiness. They are mere nominal designations, and it is the truth of the Middle Way". To Madhyamaka thinkers, only by ruling out the chains of causes and conditions and breaking away from extreme views, that is, attachment to names and appearances, can one attain the ultimate truth—Emptiness, or the Middle Way. To get rid of the attachment to both sides of emptiness and existence, the Madhyamaka School puts forward the theory of "Eight Negations", which includes neither arising nor ceasing (from the perspective of substance), neither eternal nor impermanent (from the perspective of movement), neither one nor many (from the perspective of space), and neither coming nor going (from the perspective of time). It holds that arising and ceasing, eternal and impermanent, coming and going, one and many are basic categories for all to be existent; it is also owing to these categories that human cognitions become validated. If the four categories are negated, subjective understanding and objective world are negated, this is how the truth of emptiness is revealed.

The Madhyamaka School also advocates the theory of "Two Truths", which argues that apart from emptiness—the ultimate truth (Absolute Truth), one should recognize the relative truth (Conventional Truth). To those who practice Buddhism, the absolute truth of emptiness should be told; while to the ignorant and ordinary ones, conventional truth should be told, that is, the recognition of the existence of the world and all sentient beings.

無著世親

心如工畫師，能畫諸世間，

五蘊悉從生，無法而不造。

——《華嚴經》

公元四世紀，無著受到賓頭羅的點化，每夜上昇兜率天請彌勒說法，晝間出定，向世間眾生宣說大乘。四個月間，彌勒菩薩為他解說了《華嚴》等大乘深意，並傳授了《瑜伽師地論》等經典。

無著亦根據彌勒菩薩所授的偈頌擴展為《辯中邊論》《大乘莊嚴經論》，還獨立創作了《攝大乘論》等論典，廣明大乘要義，宣揚菩薩精神。同時，無著還勸說胞弟世親學習並弘揚大乘佛法。

世親轉入大乘後，作了數量可觀的大乘論，人稱「千部論主」，其著名的著作包括《百法明門論》《唯識二十論》《唯識三十論頌》等等，系統地發展了大乘的唯識說，鑑於他們對佛法不可估量的貢獻，無著、世親兄弟二人均被尊稱為菩薩。

• 瑜伽宗

　　「瑜伽行派」又名「大乘有宗」，古印度大乘佛教的派別之一，與「中觀宗」相對。公元五世紀中，由無著、世親兩兄弟所立。相傳無著曾受到彌勒菩薩的啟示，誦出《瑜伽師地論》，為教義的根據。無著著有《顯揚聖教論》《攝大乘論》等。世親初習小乘，後隨兄習大乘，著有《唯識三十頌》等。

　　瑜伽宗和中觀宗在否定客觀現實世界方面宗旨是相同的。但瑜伽宗在否定客觀世界的同時，又肯定思維意識（阿賴耶識）的真實存在。主張「實無外境，唯有內識」、「外無內有，事皆唯識」，認為現實世界的一切都是識的幻化。

Asaṅga and Vasubandhu

The mind is like a painter,

Who can depict the whole world;

That gives rise to the five aggregates,

And there is nothing that the mind cannot create.

— The Avataṃsaka Sūtra

In the 4th century CE, Asaṅga, inspired by Piṇḍola Bhāradvāja, visited Tuṣita Heaven every night to receive teachings from Bodhisattva Maitreya. In the daytime, he came out of the meditative state and taught Mahayana

識

大乘莊嚴經論
攝大乘論
辯中邊論

百法明門論
唯識二十論

唯識三十論頌

Buddhism to all sentient beings in the world. Over a period of four months, Bodhisattva Maitreya elucidated for Asaṅga the profound teachings of Mahayana including the Avataṃsaka Sūtra (The Flower Garland Sutra), and taught classics such as Yogācārabhūmiśāstra (Discourse on the Stages of Yogic Practice).

Expanding on the hymns that Bodhisattva Maitreya taught, Asaṅga compiled the Madhyāntavibhaṅgabhāṣya and the Mahāyānasūtralāmkāraśāstra; he also created independently Mahāyānasaṅgraha to expound widely the doctrines of Mahayana and to promote the bodhisattva spirit. Meanwhile, Asaṅga convinced his brother Vasubandhu to study and promote Mahayana Buddhism.

When Vasubandhu was converted to Mahayana, he compiled a considerable number of Mahayana treatises, and thus he was called the "Owner of Thousand Treatises." Among them, famous works include Mahāyāna-śatadharma-prakāśamukha-śāstra (Mahāyāna Hundred Dharmas Introduction Treatise), Vimśatikā vijñapti-mātratā-siddhih (The Twenty Verses on Consciousness Only), and Triṃśikā-vijñaptimātratā (The Thirty Verses on Consciousness-only), which systematically developed the doctrine of vijñaptimātratā in Mahayana Buddhism. Owing to their immeasurable contributions to the Buddhadharma, Asaṅga and Vasubandhu were both venerated as bodhisattvas.

❧ Basics of Buddhism:

• Yogācāra School

The Yogācāra School is one of the Mahayana Buddhist Schools in ancient India, often compared with the Madhyamaka School. It was established in the mid-5th century CE by two brothers Asaṅga and Vasubandhu. It is said that Asaṅga was once enlightened by Bodhisattva Maitreya and recited Yogācārabhūmiśāstra (Discourse on the Stages of Yogic Practice), which became the doctrinal basis of the School. He also wrote Prakaraṇāryavācā-śāstra and Mahāyānasaṅgraha. Vasubandhu first studied the Sarvāstivāda School and later turned to Mahayana following his brother. He wrote works like Triṃśikā-vijñaptimātratā (The Thirty Verses on Consciousness-only).

Both Yogācāra and Madhyamaka Schools deny the existence of a world of external reality. However, apart from that, the Yogācāra School recognizes the existence of consciousness (ālayavijñāna). It advocates that "Reality is not from the external world but only from the internal consciousness," and "It does not exist externally but internally; everything is consciousness only," arguing that all that is in the world of reality is a projection of consciousness.

佛法東傳

信知此土有深緣，聖教三車獨得全。
誓續慧燈無盡際，時輪再轉兩千年。

—— 趙樸初

　　漢明帝夜夢金人，讓眾位大臣解夢，傅毅說：「西域有神人在，稱為浮屠，可以輕易騰空而飛，身體隨意變化，長生不老，又兼有六大神通，其力可撼動天地。陛下夢見神人，必定是因陛下恩澤遠播，神人因此特來護持陛下！」漢明帝十分開心，於是派遣蔡愔、秦景、王遵三人前去西域請佛前來。

　　蔡愔等人到了大月氏，請攝摩騰、竺法蘭來華。他們回到洛陽之後，漢明帝因攝摩騰、竺法蘭不遠萬里前來而隆重接待，並在洛陽城外建立白馬寺供養，攝摩騰於此譯出第一部漢文佛經《四十二章經》。而這裏便是漢地的第一座寺廟 —— 白馬寺，自此佛教開始流行於中土。

• 《四十二章經》

  《四十二章經》由四十二段短小的佛經組成，內容主要是闡述早期佛教（小乘）的基本教義，重點是人生無常和愛欲之弊。認為人的生命非常短促，世界上一切事物都無常變遷，勸人們拋棄世俗欲望，追求出家修道的修行生活。「四十二章」者，一經之別目，以此經分段為義，有四十二段故。「經」者，梵語修多羅，此云契經，凡佛所說真理皆可曰經。經又訓為常，以所說為常法故。此經以四十二段經文，攝佛說一切因果大義，故名四十二章經。

Buddhism Coming to the East

I am convinced that this land has strong karmic connections;

It is the only place that has all Three Vehicles of the Sacred Teachings.

I vow to sustain the light of wisdom for eternity;

May the kālacakra continue to turn for another two thousand years.

— Zhao Puchu

  Emperor Ming of the Han dynasty dreamt of a golden deity. When he asked his officials to interpret that dream, Fu Yi said, "There is a deity in the Western Regions, who is called Buddha. He can fly into the sky easily and transform his physical body at will. He has attained immortality and six supernatural powers. The reason why Your Majesty dreamt of the golden deity is because the

benevolence of Your Majesty has reached far, and the deity is coming to guard Your Majesty." Very pleased, Emperor Ming of Han dispatched Cai Yin, Qin Jing, and Wang Zun to invite the Buddha from the Western Regions.

When the delegation arrived in the Greater Yuezhi, they invited Kaśyapa Mātaṅga and Dharmarakṣa to China. Upon their return to Luoyang, Emperor Ming of Han generously welcomed Kaśyapa Mātaṅga and Dharmarakṣa who had gone through the trouble of travelling for a long distance. The Emperor also built the White Horse Monastery outside the city of Luoyang as an offering. It was at the White Horse Monastery that Kaśyapa Mātaṅga translated the Sutra of Forty-two Chapters, the first Buddhist sutra in Chinese. The White Horse Monastery is the first Buddhist monastery in China, marking the beginning of Buddhist transmission in China.

Basics of Buddhism:

- **The Sutra of Forty-two Chapters**

    The Sutra of Forty-two Chapters consists of forty-two short Buddhist texts, featuring tenets of early Buddhism (Hinayana) with a focus on the impermanence of human life and the evil of desires. It states that human life is very short and everything in the world is changing and impermanent, urging us to abandon worldly desires and pursue the life of a monastic practitioner. "The forty-two chapters" are the list of items in a sutra; the meaning of the sutra is divided into sections, and there are forty-two chapters. "Sutra", sūtra in Sanskrit, denotes "scripture" here. All the words said by the Buddha can be called sutras. Sutras are eternal teachings, on the basis that the Buddha's words are eternal principles. This sutra, with forty-two chapters of texts, explains all main points of cause and effect, and therefore it is named the Sutra of Forty-two Chapters.

羅什譯經

十喻以喻空，空必待此喻。
藉言以會意，意盡無會處。
既得出長羅，住此無所住。
若能映斯照，萬象無來去。

—— 鳩摩羅什

　　南北朝初期，佛教在漢地已有一定的影響，學佛的人也多了起來。但是由於經目繁多，譯名不統一，缺少既通華語又曉佛理的高僧，中國的僧人往往不得不通過格義的方法求助於儒道經典來解釋佛法。

　　鳩摩羅什來到中國後，系統地翻譯出了般若、十住、法華、維摩、無量壽等大乘經；還因中土戒律不完備，僧人出家不夠規範而譯出了全本的十誦律及菩薩戒本等律藏經典；此外還有《成實論》《中論》《百論》《十二門論》等大小乘論典。漢地的中觀學說也因此系統地建立起來。

　　中國佛教自鳩摩羅什以後完全脫離了對儒道的依附，在南北朝時期獨立地發展起來。鳩摩羅什的譯本，文字優雅，格調清朗，為歷朝歷代的僧俗所傳習，直至今日仍然是學佛之人的必修課本。

• 四大譯經家

　　在佛教傳入中國的近兩千年的漫長歲月中，有名字記載的佛教翻譯家有二百餘位，共譯佛教典籍兩千一百餘種、六千餘卷，他們中的傑出代表就是中國佛教史上稱作「四大譯經家」的鳩摩羅什、真諦、玄奘和不空。由於他們突出的貢獻，佛教典籍被系統地譯介到中國，從而推動了佛教在中國的傳播和發展。

　　這四位大翻譯家，其中鳩摩羅什、真諦、不空，是東來弘傳佛法的外國佛學大師。玄奘則是西行求法的中國高僧，他們雖所處的時代不同，經歷不同，但他們都以畢生的精力從事譯經事業，在各自的時代取得了光輝的成就，並在中國的翻譯史上留下了光輝的篇章。

Kumārajīva Translating the Sutras

The ten analogies are to explain emptiness,

Emptiness can only be expounded by these analogies.

To borrow other words is for better understanding of the meaning,

At the end of the meaning, there is no more to be understood.

It is like a vast net,

But there is nowhere to abide.

If one can grasp this illumination,

All phenomena are without coming or going.

— Kumārajīva

At the beginning of the Southern and Northern dynasties, Buddhism had gained considerable influence in China. More and more people started to study Buddhism. However, due to the facts that a large number of sutras were under different translated names, and there was a lack of eminent monks who knew Chinese and understood Buddhism well, Chinese monks had to interpret and categorize Buddhist terminology by relying on Confucian and Daoist classics.

When Kumārajīva came to China, he systematically translated Mahayana sutras including the Prajñāpāramitā Sūtra, the Daśabhūmikasūtra (The Ten Stages Sutra), the Lotus Sūtra, the Vimalakīrti Nirdeśa Sūtra, and the Sukhāvatīvyūhasūtra (The Infinite Life Sutra). Because Buddhist precepts were not complete and monastic codes were not standardized at that time, he also translated Vinaya classics including the Sarvāstivāda-vinaya and the Sutra of the Bodhisattva Precepts, alongside Mahayana and Hinayana treatises, such as Satyasiddhiśāstra (Treatise of Establishing Reality), Mūlamadhyamakakārikā,

Śataśāstra (Hundred Treatise), and Dvādaśanikāya-śāstra (Twelve Gate Treatise). That was how the Madhyamaka School was systematically established in China.

Since the time of Kumārajīva, Chinese Buddhism broke away from its attachment to Confucianism and Daoism and developed independently during the Southern and Northern dynasties. Owing to the elegant wording and clear style, Kumārajīva's translations had been studied and passed on by both monastics and laity throughout dynasties. Up to today, they are still must-read for people who study Buddhism.

❈ Basics of Buddhism:

• Four Great Buddhist Translators

Over the long span of the two thousand years of Buddhist transmission in China, more than two hundred Buddhist translators had their names recorded in history, who translated 2,100 Buddhist classics in over 6,000 volumes in total. The "Four Great Translators of Sutras" are the outstanding representatives in the history of Chinese Buddhism, including Kumārajīva, Paramārtha, Xuan Zang, and Amoghavajra. Thanks to their prominent contributions, Buddhist classics were systematically translated and introduced to China, which facilitated the transmission and development of Buddhism in China.

Among the four translators, Kumārajīva, Paramārtha, and Amoghavajra were foreign masters who travelled to the East to promote Buddhism, while Xuan Zang was an eminent monk from China who searched for the Dharma in the Western Regions. Though they lived in different periods and had different experiences, they nevertheless devoted their life to the career of translating sutras. Making glorious achievements in their respective period, they all left a brilliant chapter in the history of translation in China.

虎溪三笑

東林送客處，月出白猿啼，
笑別廬山遠，何煩過虎溪。

—— 李白

東晉慧遠大師（334—416），在廬山東林寺專弘淨土法門，深居
簡出，影不出山，跡不入俗。他送客或散步，從不逾越寺前虎溪。傳說
他若過了虎溪，寺後林中老虎就會發出怒吼。

一日，詩人陶淵明和道士陸修靜來訪，慧遠大師與二人談得投
機，送行時不覺過了虎溪橋。直到驚聞後山老虎發出吼叫，三人方才恍
然大悟，相視大笑而別。此「虎溪三笑」的故事，反映了佛教傳入中國
後，儒、釋、道三教交融的思想傾向，為歷代名士所欣賞。

[佛教小知識]

• 淨土宗

　　本宗的宗旨，是以修淨土者的「心行」為「內因」，以彌陀的「願
力」為「外緣」，內外相應，往生極樂淨土。因此，修持淨土法門必須
先發菩提心，也就是企求無上佛道的願心；其次是發厭離心、欣求心，
就是厭離這個眾苦煎迫的穢土而欣求清淨莊嚴的佛土之心；再來是發至

誠心、深心、回向發願心等「三心」：一、至誠心，是真實為了脫生死而求生彼國，不是為求名聞利養而現精進相的心。二、深心，對於阿彌陀佛在因地攝受一切眾生的四十八大願，抱著毫不懷疑的信心，專心一念地稱念佛號，藉由佛力加持而往生極樂。三、回向發願心，將自己所修的一切功德資糧，全部發願回向往生西方；再將功德回向一切眾生，願所有有情眾生也都往生極樂淨土。

Three Laughs at Tiger Brook

When I left the Donglin Monastery,

The moon appeared, and the apes were howling.

I bid farewell to Mount Lu telling the monk who saw me off in a smile,

Do not take the trouble to go beyond the Tiger Brook.

— Li Bai

When Hui Yuan (334-416) of the Eastern Jin promoted Pure Land Buddhism at the Donglin Monastery in Mount Lu, he lived a secluded life. He never left the mountain or interacted with the secular world. When he saw visitors off or took a walk, he never went further than the Tiger Brook in front of the monastery. Legend has it that if he went beyond the brook, the tiger in the forest behind the monastery would roar furiously.

One day, poet Tao Yuanming and Daoist Lu Xiujing came to visit. Master Hui Yuan enjoyed talking to them both so much that when he walked them out, they went beyond the Tiger Brook without being aware. Not until they heard the roars of the tiger did they suddenly realize that. They looked at one another and laughed heartily. The story of "Three Laughs of Tiger Brook," appreciated by distinguished figures in successive dynasties, reflects the trend of harmonious synthesis of the three teachings of Confucianism, Buddhism, and Daoism after the introduction of Buddhism to China.

• The Pure Land School

The aim of the Pure Land School is to be reborn in the Pure Land of Ultimate Bliss, through the mutually corresponding internal cause of "practice of the mind" and internal condition of "power of vows." Therefore, to practice Pure Land Buddhism, one must first initiate the Bodhicitta, that is, the resolve to achieve supreme Buddhahood. Secondly, one should initiate the Weary Mind and Aspiring Mind, that is, to become weary of the sufferings and torments in the impure land and aspire for the peaceful and stately Buddha Land. Then, one should initiate the "Three Minds," namely, Mind of Perfect Sincerity, Mind of Profound Resolve, and Mind of Transferring Merit to Others. First, the Mind of Perfect Sincerity is aimed at true liberation from births and deaths and for rebirth in another land, rather than diligence for fame and interest. Second, the Mind of Profound Resolve refers to absolute confidence in the forty-eight great vows made by Amitābha Buddha in the causative stage. One focuses on reciting the name of Amitābha, so as to be reborn in the Land of Ultimate Bliss with the empowerment of the Buddha. Third, the Mind of Transferring Merit to Others means transferring all merits accumulated through practice to realize the vow of rebirth in the Western Pure Land and transferring merit to all sentient beings, wishing them rebirths in the Pure Land of Ultimate Bliss.

玄奘西行

晉宋齊梁唐代間，高僧求法離長安；
去人成百歸無十，後者焉知前者難？
路遠碧天唯冷結，沙河遮日力疲殫；
後賢若不諳斯旨，往往將經容易看。

——義淨三藏

　　玄奘大師（602—664）為求取真經，利益華夏，而立下「寧可就西而死，豈能歸東而生」的誓言，義無反顧，西行求法。玄奘在印度師從戒賢法師學習了十年有餘，甚至在印度獲得了「解脫天」和「大乘天」的稱號，備受尊重。

　　玄奘歸國時，攜帶了六百五十七部經書。在唐太宗的支持下，玄奘在大慈恩寺設立譯場，翻譯出《瑜伽師地論》《攝大乘論》《成唯識論》《心經》《大般若波羅蜜多經》等大小乘經典共七十四部，一千三百三十八卷。玄奘法師依其所譯大乘經論，開創了中國的法相唯識宗，甚至影響到日本佛教的發展。

- ## 《心經》的人生智慧

　　《般若心經》就是講人生的大智慧。佛法的大智慧就是告訴我們怎樣來處理內心的煩惱、生命深處的煩惱、生活中的煩惱；就是告訴我們怎麼樣開發每個人生命深處的潛在能量。這個潛在的能量就是大智慧，就是我們人人本具的真如佛性。我們每個人在生活工作中，在處世接物中，往往有許多困惑與窘迫、煩惱與痛苦；人生道路上往往會遇到種種坎坷，種種難以逾越的困難。這些都是生命的現實，生活的現實。面對這些現實，我們應該怎麼辦呢？《心經》這本僅有兩百六十八字的無上寶典，為我們提供了生活的大智慧。

　　《心經》開宗明義告訴我們：「觀自在菩薩，行深般若波羅蜜多時，照見五蘊皆空，度一切苦厄。」只有時時以甚深的般若進行觀照，才能見到我們身心世界五蘊皆空所顯示的真理。見到了真理，開發了智慧，才能夠度一切苦厄。《心經》開宗明義的第一句，就是這本經的總綱。

Xuan Zang's Pilgrimage

Throughout Jin, Southern (Song, Qi, and Liang), and Tang dynasties,

Eminent monks left Chang'an to search for the Dharma.

A hundred had gone but no more than ten returned.

How can later generations understand the hardship of the predecessors?

Long roads and blue sky were only cold and frozen,

Sand and rivers covered the Sun while all strength was exhausted.

If the learned of later generations do not understand the purpose,

They would take these sutras lightly.

— Yijing Sanzang

To obtain genuine sutras and to benefit the Chinese people, Xuan Zang (602-664) travelled to the Western Regions in search of the Dharma without second thoughts, taking the vow to "rather die in the West instead of returning to the East alive." In India, Xuan Zang studied with Venerable Śīlabhadra for more than ten years. Highly respected, he also won titles of "Mokṣadeva" and "Mahāyānadeva."

When Xuan Zang returned to China, he carried with him 657 scriptures. With the support of Emperor Taizong, Xuan Zang set up a translation center at the Daci'en Monastery and translated seventy-four Mahayana and Hinayana classics in one thousand three hundred and thirty-eight volumes, including Yogācārabhūmiśāstra (Discourse on the Stages of Yogic Practice), Mahāyānasaṅgraha, Vijñaptimātratāsiddhiśāstra, the Heart Sutra, and the Mahāprajñāpāramitā Sūtra. Based on his translations of Mahayana texts,

Xuan Zang founded the Yogācāra School, which influenced the development of Japanese Buddhism.

• **Life wisdom in the Heart Sutra**

The Heart Sutra is about the great wisdom of life. The great wisdom of the Buddhadharma teaches us how to deal with the inner afflictions, the afflictions in the depths of life, and the afflictions in daily life. It also teaches us how to develop the potential in each of us, which is the great wisdom, the intrinsic Buddha-nature in each of us. In life or at work, we often have confusions, embarrassments, afflictions, and pains. Throughout our lives, we often encounter all kinds of ups and downs as well as insurmountable difficulties. These are the reality of being alive and the reality of life. What should we do in the face of these realities? The Heart Sutra, a supreme work consisting of only 268 words, provides us with the great wisdom of life.

The opening of the Heart Sutra says, "When the Bodhisattva Avalokitesvara was coursing in the deep Prajna Paramita, he perceived that all five skandhas are empty. Thus, he overcame all ills and suffering." Only by constantly observing with profound wisdom can we see the truth that our bodies and minds as well as all skandhas in the world are empty. Seeing the truth is developing the wisdom, by which one can overcome all ills and sufferings. Declared at the outset of the Heart Sutra, this sentence is the gist of the sutra.

鑒真東渡

是為法事也，不惜身命！
諸人不去，我即去耳！

—— 鑒真

742 年，受日本留學僧榮睿、普照等人之邀請，鑒真和尚以五十五歲高齡始嘗試東渡扶桑，六次東渡，五次失敗，歷經磨難，甚至雙目失明。但他矢志不渝，終於 753 年第六次東渡時成功。

鑒真和尚登陸日本之後，日本民眾夾道迎接。天皇造東大寺並設立戒壇。鑒真為皇子授菩薩戒，並為五百餘出家人授戒。自此，日本建立了正規的戒律制度，鑒真和尚亦被尊為日本律宗太祖。

此外，鑒真和尚還對日本建築、雕塑、醫藥、書法甚至飲食等方面產生了重大影響，因此被日本人尊稱為「盲聖」和「日本文化的恩人」。

• 日本佛教

　　日本佛教 (Japanese Buddhism) 為北傳佛教之一。佛教從西域三十六國傳入唐朝，再經唐朝傳入日本，已有一千四百餘年的歷史。日本佛教的發展、演進，可略分為：飛鳥時代 (546—645)、奈良時代 (645—781)、平安時代 (782—1192)、鎌倉時代 (1192—1333)、室町時代 (1333—1600)、江戶時代 (1600—1868)、明治維新之後 (1868 至今) 七個時期。日本在統計上約有七萬五千座寺院、三十萬尊以上的佛像。世界最古老的木造寺院法隆寺，以及最古老的佛典古文書都保留在日本。現在日本佛教的概略，根據文化廳編纂的「宗教年鑑」等統計，現在日本的佛教徒大半屬於鎌倉佛教。淨土宗系（含淨土真宗）的宗派和日蓮宗系的宗派佔絕大比例，以大乘佛教佔大多數。

Jian Zhen's Eastward Sea Voyages

For the cause of the Dharma,

I am willing to sacrifice my life!

If no one is going,

I shall go!

— Jian Zhen

　　In 742 AD, invited by Rong Rui, Pu Zhao, and other Japanese monks who were studying in China, Jian Zhen tried to travel eastward to Fusang (often interpreted as Japan) by sea at the age of fifty-five. He made six

attempts and failed five times. He endured a lot of hardships and even lost his eyesight. However, his determination was so unwavering that he finally succeeded the sixth time in 753.

When Jian Zhen landed in Japan, the Japanese people greeted him along both sides of the road. The Emperor constructed the Tōdai-ji Temple and set up an ordination platform. Jian Zhen imparted Bodhisattva precepts to the Emperor, the Empress, and the Crown Prince; he also ordained more than 500 monastics. Since then, a formal Vinaya system was established in Japan, and Jian Zhen was honored as the Patriarch of Japanese Vinaya School.

In addition, Jian Zhen also had a major influence on Japanese architecture, sculpture, medicine, calligraphy, and even diet. Therefore, he is venerated by the Japanese as the "Blind Sage" and "Benefactor of Japanese Culture."

⬚ Basics of Buddhism:

• **Japanese Buddhism**

Japanese Buddhism is one of the branches of the Northern Transmission of Buddhism, which was introduced from the Western Regions consisting of thirty-six states to Japan via China in the Tang dynasty. It has a history of more than 1,400 years. The development and evolution of Japanese Buddhism can be divided into seven periods, namely Asuka period (546-645), Nara period (645-781), Heian era (782-1192), Kamakura period (1192-1333), Muromachi period (1333-1600), Edo period (1600-1868), and post-Meiji Restoration (1868-present). In Japan, it is estimated that there are about 75,000 temples and more than 300,000 Buddhist statues. The world's oldest monastery constructed in wood, the Horyuji Temple, as well as the oldest ancient Buddhist scriptures are kept in Japan. In terms of Buddhism in contemporary Japan, according to the statistics of the Yearbook of Religions compiled by the Ministry of Culture, most of the Japanese Buddhists belong to Kamakura Buddhism. Pure Land School (including Shin Buddhism) and Nichiren School are dominant in proportion, with Mahayana Buddhism accounting for the large majority.

禪淨雙修

> 有禪有淨土，猶如戴角虎；現世為人師，當來作佛祖；
>
> 無禪無淨土，鐵牀並銅柱；萬劫與千生，沒個人依怙。

—— 永明延壽

永明延壽是唐末五代時的禪宗高僧，他以心性為佛法的中心，整合了禪宗、天台宗、華嚴宗、法相宗等四家的觀點，綜合成為百卷本的《宗鏡錄》。

永明延壽認為禪宗重在修心，修心就是修淨土。所謂「色不自色，因心故色」，《維摩詰經》云：「欲得淨土，當淨其心。隨其心淨則佛土淨。」反過來說，「心不自心，因色故心」—— 修淨土也是修心啊！如此修行，可見自性彌陀，禪與淨土當是不二的。

「有禪有淨土，猶如戴角虎。現世為人師，來生作佛祖。」禪宗側重自力，淨土宗著重他力。修行者若能於自力之基礎上借助他力，融自他二力為一體，將可達不可思議的勝妙境界。此種修行方法稱為「禪淨雙修」，亦成為明清以來佛教修行之主導方式。

• 自力與他力

　　自他二力是相輔相成的，由於自力引發他力的感應，由於他力而加強了自力的力量。佛法是重自力的，是重在自求解脫，開發本有之佛性的。但佛菩薩的悲願，濟度眾生，護念眾生，自是一種他力，而這種他力的感應，就像俗語說的：「自助而後天助」，是應我們自身力量之所感。完全的他力，近乎迷信而沒有智慧，這是神教、是外道；完全的自力，則又不太保險，是以，禪淨雙修的法門，彌補了此一偏差的不足。

Combined Practice of Chan and Pure Land

With Chan and Pure Land, it is like a tiger with horns,

One can be a teacher in this life and become a Buddha in the next.

Without Chan or Pure Land, it is like iron bed or copper columns,

For ten thousand kalpas and thousand lifetimes, no one can rely on them.

— Yongming Yanshou

　　Yongming Yanshou was a prominent monk of the Chan School during the late Tang dynasty and the Five Dynasties. Regarding "mind-nature" as the center of the Buddhadharma, he integrated views of Chan, Tiantai, Huayan, and Yogācāra Schools and compiled the Records of the Source Mirror of a hundred volumes.

　　Yongming Yanshou believed that the key of the Chan School is cultivation of the mind and cultivation of the mind is to practice the Pure Land School. As the saying goes, "Form has no intrinsic form; it exists because of the mind." The Vimalakīrti Sūtra states, "If one wants to reach the Pure Land, they should first purify their mind. When the mind is pure, the Buddha-land is pure." The other way around, "Mind is not the intrinsic mind; it exists because of the form." In fact, practicing the Pure Land School is to cultivate the mind. In this way, one can see the intrinsic nature of Amitābha Buddha. Therefore, Chan and Pure Land are not two.

"With Chan and Pure Land, it is like a tiger with horns. One can be a teacher in this life and become a Buddha in the next." The Chan School puts emphasis on one's own strength, while the Pure Land School focuses on external strength. If practitioners use external strength in addition to their own strength, uniting the two as one, they can reach the wonderful state that is beyond thought and words. This method of combined practice of Chan and Pure Land has become a dominant Buddhist method since Ming and Qing dynasties.

Basics of Buddhism:

• Internal strength and external strength

Internal strength and external strength complement each other. Internal strength affects external strength and causes it to respond; external strength enhances the power of internal strength. The Dharma focuses on one's own strength, liberation through one's own efforts, and development of intrinsic Buddha-nature. However, Buddhas and bodhisattvas lead all sentient beings to liberation and protect all sentient beings, which naturally is the external strength. As the saying describes, "One helps oneself and the divine helps." Sympathetic resonance with such external strength is a response to our own strength. Total reliance on external strength is like superstition and lacks wisdom. It is theism, not Buddhism. Completely relying on one's own strength does not guarantee success. Therefore, the method of combined practice of Chan and Pure Land makes up for those shortcomings.

人間佛教

仰止唯佛陀，完成在人格，人成即佛成，是名真現實。

—— 太虛法師

「佛法在世間，不離世間覺，離世覓菩提，恰如求兔角。」六祖慧能大師曾給世人留下這樣的教導，提醒修行者們，出世的理想不能脫離現實的生活。百丈懷海禪師進而引入了農禪，將勞作與禪相結合，反映出佛教貼近生活的一面。

清末民初，正值國內戰亂之時，中國佛教出現空前危機。以太虛法師為代表的高僧大德紛紛奔走呼籲，提倡佛教改革，呼籲佛教適應時代的發展。太虛法師認為中國佛教的末流只重視兩件事：一、死；二、鬼 —— 這使得學佛成了學死。為了對治這一問題，太虛法師提倡「人生佛教」，主張「學佛就是學做人」，呼籲佛教重視現實的人生！

印順導師進一步開展人間佛教之理念，而趙樸初居士、星雲大師、證嚴上人和聖嚴法師則落實人間佛教理念於社會實踐，在農禪並重的傳統中國佛教精神主導下，莊嚴國土、利樂有情，建設人間淨土。

- 人間佛教

　　用佛教來解決人生問題，佛教要為活人服務，與世俗社會緊密聯繫。成佛在人間，人成佛成，是為真現實。這就是人間佛教的思想。經過趙樸初居士等人的完善，愛國愛教也成為「人間佛教」的重要組成部分。義學的研究概念並不否定人間菩薩道的善巧運用，但更不忘記解脫道的究竟把握。以人為本的經驗不是不可以，但不完整且太狹隘。佛出現在人間，但不以人間為限，換句話說，不能以人的經驗來解釋對佛法的理解。

Humanistic Buddhism

While the Buddha is the focus of our emulation,

Accomplishment of Buddhahood would depend on one's character;

If one cán be a noble person, one can become a Buddha.

This is the true reality.

— Tai Xu

　　"The Dharma is in the world, enlightenment is not apart from the world. Looking for Bodhi out of this world is like searching for a rabbit's horn." These are the teachings from Hui Neng, the Sixth Patriarch of the Chan School, reminding practitioners that the ideal of transcending this world cannot be separated from life in this world. Chan Master Baizhang Huaihai further introduced the Chan of farming, combining labor and Chan, reflecting the mundane aspect of Buddhism.

At the end of the Qing dynasty and the beginning of the Republic of China, in the middle of civil wars, Chinese Buddhism had an unprecedented crisis. Tai Xu carried on Householder Yang Renshan's thoughts on reviving Chinese Buddhism. He wrote books and put forth theories, travelling to advocate Buddhist reform and to urge the Buddhist community to adapt to changing times. Tai Xu argued that the end of Chinese Buddhism will be preceded by attention on only two things: one is death, and the other ghosts, which made Buddhism a subject of death. In order to deal with this problem, Tai Xu advocated "Humanistic Buddhism" and "learning Buddhism is learning to be a human," calling on the Buddhist community to value life in reality.

Yin Shun further developed the theories of Humanistic Buddhism, while Householder Zhao Puchu, Hsing-yun, Cheng Yen, and Sheng-yen implemented the theories of Humanistic Buddhism in social practices. Guided by the traditional Chinese Buddhist spirit that emphasizes both farming and Chan, they have adorned this world, benefitted sentient beings, and constructed a Pure Land in this world.

❈ Basics of Buddhism:

- **Humanistic Buddhism**

    In helping to solve problems in life, Buddhism must serve the living and be closely connected with the secular society. It is in this world that Buddhahood is achieved; by becoming a good and noble human being, one becomes a Buddha. It is a true reality, and it is the thoughts of Humanistic Buddhism. Through further improvement by Zhao Puchu and others, "love the country, love Buddhism" has also become an important part of Humanistic Buddhism. The study of doctrines does not deny skillful applications of the Bodhisattva path on earth. Nor does it depart from the ultimate goal of the Path to Liberation. Human-centered experience makes sense, but it is incomplete and narrow. The Buddha appeared in the world, but he was not confined to this world. In other words, we are not able to explain the Dharma with human experience.

木杯渡水

何年顧虎頭，滿壁畫滄州。赤日石林氣，青天江海流。
錫飛常近鶴，杯渡不驚鷗。似得廬山路，真隨惠遠遊。

—— 杜甫

　　根據《高僧傳》記載，劉宋杯渡禪師，相傳常乘木杯渡水，故以「杯渡」為名。428 年，杯渡禪師乘木杯渡海南下到達新安，其登陸的地點大約就在今天香港的屯門附近。

　　那時的屯門乃是兵家屯兵之要塞，但這裏的人尚未接觸過佛法。杯渡禪師於是隱居在離軍營較高的山中，並以佛法神通度化迷津，信奉者絡繹不絕。

　　其當時居住的岩洞便是今日屯門青山寺的杯渡岩，後人於是建「杯渡寺」以為紀念，是為佛教傳入香港之始。

[佛教小知識]

- **香港三大古寺**

　　青山寺、凌雲寺、寶蓮禪寺為香港三大古寺。青山寺位於屯門，又名青山禪院，禪院創建於一千五百年前的東晉末年，亦是「新安八景」之一的「杯渡禪蹤」所在地，於 1985 年評為一級歷史建築，據考證應為香港佛教發源地。凌雲寺創建於唐初，開元初年（約 713 年）開鑿佛像，寺宇又有擴建。1911 年妙參法師從羅浮山來此弘化。1925 年，寶蓮寺傳戒，紀修老和尚請妙參為戒壇尊證，傳戒圓滿後，決定以後由寶蓮禪寺、青山寺、凌雲寺每年輪流舉辦，寶蓮禪寺才有了每隔三年傳一次戒的傳統。戰後，青山寺、凌雲寺傳戒相繼停辦，唯獨寶蓮禪寺從 1925 年至今（除抗日戰爭時中斷外），一直依循祖制，每隔三年傳一次戒，寶蓮禪寺因而成為戰後香港唯一的傳戒道場。

Chan Master Bei Du Crossing the Waters in a Wooden Cup

What year did "Tigerhead" Gu Kaizhi

fill this wall with a painting of Cangzhou?

Red sun, the vapors of rock and forests,

blue skies, the current of lakes and rivers.

The tin staff flies always close to the crane,

the wooden cup crosses not alarming the gulls.

It seems that here I have found the road to Mount Lu

and truly roam together with Huiyuan.

— Du Fu

According to the Biographies of Eminent Monks, Chan Master Bei Du (Pui To in Cantonese) of the Liu Song period in the Southern and Northern

dynasties was often seen crossing the waters in a wooden cup. That was why he was called Bei Du, which is a combination of words respectively meaning "cup" and "ferry." In 428, Chan Master Bei Du arrived in Xin'an from Hainan, and the landing site was around Tuen Mun in Hong Kong today.

At that time, Tuen Mun was a military fortress, and the people there had not encountered the Dharma. Chan Master Bei Du stayed in seclusion in the mountains above the military camp, teaching the unenlightened with the Dharma and miraculous deeds.

The cave Bei Du resided at that time is the location of Tsing Shan Monastery in Castle Peak today. Later generations built the Beidu Monastery, present-day Tsing Shan Monastery, to commemorate him. It marked the beginning of the introduction of Buddhism to Hong Kong.

❈ Basics of Buddhism:

• **The Three Ancient Monasteries in Hong Kong**

Tsing Shan Monastery, Ling Wan Monastery, and Po Lin Monastery are the three great ancient monasteries in Hong Kong. The Tsing Shan Monastery is located in Tuen Mun, also known as Tsing Shan Chan Temple. The monastery was founded 1,500 years ago during the late Eastern Jin dynasty. It is also where the "Chan traces of Pui To," one of the "Eight Scenes of Xin'an," is located. It was rated as a Grade I Historical Building in 1985, and research has indicated that it is the birthplace of Buddhism in Hong Kong. Ling Wan Monastery was founded in the early Tang dynasty. In the early years of Kaiyuan (circa 713), Buddha statues were made, and monastery compounds were expanded.

In 1911, Venerable Miao Can came from Mount Luofu to promote Buddhism in Hong Kong. In 1925, an ordination ceremony conferring precepts took place at the Po Lin Monastery, and Venerable Ji Xiu invited Venerable Miao Can as one of the reverend witnesses of the ordination ceremony. After the precepts had been conferred, it was decided that Po Lin Monastery, Tsing Shan Monastery, and Ling Wan Monastery would take turns to host the annual ordination ceremony. That was how Po Lin Monastery began the tradition of holding the ordination ceremony every three years.

After the war, Tsing Shan Monastery and Ling Wan Monastery both stopped hosting ordination ceremonies. Only Po Lin Monastery continues to host the ordination ceremony every three years, a tradition that has lasted from 1925 to the present-day, and this is why Po Lin Monastery became the only monastery where precepts can be conferred in post-war Hong Kong.

七重寶樹隨緣現；四色蓮花稱意開。

—— 趙樸初

　　清朝末年，有不少以清修為樂的佛教修行者，自發來到香港山林，建立起一個個「小茅蓬」，過着簡單樸素的農禪生活。據統計，到 1941 年的時候，僅在大嶼山地區修築的大小茅蓬就大約有九十四間之多。

　　1906 年，大悅、頓修和悅明三位禪師從江蘇省鎮江市金山江天禪寺輾轉遊歷來到香港大嶼山，他們在此發現了一片高山平地，於是便於蔓草叢中披荊斬棘、開山種地，築立起小石屋。隨後，十方的雲水僧聞風而至，合力蓋搭起一間大的茅蓬，並因之命名為「大茅蓬」。「大茅蓬」在「茅蓬佛教」時代處於領導地位，它即是今日寶蓮禪寺的前身。

　　1924 年，紀修大和尚由金山江天禪寺來港，被大眾禮請任「大茅蓬」的第一任住持，「大茅蓬」也隨後更名為「寶蓮禪寺」。是時，內地僧眾前來清修者絡繹不絕，當地的許多「小茅蓬」亦向「禪寺」靠攏，漸漸形成了以「寶蓮禪寺」為核心的統一的「茅蓬佛教」中心。

　　在香港佛教近代史上，大悅、頓修、悅明三位禪師是寶蓮禪寺的開山祖師，他們最早將近代江浙叢林制度帶入香港，從而奠定了香港佛

教「農禪生活」的模式，開闢了香港近代佛教叢林的先河。香港佛教也
由此道接千載，傳播至今。

- **農禪並重**

　　印度僧人通過「乞食」來獲得信徒的日常供養。後來佛教傳入我國，經過實踐，發現這種「乞食」方式不適用當時的國情，故而佛教的大德法師開始尋求新的方式。

　　「農禪並重」最初孕育發端於四祖道信。《傳法寶記》記載，道信「每勸門人曰：努力勤坐，坐為根本。能作三五年，得一口食塞飢瘡，即閉門坐」。道信號召門人都去從事生產勞動，去墾荒耕田，劈柴燒火，解決吃飯問題，認為它是坐禪的基本保障，是修行不可或缺的重要組成部分。後來，禪宗僧侶融禪於農、以農悟道的生活習慣和修行方式，促進了農禪制度的形成與發展，「農禪並重」成為中國佛教的優良傳統，由寶蓮禪寺的開山祖師們傳入香江，直至今日。

Practicing Buddhism in Thatched Huts

Seven rows of treasure trees will appear according to conditions;
Four-colored lotuses will blossom in accordance with your wish.

— Zhao Puchu

　　At the end of the Qing dynasty, there were many Buddhist practitioners who were happy to practice alone. They spontaneously came to the forests of Hong Kong and set up small thatched huts where they could live a simple life integrating farming into Chan. According to statistics, by the year 1941, just in Lantau Island, there were around ninety-four thatched huts of different sizes.

In 1906, the three Chan masters—Da Yue, Dun Xiu, and Yue Ming—came to Lantau Island after an arduous and long journey from Jiangtian Chan Monastery in Jinshan, Zhenjiang City, Jiangsu Province. They found a flat highland where they built a small stone house by clearing out a way through creeping weeds and clearing a piece of virgin land for farming. Later on, they were quickly followed by itinerant monks from different places. They built a large thatched hut together and named it the "Big Thatched Hut." The "Big Thatched Hut" was in a leading position during the period of "Thatched-Hut Buddhism" and is the predecessor of today's Po Lin Monastery.

In the year 1924, Ji Xiu came to Hong Kong from Jiangtian Chan Monastery of Jinshan. At the request of the assembly, he became the first abbot of the "Big Thatched Hut" and renamed it as Po Lin Monastery. Then, monks from the mainland streamed in to practice there, and many local "little thatched huts" were built close by the Monastery. These gradually formed a center for "Thatched-Hut Buddhism," with Po Lin Monastery as the center.

In the modern history of Buddhism in Hong Kong, the three Chan masters—Da Yue, Dun Xiu, and Yue Ming, known as the founders of Po Lin Monastery, were the first to introduce the modern monastery administration of Jiangsu and Zhejiang provinces to Hong Kong. This established the mode of Buddhism in Hong Kong—that is, integrating agricultural work into Chan, and Po Lin Monastery became the forerunner of modern Buddhist monasteries in Hong Kong. Since then, Buddhism in Hong Kong has continued to be transmitted to this day for more than a century.

• **Combining Chan with Farming**

Indian monks used to obtain the daily offerings of food from believers through "mendicancy." Later, when Buddhism was introduced to China and the same was practiced, it was found that this "mendicancy" method was not suitable under Chinese conditions at that time. Therefore, some Buddhist masters began to seek new ways for their provisions.

The idea of "combining Chan with farming" was originally initiated by Dao Xin, the Fourth Patriarch of the Chan School. As the Annals of the Transmission of the Dharma Treasure recorded, Dao Xin "often encouraged his disciples thus: Practice sitting meditation diligently, as it is the foundation of cultivation. Spend three to five years on farming for food so that you could cure your hunger with something to eat. After that, you should do sitting meditation in seclusion." Dao Xin called on all his disciples to engage in productive labor, like clearing land and tilling fields, chopping firewood and making fires for cooking so they could feed themselves. In his opinion, this was the basic assurance for sitting meditation and an indispensable part of their Buddhist practice.

Later on, monks of the Chan School integrated Chan into farming and sought to awaken to the truths of Buddhism through agricultural work. Such habits of life and ways of practice brought about the formation and development of the Agricultural Chan system, and as a result, "combining Chan with farming" became a fine tradition of Chinese Buddhism. This tradition was introduced by the founding masters of Po Lin Monastery and has been practiced in Hong Kong till this day.

佛誕假期

千載勝緣逢盛世，好將佛事助文治。
心光常注近及遠，事業毋忘後視今。

—— 趙樸初

　　佛教傳入中國後，人們相信世尊誕生的日期是農曆的四月初八。慶祝佛誕的活動從魏晉時期便開始在民間流傳，南北朝時更顯豐富多采，在唐朝成為一年中最隆重的佛教節日之一。

　　1950 年的世界佛教大會之後，亞洲很多個國家或地區紛紛定立佛誕日或衞塞節為公眾假期。香港在被英國統治的近一百年間，只許官方慶祝西方的宗教假期，佛教徒只好在寺院、精舍內自行慶祝佛誕。佛誕既然不屬於全民的假日，公眾在思想意識上就不會重視佛教的教育意義。為此，香港佛教聯合會在覺光長老的帶領下連續四十多年不斷上書英屬香港政府，要求確定每年農曆四月初八佛陀誕生日為公眾假期，然而這一訴求卻從未得到殖民政府的任何回應。

　　1997 年，香港回歸祖國，成立了特別行政區政府，實行「一國兩制」，高度自治，宗教平等，信仰自由。考慮到香港市民的切身利益，1999 年，香港政府立法將佛誕定為公眾假日，為香港佛教奠下新的里程碑。

- **南傳「衛塞節」**

衛塞節 (Vesak) 又稱佛誕日，是斯里蘭卡、泰國、緬甸等南傳佛教國家紀念佛陀誕生、成道、涅槃的節日。在 1999 年的第五十四屆聯合國大會上，衛塞節獲得聯合國承認，成為「聯合國衛塞節」(United Nations Day of Vesak)。

而今，每年五月的月圓之日，各國佛教徒都會舉行盛大的慶典，點平安燈、供花祈福、慈善佈施、祈求吉祥如意、國泰民安。

The Buddha's Birthday as a Public Holiday

There happens to be an extremely rare condition in this flourishing era,

Which offers a chance for Buddhist works to facilitate cultural achievements.

The light from a Buddha's mind always shines near and far,

And later generations will look back at what we do today.

— Zhao Puchu

After Buddhism was introduced to China, people believed that the birthday of the Buddha was the eighth day of the fourth lunar month in the Chinese calendar. The celebration of the Buddha's birthday began in the Wei and Jin Dynasties and became more festive in the Northern and Southern dynasties. It even became an official holiday for a time in the Tang dynasty.

After the World Fellowship of Buddhists Conference in 1950, many countries or regions in Asia established the Buddha's Birthday or Vesak as a public holiday. In nearly a century of British rule, Hong Kong was only allowed the official celebration of Western religious holidays. Buddhists in Hong Kong had to celebrate the Buddha's birthday in a Buddhist monastery or vihara by themselves. Since the Buddha's birthday was not a public holiday, the public would not pay much attention to the educational significance of Buddhism. To change this, the Hong Kong Buddhist Association, under the leadership of the Most Venerable Kok Kwong, had been petitioning the British Hong Kong Government for more than forty years to officially declare the Buddha's birthday on the eighth day of the fourth lunar month a public holiday. However, this appeal was never responded by the colonial government.

In 1997, Hong Kong returned to the motherland, and a special administrative region government was established to implement the "one country, two systems" policy which offers a high degree of autonomy, equality of religions, and freedom of belief. With the vital interests of the people of Hong Kong in mind, the Hong Kong Government legislated to make the Buddha's birthday a public holiday in 1999, which marked a new milestone for Buddhism in Hong Kong.

✂ Basics of Buddhism:

• Vesak in Theravadin Countries

Vesak, also known as the Buddha's Birthday, is celebrated in Theravadin countries, including Sri Lanka, Thailand, and Myanmar, in order to commemorate the birth, enlightenment, and nirvana of the Buddha. At the 54th UN General Assembly in 1999, Vesak was recognized by the United Nations as the "United Nations Day of Vesak."

Nowadays, on the full moon day in May every year, Buddhists from all over the world will hold a grand celebration, lighting the lamps of peace, making offerings of flowers, doing charity, and giving donations, in order to for auspiciousness, good fortune, prosperity of the country, and peace for the people.

龍華三會

佛寶讚無窮，功成無量劫中。
巍巍丈六紫金容，覺道雪山峰。
眉際玉毫光燦爛，照開六道昏蒙。
龍華三會願相逢，演說法真宗。

—— 佛寶贊

　　五十六億七千萬年之後，彌勒菩薩從兜率天降於人世。長大之後，他有感於諸行無常，自斷鬚髮，出家修行，於華林園中龍華樹下成道。諸帝釋梵天王祈請彌勒說法。

　　在大眾的跟隨下，彌勒進入翅頭末城，開始講述四聖諦、三十七道品和十二因緣。這時上根的九十六億人全都證得了阿羅漢果，即是彌勒佛的初轉法輪；彌勒佛又回到華林園的重閣講堂重說四諦、十二因緣等法，是為龍華二轉法輪。這時又有中根九十四億人得阿羅漢果；彌勒佛的第三次大會上，再有下根九十二億人得阿羅漢果。

• 彌勒菩薩

彌勒佛 (Maitreya)，意譯為慈氏，在大乘佛教經典中，常被稱為阿逸多菩薩摩訶薩，是世尊釋迦牟尼佛的繼任者，未來將在娑婆世界降生修道，成為娑婆世界的下一尊佛（也叫未來佛），即賢劫千佛中第五尊佛，常被稱為「當來下生彌勒尊佛」。被唯識學派奉為鼻祖，其龐大思想體系由無著菩薩、世親菩薩闡釋弘揚，深受中國大乘佛教大師支謙、道安和玄奘的推崇。在一些漢傳佛教的寺院裏，常見到袒胸露腹、笑容可掬（或大肚比丘）的彌勒佛像，這是以布袋和尚為原型塑造。此在佛教作為表法教育，表示「量大福大」，提醒世人學習包容。其中大肚能容，容天下難容之事；開口便笑，笑世間可笑之人。

Three Great Assemblies under the Dragon-Flower Trees

May the Buddha the most precious be praised without end.

His success was achieved through countless eons.

Majestically, sixteen feet tall and purplish gold in color,

He realized enlightenment by snowy mountain peaks.

Between eyebrows his white curls emit rays with brilliance

To shine and pierce the darkness of the six paths of existence.

In the three assemblies, under dragon-flower trees, we wish to meet

When the truth of the Dharma is preached.

— Verse of Praising the Buddha

After 5.67 billion years, Maitreya Bodhisattva will descend to the human world from Tuṣita Heaven. When he grows up, he will realize the impermanence of all phenomena, shave off the beard and hair by his own, renounce the secular life to practice Buddhism, and finally attain enlightenment under the dragon-flower tree at Flower Grove Garden. Then the Śakra Devānām-Indra and Brahmā will pray to Maitreya Buddha and request Him to teach the Dharma.

Followed by his disciples, Maitreya will enter the city of Ketumati and begin to teach them the Four Noble Truths, the Thirty-seven kinds of practices for the attainment of enlightenment, and the Twelve Links of Dependent Arising. On this occasion, 9.6 billion people of superior capacity will all realize the state of an arhat. This will be the first time for Maitreya

Buddha to turn the Dharma wheel. Later, Maitreya will return to the Flower Grove Garden to teach again on doctrines such as the Four Noble Truths and the Twelve Links of Dependent Arising, which will be the second turning of the Dharma wheel, and 9.4 billion people of medium capacity will attain arhatship. In Maitreya Buddha's third great assembly, 9.2 billion people of lower capacity will attain arhatship.

▓ Basics of Buddhism:

- **Maitreya Bodhisattva**

Maitreya Buddha, meaning the compassionate one, is often referred to as Ajita bodhisattva-mahāsattva in Mahayana Buddhist scriptures. He is considered the successor to Śākyamuni Buddha. In future, Maitreya will descend to the Saha World to cultivate the Way and become the next Buddha (also called the Future Buddha) of the Saha world. He is the fifth Buddha among the thousand buddhas of the bhadrakalpa and is often called "Maitreya Buddha, of future birth." Maitreya is regarded as the founder of the Yogācāra School, whose versatile logical system was largely formulated and carried out by Asaṅga Bodhisattva and Vasubandhu Bodhisattva, and was further highly praised by masters of Chinese Mahayana Buddhism— Zhi Qian, Dao An, and Xuan Zang. In some temples of Chinese Buddhism, it is common to see the smiling and bare-chested Maitreya statues with a big abdomen, of which the prototype is Monk Budai (or Big-belly Maitreya). In Buddhism, this is a way to manifest the Dharma, which means "the greater the capacity of one's mind, the more merits one will obtain." It is to encourage people to learn to be magnanimous, just like Maitreya, whose big belly can tolerate all the things that are difficult to tolerate, whose big grin is symbolic of how he would laugh off the follies of people in this world.

無盡燈

Part Three:

Everlasting Lamp

教外別傳

法本法無法，無法法亦法，
今付無法時，法法何曾法。

—— 佛陀

　　就如所有其他的教化一般，佛法的宣導，基本上都是要透過語言文字來表達其內容，才能讓人得沾法益，繼而廣為傳播。佛在世時應機施教，口傳正法，直至他入滅之後，弟子才把佛陀的法教結集起來，成了日後的三藏十二部經教。但我們不要忘記，佛陀初證大道的時候，曾

認真考慮過言語文字對開示正法的局限性，而每個人在詮釋與理解上，又都可能出現誤差，故當面對稀有難遇、上根利智的人，可以不用言說、直接以心傳心的話，佛陀就會默然傳法。

一次在靈山會上，佛陀就曾一言不發，信手拈起一支花展示眾前，而當時就只有大迦葉尊者破顏微笑。佛陀這便說道：「吾有正法眼藏，涅槃妙心，實相無相，微妙法門，不立文字，教外別傳，付囑摩訶迦葉。」這就是禪宗「拈花微笑」的公案，代表着心燈相傳，法脈相承，綿綿無盡之意。

※※ ［佛教小知識］ ─────────────────────────

• 心法 ── 千聖不傳

砍柴出身的惠能，在南方弘揚禪法，天下歸心，神秀十分不解，派遣得意弟子志誠前往曹溪山一探究竟。志誠來到惠能身邊，真心誠意向惠能求法，惠能卻說：「吾若言有法與人，即為誑汝。但且隨方解縛，假名三昧。」惠能明確告訴世人，「我如果說有教法給人，那就是騙你。只是為了隨順方便替大家解除執縛，而假託個名稱叫做『三昧』。」《菩提達摩大師碑》將心法稱為「說無說法」，也說明了同樣的道理，「及乎杖錫來梁，說無說法。……帝后聞名，欽若昊天。嗟乎，見之不見，逢之不逢，今之古之，悔之恨之，朕以一介凡夫，敢師之於後。」

惠能臨終時，弟子再一次問他：「師從此去，早晚可回？」惠能回答道：「葉落歸根，來時無口。」六祖惠能再一次提醒大家，他一生都沒說過甚麼法，只是教導人們覺悟這種心法的方法而已，因為無上心法「言語道斷，心行處滅。」《壇經》甚至直截了當地說：「諸佛妙理，非關文字。」禪宗因而把心法說成是「千聖不傳」之法。

A Special Transmission Outside the Scriptures

In essence, Dharma is no-Dharma,

No-Dharma is insubstantial either.

Now to pass the no-Dharma on,

Is there ever a dharma?

— The Buddha

Just like all other teachings, the transmission of the Dharma mainly relies on language and words so that it can benefit people and spread widely. During his lifetime, the Buddha taught people according to their capacities and expounded the Dharma through oral transmissions. Not until he entered nirvana that his disciples compiled his teachings into the Tripiṭaka and the twelve divisions of the canon. But we should remember that soon after his attainment of enlightenment, the Buddha seriously considered the limitation of language and words for expounding the true Dharma, and he knew there might be errors in individual interpretation and understanding. Therefore, whenever he encountered someone of extraordinary talent and spiritual maturity, a rare occasion indeed when words became redundant, the Buddha would transmit the Dharma in silence, directly from mind to mind.

Once in the assembly at the Gṛdhrakūṭa (the Vulture Peak), the Buddha said nothing but casually picked up a flower to show it to the audience; at that moment, only the Venerable Mahākāśyapa smiled. Then the Buddha said, "I possess the true Dharma eye, the marvelous mind of Nirvana, the true form of the formless, the subtle Dharma Gate that does not rest on words or letters but is a special transmission outside of the scriptures. This I entrust to

Mahākāśyapa." This is a Chan koan named "Flower Sermon," representing the passing down of the mind-lamp and the unbroken transmission of the Dharma lineage.

✿ Basics of Buddhism: ─────────────────────────

- **The Dharma of mind cannot be transmitted by even a thousand sages**

Once a woodcutter, the Chan Patriarch Hui Heng taught Chan in Southern China and attracted followers from all over the country. Puzzled by Hui Neng's success, Shen Xiu (a senior disciple of Hui Neng's master) sent one of his favorite students, Zhi Cheng, to Mount Caoxi where Master Hui Neng resided, in order to find out the reason behind it. Zhi Cheng came to Hui Neng and asked sincerely about the Dharma. Master Hui Neng said, "To say that I have the Dharma to teach you would be lying to you. What I do is simply to untangle you whenever conditions allow, and [once untangled], give it a name of samādhi." This was what Hui Neng clearly told the worldlings. The inscription on the monument in memory of Great Master Bodhidharma also referred to the Mind-Dharma as "the unspeakable Dharma." On the monument, it reads, "[Bodhidharma] came to visit the State of Liang with his rod and spoke the unspeakable Dharma. Later on, [Emperor Wu of Liang] heard about the Master's reputation and respected him greatly. He regretted that although he had seen the Master in person, he did not know who he truly was; and although he had met him, he did not learn from him. The emperor sighed, 'What a great regret! How would I, an ordinary man, dare to claim such an accomplished master as my teacher.'"

When Hui Heng was dying, his disciples asked him again, "Master, now that you are leaving us, will you be back sooner or later?" Hui Neng answered, "Leaves fall and return to the roots. When I came, I spoke no words." Hui Neng reminded people again that he had not taught any Dharma all his life, but had only led people to realization of "the Dharma of mind," for this supreme mind-Dharma "cuts off the channel of language and annihilates the locus of mental functioning." The Platform Sutra points out directly that "The wondrous principle of the Buddhas has nothing to do with words." Thus, the Chan School considers mind-Dharma as the "ultimate attainment of awakening realized through one's own efforts that cannot be transmitted by even a thousand sages."

不立文字

空門不肯出，投窗也太癡；
百年鑽故紙，何日出頭時？

—— 古靈禪師

　　曾有兩師兄弟在柏樹下參禪，一粒柏樹籽掉到師弟的頭上，他這便問師兄說：「柏樹籽可有佛性？」師兄答道：「當然有佛性！」接下來的對話就是「柏樹籽何時能成佛？」

　　師弟問：「那虛空何時落地？」

　　師兄答：「柏樹籽成佛時。」

　　以上的對答永無定論，往往令一般人摸不着頭腦。禪宗大德意識到文字言語的局限性，主張藉教悟宗，透過禪定的修行，衝破文字語言的束縛，用心去悟道，故而有「不立文字」之說。

[佛教小知識]

- **文字障**

　　文字障指讀經律論的時候過於執着於文字，而不能透過文字了解真實奧義，又或者過於執着於自己以往的成功經驗，自己以往證得的念想，那麼這些原來的成就，反而成為了阻止自己了解大道的障礙。

No Dependence upon Words

Though the door is open, it prefers to stay in,

What a fool to have hit the window over and again.

Read for ages and get lost in ancient pages,

When will the awakening ever take place?

— Gu Ling

Once upon a time, there were two disciples meditating under a cypress. Suddenly, a seed fell onto the junior's head, so he asked the senior practitioner, "Is there Buddha nature in a cypress seed?" His senior answered, "Of course there is!" The conversation that followed was all about "when the cypress seed will become a Buddha?"

The junior disciple asked, "When will the great void fall to the ground?"

His senior answered, "When the cypress seed becomes a Buddha."

Chan dialogue like this is often confusing and yields no definite conclusions. The great masters of Chan realized the limitation of language, so they encourage one to realize enlightenment through reading the scriptures and practicing meditation so that one can break through the bondage of language and awaken the mind to the Way. The saying of "not dependent upon words" thus came into being.

- **Impediment of words**

    "Impediment of words" refers to rigid attachment to words when one reads sutras, vinaya, and sastras, to the extent that it blocks the reader from understanding the true meaning beyond the words. Or, one might be too attached to previous successful experience and realization that it becomes an impediment to realization of the Way.

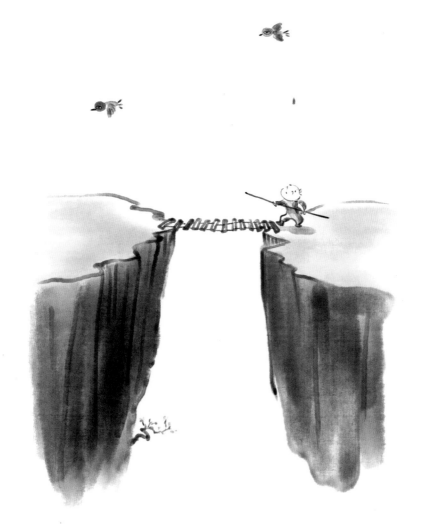

直指人心

念正天堂路，念邪地獄門；
萬法由心生，萬事由心滅。

——古德

有一位將軍問白隱禪師：「真的有天堂、地獄嗎？」白隱禪師看了他一眼，自言自語地說，「這人看起來像個屠夫，那裏適合當將軍？」將軍聽得血脈噴張，「唰」一聲就把刀抽了出來，怒不可遏地吼道，「你敢小看我，我宰了你！」

禪師慢悠悠地說，「你看，地獄之門不是打開了嗎？」將軍猛然醒悟，連忙收起刀，跪在地上向禪師陪罪，「請原諒我的莽撞！」禪師這時微笑說，「你看，天堂之門不是打開了嗎？」

這則公案告訴人們，禪師不用論證天堂與地獄的存在與否，只用「直指人心」的方法直接讓將軍領略到自心一念天堂、一念地獄的轉變。天堂與地獄、眾生與佛，煩惱與菩提、愛與恨、苦與樂、得與失、是與非、正與邪、好與壞，並非絕對的差別對立，其區別只在一念之間的迷與悟。譬如說，從地獄到天堂的時間其實很快，快到一念之間：一念迷，怒火中燒，殺人放火，無惡不作，苦海無邊；一念悟，海闊天空，快快樂樂，歡喜自在。

- **一念轉境，自在快樂**

在一般人的心目中，佛陀是法力無邊、神通廣大的教主。其實不然，在佛陀一生中，令他「頭痛」的人和事從未間斷過。譬如說，有些弟子不聽話，佛陀因而制定了不少戒條；有些人因為心懷嫉妒而與佛陀為難，在盛大的集會上辱罵佛陀；別有用心的人故意誤導民眾，令佛陀和弟子們三個月沒有供養，只能靠吃馬麥度日；在佛陀晚年，他的堂弟提婆達多幾次想謀害他；憍薩羅國琉璃王為了個人恩怨，入侵迦毗羅衛國，使釋迦族遭受滅族之災……

值得我們思考的是，成了佛的人，應該永遠快樂才對，但是面對滅族之災，如果佛陀仍然很開心，不為所動，真有點不合常理。其實，普通人心隨境轉，一顆心很容易受身外之物的影響，情緒隨之而波動。比如，在廣告等促銷方式的鼓動和商業對利益的追求之下，新的產品不斷的出現，人們的需求變得越來越多，慾望也越疊越高。當這種永無休止的慾望得不到滿足時，痛苦由此而生。同樣，當別人講我們不好時，我們便生氣、難過。因此，受環境左右的心，隨環境之改變，時而焦躁，時而憂心，時而恐懼，時而絕望，當然，有時也會得意忘形。然而其結果都一樣：痛苦不堪。

在佛教看來，一個快樂而有智慧的人，不是身邊沒有令他困擾的人和事，而是他面對困擾時不受外境的左右，不會「寢不安席，食不甘味」，其心態依然能夠保持從容而不慌亂。這就是佛教所講的「境隨心轉」的境界，一個人若能領悟到這一點，便會把別人的誤解看成是磨練自己心智、昇華自己人格的契機，於一念之間，化煩惱為菩提。這樣也就能做到隨緣不變、不變隨緣，以平常心看淡世間的悲歡離合、炎涼冷熱，不以物喜、不以己悲的平和心境自然生起，不為外界影響。佛門的這種「境隨心轉」的人生智慧，使得我們能與佛同行，笑對煩惱，即使一個人有麻煩時，也能擁有快樂的心境，這才是修行的真功夫。

Pointing Directly at the Mind

Virtuous thoughts lead to heaven;

Vile thoughts lead to hell.

All dharmas arise from the mind;

All things cease with the mind.

— An ancient sage

A general asked Chan Master Bai Yin, "Do heavens and hells really exist?" Bai Yin glanced at him, then turned and talked to himself, "This man looks like a butcher. How could he be a general?" The general was outraged. He took out his sword, shouting loudly, "How dare you look down upon me? I'll kill you!"

Then, the Chan master spoke calmly, "See, the door to Hell just opened." The general was awakened by these words. He quickly withdrew his sword, knelt before the master, and asked for his forgiveness. "Please forgive my impetuousness," the general pleaded. The Chan master then smiled, "See, the door to Heaven is now open."

In this story the Chan master was not trying to justify the existence of heavens or hells; he just used the method of "pointing directly at the mind," and the general understood that "Heaven and Hell alters within an instant of thought." Heaven and Hell, sentient beings and Buddha, afflictions and enlightenment, love and hatred, suffering and pleasure, gain and loss, right and wrong, good and evil—their relative differences are not absolutely opposing; their differences lie in the moment of thought being deluded or awakened. The example above demonstrates that the change from Heaven to Hell is actually as fast as an instant of thought: With one thought of delusion, rage can arise to commit murder, arson, and all other sorts of crimes that lead to endless sufferings; with one thought of enlightenment, there would be joy, happiness, and freedom as boundless as the sea and the sky.

Basics of Buddhism:

- **Free the mind from surroundings to experience freedom and joy**

Many consider the Buddha an omnipotent master with infinite superpowers. This may not be the case. During the Buddha's lifetime, he had to deal with constant "headaches." Sometimes when certain disciples misbehaved, the Buddha established the precepts accordingly; sometimes out of jealousy, people reproached the Buddha in front of a grand assembly; and on one occasion, there were people w' purposely misled the villagers to stop their offerings of alms to the Buddha and his disciples so they had to live on barley for three months. In later years of the Buddha's life, his cousin Devadatta made several attempts to murder him; because of personal grievances, King Virūḍhaka of Kośala invaded Kapilavastu and slaughtered the Śākya clan... .

We might wonder whether those who have attained Buddhahood are always happy. If the Buddha remained happy and unmoved in face of the catastrophe of his clan, it would seem unreasonable. Actually the state of mind of an ordinary person is easily influenced by external circumstances, and their emotions are in turn affected. For instance, in pursuit of greater profits, more and more new products are launched on the market, each accompanied by enticing promotional and advertising campaigns. These would encourage consumers to want more and turn on their insatiable desires. When wants are not met and desires unsatisfied, suffering arises. Similarly, when we are being badmouthed, we get angry or feel sad. Our mind, conditioned by external circumstances, would be sometimes restless, sometimes worried, sometimes terrified, and sometimes hopeless. Of course, there are also times when our mind gets overjoyed or inflated, the result of which is all the same: terrible pain.

From the Buddhist point of view, a happy and wise person is not someone who experiences no troubles or difficulties in life, but someone who remains unaffected by what happens around him. He would not "stay awake through the night or lose his appetite." Rather, he remains calm and poised. This is what is called in Buddhism "free the mind from surrounding conditions." If one can understand this, he would take people's misunderstandings of him as an opportunity to hone his mind and personality; he would transform afflictions into enlightenment at the turn of a thought. He will then be able to hold his ground while the environment changes, and accord with karmic conditions without losing himself in the process. He will be able to see through the vicissitudes of life with an ordinary mind and attain tranquility without being disturbed by personal gain or loss. With the life wisdom taught by the Buddha, that is, freeing the mind from external conditions, we can follow the path of the Buddha, smile at afflictions, and stay happy even when facing troubles. This marks the real practice of Buddhism.

見性成佛

> 我有明珠一顆，久被塵勞關鎖。
> 今朝塵盡光生，照破山河萬朵。

—— 茶陵鬱禪師

　　一個富翁害怕家道中落，就在愛兒的衣服裏縫了一顆明珠，估量着就算將來家產沒有了，也可以變賣這顆明珠維持生活，萬萬想不到兒子後來竟淪為乞丐，不知道衣服裏藏有價值連城的明珠。後經親友告知，才取出寶珠，置田買房，過上富裕生活。

　　這是《法華經》七喻中的「衣珠喻」，以乞兒比喻小根之人，以明珠比喻佛性，小、中根機的人與大根機的人一樣，本來都具有相同的佛性，無二無別。佛陀對所有根機的人都是說同樣法 —— 見性成佛的般若大法，眾生隨其領悟能力之不同而得到不同的利益。正如《維摩詰經》云：「佛以一音演說法，眾生隨類各得解。」

[佛教小知識]

• 見性成佛

　　茶陵鬱在其悟道詩中將「真如自性」比喻為心中的明珠，本來清淨，任何灰塵都無法污染它，是成佛的基因。只因一念之差，眾生迷失本性，如同灰塵覆蓋明珠，自性的智慧之光無法顯現出來，邪見橫行，心魔控制着我們的身心，起惑造業，苦海無邊。一念悟，起正見，遮蔽在自性上貪瞋癡等煩惱塵，立可轉染成淨，轉邪成正，轉凡成聖，明心見性。正如惠能説，「性中各自離五欲，見性剎那即是真。今生若遇頓教門，忽悟自性見世尊。」換而言之，真如自性，人人本具，是成佛的基因。覺悟自性，取決於人在悟性上如何下功夫。

Seeing One's Intrinsic Nature is Accomplishment of Buddhahood

There is a bright pearl within me,

Buried for a long time under dust.

Today, the dust is gone and the light radiates,

Shining through all the mountains and rivers.

— Cha-Ling Yu

A millionaire was worried that the family fortunes would decline, so he sewed an invaluable pearl into the clothes of his beloved son. He thought that even if one day the family property were gone, his son would sell the pearl and make a living. Unfortunately, his son did lose everything later and became a beggar. He did not know about the pearl until his relatives told him about it. Then, the son took out the pearl, sold it to purchase some lands and houses, and lived a rich life.

This is the pearl metaphor in the Lotus Sutra. The pearl is analogous to Buddha nature, while the beggar the people of small spiritual capacity. People of small and medium spiritual capacities possess the same Buddha nature as people of superior capacity. The Buddha preaches the same Dharma to people of all spiritual capacities, that is, the great Dharma Prajna that leads sentient beings to see their own intrinsic nature and attain Buddhahood. Everyone benefits from it differently according to their capacities of penetrating the Dharma. Just as the Vimalakīrti Nirdeśa Sūtra says, "The Blessed one expresses himself in a single sound, and beings, each according to his category, grasp its meaning."

※ Basics of Buddhism:

- **Seeing one's intrinsic nature is accomplishment of Buddhahood**

In his enlightenment poem, Cha-Ling Yu compared one's intrinsic nature to a pearl in the mind. The pearl is pure by nature and undefiled by dust. It is the gene of Buddhahood. However, out of illusion, all sentient beings turn ignorant of who they are, like the pearl covered by dust, and the radiance of innate wisdom is concealed. Wrong views prevail, and Mara takes command of our body and mind. Driven by delusions, people commit karmic deeds and suffer endlessly in samsara. Upon one awakened thought, right views arise and the dust of afflictions such as greed, aversion, and ignorance are instantly purified, the wrong is corrected, the ordinary turns noble, and one's intrinsic nature realized. As Hui Neng said, "Each of you give up the five desires within your nature. Truth is known the moment we realize the Essence of Mind. If you encounter this direct teaching in your lifetime, immediately you will realize the intrinsic nature and see the World-honored One." In other words, everyone is endowed with the true suchness of one's intrinsic nature, which is the foundation for the attainment of Buddhahood. To become enlightened on one's intrinsic nature depends on how one cultivates on basis of one's potential for enlightenment.

達摩西來

達摩西來一字無，全憑心地用工夫；
若要紙上談人我，筆影蘸乾洞庭湖。

—— 古德

　　菩提達摩，簡稱達摩，於南北朝劉宋 (470—478) 年間來到中國。達摩是釋迦佛的第二十八代弟子，從印度西來中土弘揚佛法，是中國禪宗的初祖。

　　有說達摩見到當時南朝的梁武帝時，武帝問他：「我即位以來，尊崇佛法，建寺寫經、度僧無數，且問可有功德？」達摩答：「沒有功德。」梁武帝心中不悅，繼續問：「甚麼是聖諦第一義？」達摩答曰：「廓然無聖！」

　　這段絕不投機的對話，正好反映了後來古德所說的「達摩西來一字無，全憑心地用工夫」，無怪不立文字、直指人心的風格，就成了日後中國禪宗的特色。

　　當達摩發覺梁武帝無法領悟心地法門，便轉投北魏的少林寺，在那裏面壁九年、傳佛心印，令禪法大行於中土，至宋朝時更遠播朝鮮、日本等地，至今流傳不絕。

• 功德與福德

　　達摩從印度到中國的第二年，被虔誠信佛的梁武帝迎請到宮中。梁武帝問達摩，「我自從當了皇帝後，大造佛寺，寫佛經，培養發展僧人，不可勝計，敢問有何功德？」

　　按照世俗看法，梁武帝建佛、寫經、度僧，不可勝計，應該是有大功德的。普通信眾哪怕在佛寺功德箱內投下一文錢，都認為有功德，何況梁武帝投入那麼多錢財呢！出乎常人意料的是達摩竟說：「這些並沒有甚麼功德」。梁武帝大惑不解，於是質問道：「何以沒有功德？」達摩解釋說：這些只是世間的福德。為了表面的虛榮或回報而行善，是福德。這樣，行善之人往往因自己的善行而自大。功德則不同，行善佈施的目的不是為了一己之私，而是在幫助別人的同時，去除自己的執着心，提升自我，方能遠離苦惱。

The Arrival of Bodhidharma

Bodhidharma travelled from the West but brought no words,

The real practice occurs only in the mind.

If things are to be talked about on paper,

The entire Dongting Lake will be dried for ink.

— An ancient sage

　　Bodhidharma, or simply called Da Mo, came to China during the Liu Song of the Southern and Northern dynasties (470–478). As a disciple of

the twenty-eighth generation of the Buddhist lineage, he came from India to China to disseminate Buddhism. He is considered the first patriarch of the Chan tradition in China.

It is said that when Bodhidharma met Emperor Wu of Liang, the emperor asked him, "After ascending the throne, I advocated Buddhism, built temples, copied sutras, and helped countless monks. Have I acquired any merits?" Bodhidharma answered, "No merit at all." Emperor Wu of Liang was displeased. He asked again, "What is the ultimate reality by the noble truth?" Bodhidharma answered, "Vast Emptiness, Holy Nothing!"

This disagreeable conversation shows exactly what an ancient sage said, "Bodhidharma travelled from the West but brought no words. The real practice occurs only in the mind." No wonder that later on, the Chinese Chan

School developed a unique style of "not dependent upon words, and pointing directly at the mind."

Realizing that Emperor Wu of Liang couldn't understand the mind-ground method, Bodhidharma then went to Shaolin Temple of the Northern Wei dynasty, where he sat facing the wall for nine years and passed on the mind seal of the Buddha's teaching. As such, the Chan lineage became widely popular in China and in the Song dynasty, it even spread to regions such as Korea and Japan, where it has flourished to the present day.

Basics of Buddhism:

• Virtues Vs Merits

In the second year of Bodhidharma's arrival in China, he was invited to the royal palace by Emperor Wu of Liang, who was a devoted Buddhist. The emperor asked him, "After ascending the throne, I advocated Buddhism, built temples, copied sutras, and helped countless monks. Have I acquired any merits?"

If we follow secular thinking, Emperor Wu of Liang should have acquired great merits by building Buddhist temples, copying sutras, and helping monks. For an ordinary Buddhist, offering a cent to a temple is considered a meritorious deed, not to mention that the emperor had offered so much. But surprisingly, Bodhidharma said, "No merit at all." Confused as Emperor Wu of Liang was, he questioned, "Why?" Bodhidharma explained, "What you did is only meritorious by secular standard, good deeds performed to please the ego or to earn some rewards in return. As such, people often become more self-conceited because of their good deeds. Virtuous deeds are different. They are motivated not by personal benefits, but the benefits of all. While extending the help, the person eliminates his self-grasping, becomes a better person, and is gradually freed from pain and sufferings."

慧可求法

趙州八十猶行腳，只為心頭未悄然；

及至歸來無一事，始知空費草鞋錢。

—— 張無盡

達摩祖師在嵩山面壁期間，有位年輕人慧可前來求法，在雪地裏苦候到天明，並且還以斷臂的方式表達赤誠之心。達摩祖師知其意志堅定，便問，「諸佛求道為法忘形，你今斷臂，求又何在？」

年輕人答道，「我心未寧，乞師與安。」

達摩反問，「你的心在何處？拿來吧，我替你安。」慧可找了半天也找拿不出自己的心。正在為難之際，達摩意味深長地說，「不用找了，我已替你安好了。」

慧可豁然大悟：無論妄心、淨心、真心，皆緣生緣滅，無心可得，自然無心可安，這不安而安，即是最上乘的安心之法。

─── [佛教小知識] ───────────────

- **參訪善知識**

有人向唐朝趙州從諗禪師請教，「末劫時，還有沒有『這個人』？」我們的肉身是否會隨星球的壞、空而毀滅？趙州禪師回答，「會壞」。

那人又問，「那麼，我們的業識又去何處？」

「隨他去！」趙州回答後，內心也產生了困惑，覺得不妥，無法安心修道。於是，八十歲高齡的趙州禪師跋山涉水，參訪善知識，尋找答案。

古往今來，禪門修道人心有疑問，參訪善知識，化解心中疑慮，這種做法極為普遍，成為佛門的優良傳統。當初六祖惠能也是因為聽聞《金剛經》，心有所悟，不遠千里，去黃梅參訪五祖弘忍這位大善知識，「一聞言下便悟，頓見真如本性。」真如本性，無形無相，普通根性的人難以一下子參透，也是可以理解的。六祖惠能提醒大眾，「若自不悟，須覓大善知識、解最上乘法者，直示正路。」這是參禪悟道的關鍵。

Hui Ke Seeking the Dharma

At the age of eighty, Master Zhaozhou was still wondering,

All because of the still restless mind.

Upon returning having found nothing,

It was realized that money paid for the worn shoes was spent in vain.

— Zhang Wujin

While Bodhidharma was meditating in Mount Song, a young man named Hui Ke came to seek the Dharma. The young man waited outside the cave in the snow throughout the night until dawn. He even showed his sincerity by cutting off one of his arms. Bodhidharma understood his resolute determination and asked, "Buddhas seeking the Way would forget themselves for the sake of Dharma. Now that you have severed your arm, what for?"

The young man answered, "My mind is not at peace. I beg you, Master, to settle it for me."

Bodhidharma asked him, "Where is your mind? Bring it to me, and I will settle it for you." Hui Ke couldn't find his mind. At that moment, Bodhidharma said, "No need to search for it any more. I have settled it for you."

Hui Ke was suddenly awakened: Whatever mind it may be, a deluded mind, a pure mind, or a real mind, it is not substantial but arises and perishes as conditions gather and disperse. There is no mind to attain, therefore no mind to be settled. This method of settling the mind without settling it is the supreme Dharma-door of restoring peace of mind.

Basics of Buddhism:

• Visiting wise teachers

One day, a man asked Chan Master Zhaozhou Congshen, "At the end of the kalpa, will there be 'this person'? Will our physical body be destroyed together with the decay and disappearance of the Earth?" Zhaozhou replied, "Yes."

Then the man asked again, "If so, where will our karmic consciousness go?"

"Go with it!" After giving this answer, Zhaozhou felt perplexed and uneasy to the extent that he couldn't continue with his practice in peace. Thus, at the age of eighty, he travelled a long journey and visited wise teachers searching for answers.

Throughout history, it has become a wonderful tradition for Chan practitioners who have doubts to visit wise teachers in order to dispel their doubts. The Sixth Patriarch Hui Neng also went on a journey to Huangmei to visit the Fifth Patriarch Hong Ren after hearing The Diamond Sutra, and "I became enlightened as soon as I heard him speak. I suddenly saw the fundamental nature of suchness." The fundamental nature of suchness is without form or image, which cannot be penetrated by ordinary people, and this is understandable. The Sixth Patriarch Hui Neng reminded us, "If you do not become enlightened by yourself, then you must seek a great spiritual compatriot, someone who understands the Dharma of the Supreme Vehicle, to indicate directly the correct path for you." Seeking the right teacher is critical for Chan practice and the attainment of enlightenment.

漸悟神秀

> 身是菩提樹，心如明鏡台。
> 時時勤拂拭，莫使有塵埃。

—— 神秀

常為菩提樹澆水、施肥、修除旁枝，它才能茁壯成長；我們的身、口如同菩提樹一般，應常以「持戒」來修正我們的一言一行，使之合與規範。同樣，我們的心原本如同明鏡台一樣明亮，應以「修定」來清除我們心靈深處的私心、雜念等塵埃，保持本性的清淨。

神秀修道方法的要點是「時時勤拂拭」，主張修行要循序漸進。這種漸悟式的修行方式，對普通根機的修道人十分適合。然而，神秀將身、心比做菩提樹與明鏡台，塵埃比做煩惱，字裏行間流露出他仍在有分別的心境上下工夫，於惠能「無住生心」的頓悟法門仍有一段距離，因而失去繼承五祖衣缽的資格。

[佛教小知識]

• 北宗禪

禪宗五祖弘忍之門下大通神秀，以弘法於北方，故稱北宗。五祖入寂後，神秀遷至江陵當陽山（湖北），力主漸悟之說，其教說盛行於長安、洛陽等北地。而在南方，六祖惠能則於韶州（廣東）曹溪山說法教化，主張頓悟之思想，蔚成南宗禪，中國禪宗史上乃有所謂南宗北宗、南頓北漸等名稱。

Shen Xiu's Gradual Enlightenment

The body is the bodhi tree,

The mind is like a bright mirror's stand.

Be always diligent in rubbing it—

Do not let it attract any dust.

— Shen Xiu

The bodhi tree will thrive if it is constantly watered, fertilized, and pruned. Likewise, our physical action and speech should be amended through precepts so that they can comply with the disciplines. Similarly, our minds were originally as pure as the stand of a bright mirror. We should practice concentration to remove the inner dust such as selfish motives and distracting thoughts to maintain the purity of our primordial nature.

With its essence being the frequent removal of dust, Shen Xiu's approach focuses on a gradual process of cultivation. The method of gradual enlightenment is quite suitable for practitioners of average spiritual capacity. Shen Xiu's analogies comparing the body and mind to the Bodhi-tree and mirror stand, and dust to afflictions indicate that he was still practising within

身是菩提樹
心如明鏡臺時
時勤拂拭
勿使惹塵埃

a discriminating state of mind. As his approach was yet to be comparable to Hui Neng's sudden enlightenment approach, Shen Xiu lost his chance to inherit the Dharma lineage transmitted by the Fifth Patriarch.

Basics of Buddhism:

• The Northern Chan School

Shen Xiu, one of the chief disciples of Hong Ren, the Fifth Patriarch of the Chan School, promoted the Dharma in northern China, which was hence referred to as the Northern School. After the Fifth Patriarch passed away, Shen Xiu moved to Dangyang Mountain in Jiangling (Hubei Province) and disseminated the teaching of gradual enlightenment, which was prevalent in the north such as Chang'an and Luoyang. Hui Neng, the Sixth Patriarch, spread the Dharma in Caoxi Mountain of Shaozhou (Guangdong Province), fostering the teaching of sudden enlightenment, hence referred to as the Southern School of Chan. As such, in the history of Chan tradition, there are names such as the Southern School and the Northern School, or terms such as Sudden South and Gradual North.

頓悟惠能

菩提本無樹，明鏡亦非台。
本來無一物，何處惹塵埃。

—— 六祖惠能

　　雖說北宗的神秀是五祖弘忍的首座弟子，但最後被傳授禪宗衣缽
的，卻是南宗的惠能。六祖惠能並不是滿腹經綸的學士，他本來就只是
嶺南的一個樵夫，家境貧窮，與母親相依為命，一次在賣柴的路上聽見
有人唸誦金剛經，至「應無所住而生其心」，便當下悟道，繼而前往黃
梅找五祖，在他座下出家。

　　那為甚麼最終竟是惠能被五祖傳授衣缽而非神秀呢？五祖就是因
為讀了惠能以下的偈頌，而認定他的悟境超於神秀，故而確立他為接班
人的地位。

　　「菩提本無樹，明鏡亦非台，本來無一物，何處惹塵埃？」

　　惠能悟道偈中的「本無樹」與「亦非台」道出這樣一個道理：現
象世界中的萬物，皆緣生緣滅，瞬息萬變，空無自性，「本來無一物」，
從哪裏能找到一個固定不變的塵埃供人們去「時時拂拭」呢？只要覺悟
到本無一物的清淨自性，便可立地成佛。這就是惠能的頓悟法門，為中
國禪宗從理論和方法上找到了一條超塵脫俗的快捷方式。

• 南宗禪

「南宗禪」與「北宗禪」相對，因慧能在江南布傳法，所以叫南宗禪。禪宗從五祖弘忍處分為慧能與神秀兩支，神秀在北方傳承，所以有「南能北秀」的說法。「南宗禪」的禪風完全擺脫之前的佛法學說，不拘束於名相，不滯於言句，提倡修證不二、迷悟一如；稱自己本覺之妙心乃本成本明，並不存在真實的煩惱妄念，所以宣導「一超直入如來地」的頓悟學說，又稱祖師禪。「南宗禪」到後世極盛，分化出五家七宗的分派，所以一般尊南宗為禪之正宗，尊慧能為禪宗第六祖。南宗禪，主張「明心見性」、「直指人心」、「頓悟成佛」。南宗的頓悟，認為只要消除妄念、性體無生，則立刻成佛。沒有必要緩緩靜修。慧能的弟子神會比喻這種頓悟為「利劍斬束絲」。他說：譬如一縷之絲，其數無量，若合為一繩，置於木上，利劍一斬，一時俱斷。絲數雖多，不勝一劍。發菩提心，亦復如是。因為煩惱妄念可以「一時俱斷」，所以剎那之間成佛就是完全有可能的。

Hui Neng's Sudden Enlightenment

Bodhi is fundamentally without any tree;

The bright mirror is also not a stand.

Fundamentally there is not a single thing—

Where could any dust be attracted?

— Hui Neng, the Sixth Patriarch

Although Shen Xiu of the Northern School was the chief disciple of the Fifth Patriarch Hong Ren, it was Hui Neng of the Southern School who inherited the Dharma lineage of the Chan School. Hui Neng was not an erudite scholar but a woodcutter from Lingnan, who was born in a poor family and lived with his mother. One day, on the way to sell wood, Hui Neng heard someone chanting the Diamond Sutra. When it came to the sentence "The mind should arise but without any attachment," Hui Neng became enlightened suddenly. Then he went to Huangmei for the Fifth Patriarch and renounced his secular life there.

Why did Hui Neng inherit the Dharma lineage of the Fifth Patriarch rather than Shen Xiu? It is because the Fifth Patriarch had read the verse of Hui Neng and affirmed that his understanding of the Dharma is superior to that of Shen Xiu. He therefore chose Hui Neng as his successor.

Bodhi is fundamentally without any tree;

The bright mirror is also not a stand.

Fundamentally there is not a single thing—

Where could any dust be attracted?

The verses in Hui Neng's enlightenment gatha, the "fundamentally without any tree" and "not a stand," reveal the truth: All worldly phenomena arise and cease following the law of dependent origination. They change every moment and are insubstantial in nature. If "fundamentally there is not a single thing," where can we find a permanent dust to remove? So long as one realizes that one's intrinsic nature is pure and free from all bondages, one will instantly become a Buddha. This is Hui Neng's Sudden Enlightenment Dharma-door. Hui Neng discovered a direct path to enlightenment in theory and practice for Chinese Chan Buddhism.

• The Southern Chan School

The Southern Chan School, as opposed to the Northern Chan School, is so named as Hui Neng transmitted the Dharma in the south of Yangtze River. From the Fifth Patriarch Hong Ren, the Chan School of Buddhism was divided into two sects, one represented by Hui Neng and the other by Shen Xiu, who spread the Dharma in the north. Thus, they are also called "Neng of the South and Xiu of the North." The Chan style of Southern School is totally different from the previous Buddhist doctrinal style; it is not restrained by names and appearances or words and sentences. It advocates the non-duality of cultivation and realization, and that delusion and enlightenment are one. It claims that the awakened wondrous mind is originally bright and perfect, and the so-called afflictions or delusive thoughts are indeed insubstantial. Thus, the Southern Chan School fostered the teaching of sudden enlightenment which leads practitioners to "instantly enter the realm of Tathāgata." This is also known as Patriarch Chan. The Southern Chan School was very popular in subsequent years, having evolved into the Five Houses and Seven Schools. It was famous for being the authentic lineage of Chan Buddhism and Hui Neng was honored as the Sixth Patriarch of the Chan tradition in China.

The Southern Chan School calls for "discovering one's true mind and seeing one's intrinsic nature," "directly observing one's own mind," and "attaining sudden enlightenment for realization of Buddhahood." Sudden enlightenment as preached by the Southern Chan School suggests that Buddhahood is instantly attained when the mind is free from delusions and the non-arising of essential nature is manifested, and therefore it is not necessary to cultivate in a gradual manner. Shen Hui, the disciple of Hui Neng, compared sudden enlightenment to cutting a bundle of threads with a sharp sword. He explained that if pieces of threads are bundled together and put on the table, they can be cut off altogether by a sharp sword even if they are numerous in number. It is the same when Bodhicitta arises, because afflictions and deluded thoughts can be cut off instantly altogether. Therefore, it is quite possible to become a Buddha in an instant.

道由心悟

前念迷，即凡夫；

後念悟，即佛。

——《六祖壇經》

據《景德傳燈錄》記載，年輕的馬祖道一整天靜坐不動，看心觀靜，期盼有朝一日妄心不起，開悟成佛。其師懷讓禪師十分憂慮，故意問他，「坐禪圖甚麼？」道一回答，「圖作佛」。

懷讓一言不發，就拿出一塊磚頭，在道一身旁的石頭上磨了起來。好奇心驅使道一向前詢問所以然。懷讓回答，「磨作鏡」。道一頓覺好笑，「磨磚豈得成鏡耶？」

這時懷讓抓住機會反問，「磨磚不能成鏡，坐禪豈得成佛耶？」道一仍滿臉疑慮地問，「如何才能開悟成佛？」懷讓開導他說，「如果一個人所駕的車停下來，要使車繼續行走，你是打車還是打牛？」道一聞言大悟。要使車子順利到達目的地，如果車子不走了，問題不在車子，而在牛；同理，惠能告誡世人，「道由心悟，豈在坐也？」

參禪悟道時，若過於執着於坐禪的儀式，是心外求法，故惠能說，「若言如來若坐若臥，是行邪道。」只有從心入手，去除一切執着，「無所從來，亦無所去，無生無滅」，頓悟自心本來清淨，與佛無異，此心即佛，這就是「如來清淨禪」。

• 心佛眾生，三無差別

> 不悟，即佛是眾生；
>
> 一念悟時，眾生是佛。

——《壇經》

　　眾生本具清淨心，與佛無二無別，其差別只在迷悟兩字而已。一念無明生起，貪心生起，迷失了自性便成了眾生，而通過修行悟到自性，便成了覺悟的人，即是佛。《六祖壇經》因而說，「不悟即佛是眾生；一念悟時，眾生是佛」。眾生與佛的根本區別就是一念之間的迷與悟。《六祖壇經》以當下這一念巧妙地將《楞伽經》的「自性清淨」思想與般若經典中的空、有不二的「中道實相」結合在一起，以「前念迷即凡夫，後念悟即佛」、「前念着境即煩惱，後念離境即菩提」等教法，闡釋禪修

的關鍵是六祖當下一念的轉迷成悟。一切佛法都在人自心之中，佛也不例外。以此啟迪人們的自覺意識，增強世人自我解脱的自信。《六祖壇經》為身處紅塵中身心疲憊的「俗人」，指出了一條自性自悟的精神解脱之路。

Enlightened to the Way through the Mind

With a preceding moment of deluded thought, one was an ordinary person, but with a succeeding moment of enlightened thought, one is a buddha.

— The Platform Sutra

According to The Jingde Record of the Transmission of the Lamp, the young Mazu Daoyi sat still all day long observing the mind hoping that one day the deluded thoughts will no longer arise, then he will be enlightened and become a Buddha. His master Huai Rang was concerned about this and asked him, "What is your purpose of sitting meditation?" "To become a Buddha," replied Dao Yi.

Without saying anything, Huai Rang took a brick and ground it on the stone beside Dao Yi. Out of curiosity, Dao Yi asked the reason why. "To grind it into a mirror," replied the Master. "How can a brick be ground into a mirror?" laughed Dao Yi.

Huai Rang took this opportunity to ask him, "If a brick cannot be ground into a mirror, then how can sitting meditation lead one to

Buddhahood?" Filled with doubt, Dao Yi asked, "How can I be enlightened and become a Buddha?" Huai Rang explained, "If an ox cart stopped and the driver wants it to move again, will the driver whip the ox or the cart?" Upon hearing these words, Dao Yi was enlightened. If the carriage stops moving towards the destination, the problem lies in the ox rather than the cart. Similarly, Hui Neng exhorted sentient beings, "One is enlightened through the mind rather than through sitting meditation."

When one meditates for enlightenment with an excessive attachment to the ritual of sitting meditation, he or she is seeking the Dharma outside the mind. Thus, Hui Neng said, "To say that the Tathāgata sits or lies down is to practice a false path." One should eliminate all attachments from his own mind, for suchness never comes or goes, neither arises nor vanishes. In sudden enlightenment, one sees the mind is innately pure and not different from the Buddha's mind, and that the mind is Buddha. This is the lineage of the Pure Tathāgata Chan.

Basics of Buddhism:

- **The mind, the Buddha, and sentient beings are the same**

  If one is unenlightened, then the buddhas are sentient beings.

  When one is enlightened for [even] a single moment, then sentient beings are buddhas.

  — The Platform Sutra

Sentient beings originally possess a pure mind that is no different from that of the Buddha. It is the delusion or enlightenment of their minds that makes the difference. When a thought of ignorance and craving arises, one loses one's intrinsic nature and becomes a sentient being. However, if one realizes his or her intrinsic nature through cultivation, one becomes an enlightened person—a Buddha. It is therefore said in the Platform Sutra, "If one is unenlightened, then the buddhas are sentient beings. When one is enlightened for [even] a single moment, then sentient beings are buddhas."

The fundamental difference between sentient beings and Buddhas is whether one is deluded or enlightened in a flash of thought. By using the thought in the current moment, the Platform Sutra skillfully combines the teaching of pure intrinsic nature in Lankāvatāra Sūtra with the truth of Middle Way of non-duality between emptiness and existence in the Prajna scriptures. It emphasizes that the key to meditation is to transform delusion into enlightenment through such teachings as "With a preceding moment of deluded thought, one was an ordinary person, but with a succeeding moment of enlightened thought, one is a buddha" and "To be attached to one's sensory realms in a preceding moment of thought is affliction, but to transcend the realms in a succeeding moment of thought is bodhi." By explaining that all the teachings are within the minds of sentient beings as well as Buddhas', it inspires the awareness for enlightenment and boosts the confidence to set themselves free. The Platform Sutra leads struggling sentient beings in the secular world to enlightenment and self-liberation.

心無罣礙

前念著境，即煩惱；

後念離境，即菩提。

——《六祖壇經》

人人都渴望活得自在，但要活得自在，首先就要心安。可是人的心，往往因為生活的逼迫、感情的牽扯、人我是非的挑動，被弄得百般煎熬、忐忑不安。要從此等煩惱中解脫出來，令得心安，談何容易？但我們可以肯定，自心一天仍是隨境而生、為逐境而存的話，那我們的心就永遠難以安然。

有僧人問石頭希遷禪師：「如何是解脫？」

禪師追問：「是誰束縛了你？」

僧人又問：「如何是淨土？」

禪師又反問：「是誰污染你了？」

僧人再問：「如何是涅槃？」

禪師答道：「是誰讓你在生死中輪迴？」僧人豁然大悟。

歸根究底，沒有其他人能幫我們徹底消除煩惱，要達至解脫，得靠自己。也許我們無法一下子就空掉心中的罣礙、不為外境所轉，但正如《六祖壇經》所云：「前念著境即煩惱，後念離境即菩提。」就讓我們先從每一個念頭做起吧！

• 迷悟一念間

　　有個失戀的人在公園裏頭，因為不甘而哭泣。一位路過的哲人不但沒有安慰她，反而笑道，「你不過是丟棄了一個不愛你的人，而他卻損失了一個愛他的人，他的損失要比你大得多，你還有甚麼可恨的呢？不甘心的人應該是他才對。」

　　世間的愛與恨、苦與樂、得與失、是與非、正與邪、好與壞、煩惱與菩提、地獄與天堂、凡夫與聖賢絕對不是對立的兩面，而是可以相互轉化的。轉化的時間很短，短到一念之間，轉化的關鍵是轉迷成悟：一念迷，萬念俱灰，淒淒慘慘，苦海無邊，而成為苦惱眾生；一念悟，海闊天空，快快樂樂，歡喜自在而成為解脫的覺者。

Mind without Obscurations

To be attached to one's sensory realms in a preceding moment of thought is affliction, but to transcend the realms in a succeeding moment of thought is bodhi.

— The Platform Sutra

Everyone wishes to live freely. But to live freely, first we should have a peaceful mind. Unfortunately, people's minds are perturbed and overwhelmed with anxiety by the pressure of making a living, entanglement of emotions, and the agitation of right and wrong between self and others. How difficult it is to extricate oneself from such afflictions and obtain a peaceful mind! But one thing is for sure: our mind will never have real peace if it is still attached and hence easily turned by externalities.

A monk asked Shitou Xiqian, a Chan master, "How is it to be free?"

The master questioned, "Who binds you?"

The monk asked again, "What is pure land?"

The master countered, "Who contaminates you?"

The monk asked again, "What is nirvana?"

The master replied, "Who makes you transmigrate in the cycle of birth and death?"

The monk was suddenly enlightened.

After all, nobody else can help us eradicate afflictions. To attain liberation, we need to rely on ourselves. Maybe we cannot instantly remove afflictions and hindrances in our mind and keep our mind unaffected by surroundings. However, we can start cultivation from purifying every thought in our mind. As it says in the Platform Sutra, "To be attached to one's sensory realms in a preceding moment of thought is affliction, but to transcend the realms in a succeeding moment of thought is bodhi." Let us start from being mindful of the arising thoughts now!

❈ Basics of Buddhism:

• **Delusion or enlightenment lies within a flash of thought**

A lady was weeping in a park because she could not accept the breakup of a relationship. A philosopher passed by. Instead of comforting her, the philosopher laughed, "You just abandoned a person who does not love you, while he lost a person who loves him. His loss is much greater than yours. He, rather than you, should be the one who weeps."

In this world, there are love and hatred, joy and sorrow, gain and loss, right and wrong, righteous and evil, good and bad, Bodhi and affliction, heaven and hell, and sages and ordinary people. These pairs are not opposite sides in absolute sense, but one can transform to the other. The transformation process can be as short as a flash of thought. And the key lies in turning the mind around from delusion to awakening. With one thought of delusion, one may be utterly disheartened, leading to a miserable life restrained in the boundless sea of suffering and thus becoming a sentient being entangled in afflictions. With one thought of enlightenment, one can possess a mindset that is as boundless as the sea and the sky, leading to a free and happy life and thus becoming an enlightened person.

百丈清規

叢林以無事為興盛，精進以持戒為第一。
煩惱以忍辱為菩提，是非以不辯為解脫。
留眾以老成為真情，山門以耆舊為莊嚴。
處眾以謙恭為有禮，濟物以慈悲為根本。

——《百丈大智禪師叢林要則》

　　自六祖惠能起，中國禪宗傳至百丈懷海，算是第九代了。百丈禪師對於中國佛教的貢獻，在於他對組織制度及叢林規式，作出了佛教史上空前的建樹。

　　佛門的「清規」，本可追溯到佛陀時代，只是當時沒有明文規定。佛教傳入中國後，至東晉道安大師時，才因應當時佛教內部的一些問題，制定了《僧尼規範》和《法門清規》。而禪宗所建立的清規，則始自百丈懷海禪師。

　　處於唐朝中葉，當時的禪僧多是居無定所的雲水僧，又或依律寺而居，故於說法行道方面，產生了諸多矛盾與不便。馬祖建立了叢林，而百丈禪師亦因應當時社會環境的變遷，為禪門的叢林僧編制了一套清規，以期有助禪宗有序持續地發展。百丈自己又推崇「一日不作、一日不食」的理念，其「農禪並重」的家風，成為了中國佛教的優良傳統，標誌着中國禪宗一代的特色。

　　奈何佛教一些大德認為，由於歷時已久，尤其於元代曾被大量刪改，現今留存的《百丈清規》版本已非其原貌。

✺✺ ［佛教小知識］

- 一日不作，一日不食

　　「馬祖創叢林，百丈立清規」。百丈懷海禪師宣導「一日不作，一日不食」的農禪生活。即使年老體弱，他每日除了領眾修行之外，仍然隨眾上山擔柴，下田種地。弟子們心有不忍，只好將禪師所用的扁擔、鋤頭等工具藏起來，不讓他勞作。

　　百丈禪師無奈，便以絕食來抗議。

　　弟子焦急地勸食，百丈禪師堅持説：「既然沒有勞作，哪能吃飯？」

　　弟子們沒辦法，只得將工具還給他，讓他繼續隨眾做農活。

　　百丈禪師「一日不作，一日不食」的禪風，成為叢林千古的楷模。

Bai Zhang Established
Monastic Regulations

A monastery will thrive if there is no dispute and conflict; the priority of diligence is observing the precepts.

Patience is taken as Bodhi (enlightenment) in transforming afflictions; non-argument is essential in liberation from right and wrong.

Honesty and earnestness is the key to rallying followers; a monastery is dignified due to the presence of virtuous elders.

Modesty and respect is the right way in treating others; compassion is essential in the distribution of resources.

— Essentials of Monastic Regulations by Chan Master Baizhang

Baizhang Huaihai is the ninth generation to inherit the Dharma lineage of the Chinese Chan School from Hui Neng, the Sixth Patriarch. In Buddhist history, he made unprecedented contributions to Chinese Buddhism for having established the organizational system and monastic regulations.

The monastic regulations in Buddhism can date back to the age of the Buddha but were not in written form. It was at the time of the Eastern Jin dynasty after Buddhism was introduced into China that Master Dao An formulated the Standards for Monks and Nuns and the Rules of Purity for Monastics, due to some issues that happened at that time inside the Buddhist community. However, the monastic regulations of the Chan School were first established by Chan Master Baizhang Huaihai.

In the mid Tang dynasty, most Chan masters were travelling and studying without fixed residence or lived by temples of the Vinaya School, which made it difficult to preach and practice Chan. As a result, Master

Ma Zu set up monasteries and Master Bai Zhang established a set of rules for Chan monasteries according to the social circumstances at that time to help the Chan School develop orderly and continuously. Bai Zhang himself upheld the philosophy of "one day without work, one day without eating." "Combining Chan with agricultural work," a special feature of the Chinese Chan School, has become an excellent tradition in Chinese Buddhism.

However, some eminent monastics believe that due to the long time it has been in circulation, and especially after it has been subjected to a large amount of omissions and deletions, the extant Baizhang Zen Monastic Regulations is no longer the original version.

✦ Basics of Buddhism:

• **One day without work, one day without eating**

Ma Zu established monasteries and Bai Zhang established monastic regulations. Chan Master Baizhang Huaihai advocated a life of cultivation in Chan and agricultural work featuring "one day without work, one day without eating." In his old age, Bai Zhang still followed others to carry wood from hills and worked in the field in addition to leading the daily practice. Worried about the master, his disciples had to hide his tools like the shoulder pole and the hoe to stop him from working.

Bai Zhang had no choice but to protest by going on hunger strike.

His disciples were worried; they pleaded him to eat. But Bai Zhang insisted, "Since I do not work, how can I eat?"

Without a choice, the disciples had to give back the tools to the master so he could continue with his farming.

The Chan style of "one day without work, one day without eating" advocated by Bai Zhang has become a time-honored model for all monastics.

一花五葉

吾本來茲土，傳法救迷情。
一華開五葉，結果自然成。

—— 達摩祖師

　　禪宗雖然發源於印度，但卻成長成熟於中國，之後更傳入韓國、日本、越南等地。

　　釋尊於靈山會上拈花，得到大弟子摩訶迦葉以會心的微笑回應，是為禪宗第一代祖師。此後相傳歷二十八世，至菩提達摩傳入中國，成為中國的禪宗初祖，又五傳之後至六祖惠能大師，則為禪宗於中國奠下了不拔的基礎。

　　由於禪修是練心之法，禪宗強調不立文字，教外別傳，直指人心，明心自會見到本然清淨之佛性，故當時師資相承、直傳心印，且又追隨者眾的流派便相繼形成，當中最主要的有溈仰、臨濟、曹洞、雲門及法眼五家。這些宗派隨機接引學人，令當時的禪風更趨盛行、廣為傳播，故有一花開五葉之稱。唐宋時代更曾發展成五家七宗，到宋以後則逐漸剩下臨濟及曹洞二宗，而清末民初時，就只有臨濟宗流傳最廣，享有「臨濟子孫滿天下」之美譽。

- 五家七宗

　　唐末五代，慧能弟子分為青原行思和南嶽懷讓兩大派。行思之後分
為曹洞、雲門、法眼三家；懷讓之後形成臨濟、溈仰二派。宋代，臨濟
再分為黃龍、楊岐二支，史稱「五家七宗」。明清以後，中國佛教以宗
派譜系而言，只有禪宗一家流布最廣，以曹洞和臨濟二分天下，至今後
嗣仍燦若繁星，成為中國漢地佛教的主流。

One Flower, Five Petals

Coming to your land, I teach the Dharma to rescue the deluded.

One flower blossoming with five petals, the fruit is produced of its own accord.

— Master Bodhidharma

The Chan School originated in India which grew and became widely known in China, and later was introduced to South Korea, Japan, and Vietnam.

When Śākyamuni Buddha twirled a flower at the assembly on Vulture Peak, the chief disciple Mahākāśyapa got the subtle message and smiled in response to the Buddha, so he became the first patriarch of Chan School. Subsequently, the Dharma was transmitted to the 28th Patriarch Bodhidharma, who had the Dharma transmitted into China. Thus,

Bodhidharma became First Patriarch of the Chan School in China. After the lineage had been passed on through five patriarchs to Sixth Patriarch Hui Neng, the Chan School flourished and built a solid foundation in China.

Because Chan practice is the approach of cultivating the mind, it emphasizes on being a "living lineage other than the literal one, not dependent upon words," and "pointing directly at the mind." With an illumined mind, one can see the innately pure Buddha-nature. Various sects of the Chan lineage were formed, and each inherited the unique style of mind transmission from master to disciple aiming directly at the mind. Chan practice became widely followed at the time. The five main sects of Chan were the Weiyang, Linji, Caodong, Yunmen, and Fayan. These sects guided the disciples towards awakening in the most unrestricted and free styles, making Chan practice more popular and accepted across the country. As such, there is a saying which goes, "One flower blossoms with five petals." Further, Chan expanded to become the Five Houses and Seven Schools during the Tang and Song dynasties. However, after the Song dynasty, Chan sects witnessed a down-turn and only the Linji and Caodong remained. By the end of the Qing dynasty and the beginning of the Republic of China, only the Linji was still widely practiced in China, with a reputation of "Linji followers are found everywhere."

※ Basics of Buddhism:

• **The Five Houses and Seven Schools (of Chan)**

In the late Tang period and during the Five Dynasties, Hui Ning's disciples were divided into two major sects: Qingyuan Xingsi and Nanyue Huairang. From Xing Si, three houses developed: Caodong, Yunmen, and Fayan. And from Huai Rang, the Linji and Weiyang sects were formed. In the Song dynasty, the Linji was further divided into two branches: Huanglong and Yangqi. Together they were called in history the Five Houses and Seven Schools of Chan. After the Ming and Qing dynasties, only Chan Buddhism stood out as the most practiced tradition in China. Particularly, the Caodong and Linji attracted almost all practitioners in the country and the number of followers split evenly between the two. Until now, descendants of the Linji and Caodong are still countless in number and shining like stars, making these two sects the mainstream in Chinese Han Buddhism today.

溈仰撥火

溈仰宗者，父慈子孝，上令下從；你欲吃飯，我便與羹；你欲渡江，我便撐船；隔山見煙，便知是火；隔牆見角，便知是牛。

——《人天眼目》

溈仰宗是禪宗一花開五葉最早形成的派別，乃溈山靈佑與其門人仰山慧寂所共同創立的。溈仰宗者，「父慈子孝、上令下從」，極為嚴謹，其接引學人，看似平衍，實則深邃奧祕、事理並行，其家風審細密切，師資唱和、體用語似爭而方圓默契，非大根器不易繼承，故此宗相傳只四代人，大概歷經一百五十年，至中晚唐時期便斷了法脈。

話說一個寒冬之夜，百丈禪師打坐時覺得非常寒冷，於是便叫當時的侍者靈佑撥弄火爐。靈佑撥了一下便說：「無火」。百丈禪師聽後便自行前去用火棍在爐中深深一撥，只見有點火花乍現，於是反問靈佑：「這不是火嗎？」這下子靈佑頓然醒悟、心開意解，急忙叩謝師父。

那點火就正如我們的心性，本自具足，只是迷時不見，悟時自現。故創立溈仰宗之後，靈佑曾言：「夫道人之心，質直無偽，無背無面，無詐妄心。一切時中視聽尋常，更無委曲。亦不閉眼塞耳，但情不附物即得。」

- 潙山靈佑

潙山靈佑（771—853），唐代高僧，俗姓趙，福建長溪（在今福州）人，為仰宗初祖。

靈佑十五歲從建善寺法常律師出家，於杭州龍興寺受具足戒，究大小乘教。後到江西參百丈懷海。有一次，懷海讓他撥爐灰，看有火沒有，他撥後說沒有，懷海往深處撥，找到火星，責備他說沒有，於是大悟。唐憲宗元和末年，至潙山弘揚禪風，村民感德，群集共建同慶寺。相國裴休前來聞道，聲譽大揚，學僧雲集，遂於此敷揚宗風達四十年之久，世稱潙山靈佑。

潙山的基本思想是「三種生」說，即把主客觀世界分為「想生」、「相生」、「流注生」，這也是他為接引學人證得大圓鏡智（佛智），達到自由無礙境地而設的三種機法。

唐宣宗大中七年 (853) 示寂，世壽八十三歲，諡「大圓禪師」。有《潭州潙山靈佑禪師語錄》、《潙山警策》各一卷傳世。

Stirring Fire, the Weiyang Style

The Weiyang Chan is characterized as such: father being affectionate and son being filial; the superior gives order and the subordinate follows; when you want to eat, I hand you the spoonful; when you want to cross the river, I ferry the boat. See the smoke over the mountain and know it is fire; see the horn over the wall and know it is an ox.

— The Eye of Humans and Gods

The Weiyang School was the first established sect among the five in Chinese Chan tradition. Weiyang was co-founded by Weishan Lingyou and his disciple Yangshan Huiji. Following the practice of "affectionate father and filial son; the superior gives order and the subordinate follows," Weiyang Chan features a strict teaching style that the disciples are guided in a seemingly plain but profound manner. Both theoretical and practical insights are emphasized by the masters. The teaching is intricate and detailed, and masters and disciples play off each other in a wonderful way, while in apparent disputes, mutual connections are made and insights passed along. The Weiyang style demands a very high spiritual capacity of the practitioner, therefore the Dharma lineage survived for only four generations over a period of about 150 years before coming to an end in the mid to late Tang dynasty.

The story goes that on a winter's night, Chan master Bai Zhang felt very cold during meditation, so he called out to his attendant Ling You to stir up the fire. Ling You stirred for a while and said, "No fire." Hearing his reply, Bai Zhang stirred deeply into the stove with a stoking stick whereupon sparks burst up. The master then asked Lingyou, "Is this not a fire?" Lingyou was suddenly awakened and got the message. Quickly, he bowed to thank his master.

Like the sparkling fire, one's intrinsic nature is complete and perfect. It is only in delusion that one does not see it. But upon awakening, the intrinsic nature manifests itself. After founding the Weiyang School, Lingyou once said, "One's mind is by nature of integrity and honesty. It does not discriminate the front and back, nor does it harbor conceit and illusion. It just sees and hears normally in every moment, and is devoid of distortive or elaborative thoughts. No need to cover the eye or the ear; [the truth] is realized by simply not grasping."

☷ Basics of Buddhism:

• **Weishan Lingyou**

Weishan Lingyou (771-853), an eminent monk of the Tang dynasty and the founding patriarch of the Weiyang Chan School, was born in Changxi of Fu Zhou region (Fujian today). His family name was Zhao.

When Ling You was fifteen, he was ordained by the vinaya Master Fa Chang in Jianshan Temple. He received full ordination at Longxing Temple in Hangzhou where he devoted himself to the study of Hinayana and Mahayana teachings. Later he came to seek instructions from Baizhang Huaihai in Jiangxi. One day, Huai Hai asked him to stir the fire stove to see if there was any fire. Ling You stirred and said, "There is no fire." Huai Hai stirred deeply into the fire stove and retrieved a small glow of ember, whereupon he showed it and upbraided, "You told me there was none?" Ling You was enlightened. During the period of Emperor Tang Xianzong's Yuanhe reign, Ling You went to Weishan mountain to propagate Chan. Villagers were touched by his morality and virtue; they assembled to build Tongqing Temple for him. The Prime Minister Pei Xiu came to Weishan mountain to listen to Chan teachings, and Ling You won considerable reputation and attracted many novice monastics from all over the country who came to Weishan. This led to the master's forty-year legacy of teaching Chan. His contributions are remembered, and he is called Weishan Lingyou by later generations.

The basic philosophy and thoughts of Weishan is the theory of "three sources" that give rise to the passions and illusions, upon which the subjective and objective worlds are conceived. The three sources are mental proliferation, worldly phenomena, and the constant influx created by interaction of the two. These are also three expediencies which he adopted to guide practitioners toward attainment of the perfect mirror wisdom (Buddha wisdom) and realization of utter freedom.

Ling You passed away at the age of eighty-three in the seventh year of Dazhong (AD 853) during Emperor Tang Xuanzong's reign. He was given the posthumous title of Chan Master Dayuan by Emperor Xuanzong. One volume each of the Selected Buddhist Writings from Chan Master Weishan Lingyou of Tanzhou and Weishan's Admonitions are in extant.

臨濟棒喝

七尺棒頭，撥開正眼；

一聲喝下，頓息狂心。

—— 古德

　　臨濟宗的開創者是義玄禪師 (787—867)，曹州南華人，出家後廣研戒律與經論，繼而到各處參學。後蒙黃檗希運禪師印可，遂於唐太宗八年 (854)，至鎮州臨濟院廣接徒眾，門風峭峻，盛於一代。

　　在黃檗門下時，義玄曾問希運禪師：「如何是佛法大意？」這一問便被禪師舉棒即打，義玄被打得莫名其妙，自問：「何錯之有？」後來經大愚禪師點醒，才恍然明白到，當頭棒喝可截斷學人的妄念，令其於猛然之間不假思索，直見佛性。

　　創立了臨濟宗之後，義玄繼承道一、希運「觸類是道」的思想，進而提出「立處即真」的主張，強調任運自在、隨緣而行，故而採用種種方便接引徒眾，更以機鋒峭峻著稱於世。義玄接化學人，每以叱喝顯大機用，故而有「臨濟喝、德山棒」之稱，這種棒喝宗風，日後亦成為了中國禪宗極具代表性的教法。

　　傳至石霜楚圓 (986—1039) 門下，臨濟宗又分出了黃龍與楊岐二派，兩者先後於公元十二三世紀被引進了日本，在那裏得到極大的發展。

• 義玄禪師

　　義玄（？—867），唐代高僧，中國禪宗臨濟宗創始人。俗姓邢，曹州南華（今山東省菏澤市東明縣）人。禪宗五家中，以臨濟宗影響最大，法脈延續最久，也以臨濟宗最具中國禪的特色，而開創臨濟這一系的，是義玄禪師。義玄的禪法，突出了人的主體性精神，強調自信，強烈反對崇拜偶像。他呵佛罵祖，機鋒峻烈，如電閃雷鳴，給人以強烈的心靈震撼。義玄作為佛家臨濟宗的創始人，有《鎮州臨濟慧照禪師語錄》傳世，世人簡稱《臨濟錄》。他有存獎等弟子二十二人。

Hitting and Shouting, the Linji Style

Hit with a seven-foot stick to open the Right Dharma-eye;
One shout to instantly bring the crazy mind to rest.

— An ancient sage

　　Chan Master Yi Xuan (AD 787-867) was the founder of the Linji School of Chan Buddhism. He was born in Nanhua District in Caozhou. After he became a monk, he first studied vinaya and the sutras and then travelled widely to learn from various teachers. After his awakening was verified by Chan Master Huangbo Xiyun, Yi Xuan, in the eighth year of Emperor Tang Taizong (AD 854), came to Linji Temple in Zhenzhou to widely receive followers. His unique teaching style made Linji Chan very popular during that era.

When Yixuan was practising under Chan Master Huangbo Xiyun, he asked what in brief is the Buddhadharma? Unexpectedly, the master hit him with a stick. Very confounded, Yi Xuan asked himself, "What did I do wrong?" Later on, Chan Master Da Yu made him realize that a sudden hit could cut off deluded thoughts, allowing him to directly see his Buddha nature.

After the founding of the Linji School, Yi Xuan inherited the Chan idea of Dao Yi and Xi Yun that "All that one comes into contact is the Way." Yi Xuan further proposed that "Reality is where you are now." He emphasized that one should act spontaneously and go along with the karmic flow. He adopted various expedient means to suit the learners and his teaching became well known for its sudden shouting to produce profound impacts. This shouting method proved very effective, hence the saying "Linji shout and Deshan stick." This style of teaching has become an iconic pedagogy of the Chinese Chan School.

When the lineage reached Shishuang Chuyuan (AD 986-1039), Linji was once again divided into two sub-sects: Huanglong and Yangqi. Both were introduced to Japan in the twelfth and the thirteenth century and flourished there.

※ Basics of Buddhism: ━━━━━━━━━━━━━━━━━━━━

• **Chan Master Yi Xuan**

Yi Xuan (?-867), an eminent monk of the Tang dynasty, was the founder of Linji School of Chinese Chan. Yi Xuan was born into a family named Xing at Nanhua in Caozhou (today's Dongming county, Heze city in Shandong province). Among the five Schools of Chan,

Linji is the most influential and with the longest Dharma lineage most representative of Chinese Chan. Chan Master Yi Xuan is the founder of the School. The Chan teachings of Yi Xuan manifest the individual spirit, emphasize self-confidence, and strongly object idol worship. He scolded the Buddhas and vilified the patriarchs, often throwing rigorous poignant remarks all of a sudden like thunder and lightning that deeply shock people's minds. His work Buddhist Writings from Chan Master Linji Huizhao of Zhenzhou, short form being Linji Records, is in extant. He has twenty-two disciples, including Cun Jiang.

切忌從他覓，迢迢與我疏；我今獨自往，處處得逢渠。

渠今正是我，我今不是渠；應須這麼會，方契得如如。

—— 洞山良價

　　曹洞宗乃中國禪宗南宗五家之一，為洞山良價 (807—869) 及其弟子本寂共同創立的。先由良價禪師在洞山創「君臣五位，偏正回互」的新禪說，後經本寂禪師在曹山解釋闡發而成的禪法。

　　相傳雲巖曇晟圓寂之後，良價每年都會於他的忌辰設齋上供，於是有僧問他：「您是在南泉普願座下悟道，為何尊雲巖作恩師而為他設供？」良價答道：「因為雲巖沒為我說破」。僧說：「那麼您是肯定雲巖要人自悟的禪風了？」良價說：「半肯定、半不肯定」。僧說：「為何不全肯定呢？」良價答道：「若全肯定，就太辜負先師了！」此公案生動地反映了曹洞的綿密家風。

　　曹洞宗的思想淵源可上溯到石頭希遷「即事而真」的見解，這樣看一切事相，自能圓轉無礙，因一切事相都能顯現理體。曹洞禪法，着重於寂靜；靈照，以徹見本源自性，故勵志於佛道生活之默照禪。

　　今天中國不少禪林都是曹洞宗法嗣所創，而曹洞宗在日本及韓國亦都非常盛行，追隨者眾。

- 洞山良價

　　良價 (807－869)，中國曹洞宗開祖，與弟子曹山本寂 (840－901) 共同創立了曹洞宗。良價禪師二十一歲時，至嵩山受具足戒。不久，謁南泉普願，深領玄旨。又訪溈山靈佑，參「無情說法」之話頭。然不契。遂依靈佑之指示往詣雲巖曇晟，舉前因緣有省，然猶涉疑滯。於是更歷參魯祖寶雲、南源道明等人。後於過水睹影時，豁然開悟。

　　唐宣宗大中 (847－859) 末，在新豐山（今江西宜豐縣同安鄉境內），建「洞山寺」。在此接引後學，弘揚大道，世稱「洞山良價」。

　　良價有弟子數百人，嗣法弟子有雲居道膺、曹山本寂、龍牙居遁、華嚴休靜、青林師虔等二十六人。弟子本寂 (840－901)，住曹山（今江西省宜黃縣北），承良價衣缽共創曹洞宗。

　　曹洞宗屬佛教南宗青原法系，中經石頭希遷、藥山惟儼、雲巖曇晟而至良價，其教法上承希遷之「即事而真」，意謂個別事物（事）顯現世界本體（真、理即佛性），理事互回（相應互涉），進而擴充五位君臣，由理事、体用關係而說明事理不二、體用無礙之理。《人天眼目》卷三謂其「家風細密，言行相應，隨機利物，就語接人」。

Meticulous, Caodong Style

Never seek from the without,

The self will only be further distanced;

As I set out on my own,

I encounter that everywhere.

That now becomes me,

Yet I am not that;

Such the way I must understand it all,

In order to accord with the Thusness.

— Dongshan Liangjie

The Caodong School is one of the five houses of Southern Chinese Chan, which was founded by Dongshan Liangjie and his disciple Ben Ji. Chan Master Liang Jie firstly founded the new Chan teaching in Mount Dong, advocating "the five ranks of ruler and minister, and the interaction of relative and absolute truth." Later through Chan Master Ben Ji from Mount Cao's further explanation, it developed into a new form of Chan teaching.

It is said that after Yunyan Tansheng passed away, Liang Jie would make offerings to him every year on his death anniversary. Some monk asked him, "You attained enlightenment under the seat of Nanquan Puyuan, but why do you revere Yun Yan as your teacher and make offerings to him?" Liang Jie answered, "Because Yun Yan didn't reveal the secret to me." The monk asked, "So do you agree with Yun Yan's Chan style that one should reach awakening by oneself?" Liang Jie said, "Half yes, half no." "Why not totally agree with it?" To this Liang Jie answered, "If I agree completely, I will be disappointing my teacher." This example shows vividly how meticulous the Chan style of the Caodong School is.

The origin of the Caodong School can be traced back to the understanding of Shitou Xiqian, that is, "phenomena are the truth." Viewing everything in this way, all are completely integrated without obstacles, as they all are embodiments of Suchness. The meditation method of the Caodong School emphasizes calmness of the heart and discernment in order to penetrate one's original nature; therefore, it focuses on the "silent illumination meditation" for self-cultivation.

Many Chan temples in today's China were established by the dharma heirs of the Caodong School. The teaching is also very popular in Japan and South Korea, with many followers.

Basics of Buddhism:

- **Dongshan Liangjie**

    Liang Jie (807-869), the founding patriarch of the Caodong School in China, established the School together with his disciple Caoshan Benji (840-901). At the age of twenty-one, Chan Master Liang Jie went to Mount Song, where he took full ordination. After that, he visited Nanquan Puyuan and deeply understood the profound implications of his teachings. Then he visited Weiyang Lingyou and meditated on the Hua Tou — "the insentient speak the dharma". However, he could not align with it. Following Ling You's advice, he then visited Yunyan Tansheng, where he gained some inspirations, yet there were still doubts. Therefore, he further visited Chan masters such as Luzu Baoyun and Nanyuan Daoming. He eventually became enlightened when he saw his reflection in the water he was crossing.

At the end of Emperor Xuanzong of Tang's Dazhong era (847-859), Liang Jie built Dongshan Chan Buddhist Temple in Xinfeng Mountain (currently in the town Tong'an, Yifeng County, Jiangxi Province). There he received and led his disciples to disseminate the Dharma, so he is generally called "Dongshan Liangjie".

Liang Jie had hundreds of disciples, among whom 26 disciples inherited his Dharma, such as Yunju Daoying, Caoshan Benji, Longya Judun, Huayan Xiujing, Qinglin Shiqian. His disciple Ben Ji (840-901) lived in Mount Cao (currently in the north of Huang County in Jiangxi Province). He took up Liang Jie's mantle and together founded the Caodong School.

The Caodong School belonged to the Dharma lineage of Qingyuan Xingsi of Southern Chinese Chan, which was passed down to Liang Jie through Shitou Xiqian, Yaoshan Weiyan, and Yunyan Tansheng. The teachings of the Caodong School inherited Xiqian's teaching— "the truth of any theory must be capable of being applied to the facts at the time," that is, individual phenomenon reflects Suchness (the truth, the ruling principle, or the Buddha nature), the principle and phenomena interact with each other (correspond and interplay), further expanding the five ranks of ruler and minister. Through the relationship between principle and phenomena, between substance and function, it shows principle and phenomena are not a dualism, and that substance and function are not mutually obstructive. As recorded in Chapter Three of Rentian yanmu (The Eye of Humans and Gods), (the Caodong School) "has a meticulous Chan style, its words corresponding with deeds, benefitting beings according to their capacities, and guiding people with suitable words."

雲門餬餅

捨身事佛在髫年，持戒空王律法嚴。
折腳睦州真諦了，脫柳雪嶺道統傳。
諸方遍歷英名震，靈樹冥通上座間。
御賜紫袍師尊貴，雲門絕唱響人天！

—— 古德

　　雲門宗是禪宗五家七宗之一，屬南宗青原法系，其開創者文偃禪師 (864—949)，初參睦州道蹤禪師發明大旨，後至雪峰參義存禪師領得玄要，之後住韶州雲門山，發揮獨妙之宗至，往來學徒不下千人，法嗣者六十一人，是謂雲門宗。

　　雲門宗的宗旨可以三句話括之：「涵蓋乾坤」、「截斷眾流」、「隨波逐浪」，世稱「德山三句」。首句意思是一切即一、一即一切，物相與法相相即，全在自身、莫向外求；第二句是直下承當、斷絕妄想之意；第三句意指因材施教、隨機度人。文偃常以一個字來截斷學生的妄想情識，禪林稱為「雲門一字關」。

　　雖然此宗門風峻險、難以接近，但不管老少賢愚問道，雲門禪師都會先供以一塊餅，教學人細心咀嚼，好讓其嘗透餬餅的滋味，以啟發他們修道要如吃餅一般，慢慢體會、逐漸提升，才能領略其深層味道，得悟最究竟的佛法。

- **文偃禪師**

  　　雲門文偃禪師 (864—949)，為雲門宗禪的創始人。文偃先在靈樹寺
  説法約八年，後在雲門寺説法約二十二年，合計在粵弘法約三十年。他
  的佛學思想有獨到之處，他接引學人的禪法更是別樹一幟，從而形成獨
  立宗派，世人稱之為雲門宗，因其弘法基地在雲門寺而得名。

Eating Rice Cakes, Yunmen Style

(He) renounced the world to serve the Buddha in childhood;

(He) strictly observed the precepts like the king of emptiness;

(He) had his leg broken in Muzhou and understood clearly the ultimate truth;

(He) removed fetters in the snowy summit and was transmitted the lineage;

(He) travelled and visited widely and established reputation as a Chan master;

(He) exhibited omniscience at the Lingshu Monastery and became the head monk;

(He) was bestowed the purple gown by the emperor and was greatly honoured;

(His teachings)—a perfect song of Yunmen, that reverberated among humans and celestials!

— An ancient sage

　　The Yunmen School is one of the Five Houses and Seven Schools of

Chinese Chan. It developed out of the Dharma lineage of Qingyuan Xingsi of Southern Chinese Chan. The founder, Chan Master Yunmen Wenyan (864-949 AD), first visited Chan Master Muzhou Daozong, from whom he was elucidated the main idea and meaning of the teaching. Then he was led to enlightenment by Chan Master Xuefeng Yicun. After that, he resided in Mount Yunmen of Shaozhou, where he was able to exquisitely develop the teaching to perfection. His disciples who came and went numbered no less than a thousand, among whom sixty-one were his dharma heirs. The Chan School he founded was thus called the Yunmen School.

The doctrines of the Yunmen School can be summarized in three sentences: "permeating heaven and earth, which refers to the inclusive and penetrating nature of the Yunmen School's teachings and is based on the realization that all things in the universe are the manifestations of Buddha-nature or true suchness without ever hindering each other," "cutting through all streams [of delusion], which means to vigorously and ruthlessly cut off all conventional ways of thinking and dualistic conceptualizing," and "following the waves and adapting to the currents, which symbolizes the therapeutic function and skillful adaptation of the teachings to all situations of students." These are generally referred to as the "three sentences of Deshan." Wen Yan often used one word to cut off the deluded conceptualization and consciousness of his disciples, which is known as "Yunmen's One-Word Barrier."

Though the style of the Yunmen School is quite challenging and hard to approach, whoever came to seek the Way, whether old or young, wise or dull, Chan Master Yun Men would always give them a piece of cake to start with. He taught them to chew the cake slowly so that they could taste its real flavour. In this way, he taught them how cultivation of the Way should be like tasting the cake, i.e., to carefully experience and gradually elevate in order to grasp the deepest meaning of the cultivation and realize the ultimate Dharma.

• **Chan Master Wenyan**

Chan Master Yunmen Wenyan (864-949 AD) is the founder of the Yunmen School. He gave the teachings initially at the Lingshu Monastery for eight years and later at Yunmen Temple for twenty-two years. He spent almost thirty years teaching the Dharma in Guangdong Province. His Buddhist ideology had specific characteristics, and he had a style of his own in receiving and guiding his disciples for their Chan practice. Thus, he established a separate Chan School, which is generally called the Yunmen School, as Wenyan disseminated the Dharma mainly at Yunmen Temple.

法眼藏鋒

通玄峰頂，不是人間。
心外無法，滿目青山。

—— 德韶禪師

　　源出南宗青原一脈的法眼宗，是中國佛教禪宗五家七宗最後產生的一個宗派，乃唐末宋初五代時期的文益 (885—958) 所創。

　　有一次，羅漢桂琛指着門前的石頭問文益：「石頭在心內還是心外？」

　　文益答：「在心內」。桂琛：「行腳之人心無羈絆，何以遊走時仍安塊石頭在心內？」文益無言以對，經月餘不得其解，後桂琛點化他道：「若論佛法，一切現成。」文益言下大悟。

　　故文益創法眼宗，宗風乃「般若無知」、「一切現成」，於他的論著中亦提出「理事不二、貴在圓融」、「不著他求、盡由心造」的宗旨。宋代越山晦岩智昭說：「法眼宗者，箭鋒相拄，句意合機，始則行行如也，終則激發，漸服人心，削除清解，調機順物，斥滯磨昏。」

　　法眼宗的發源地乃南京清涼寺，而此宗經文益、德韶、延壽三世嫡嫡相傳，在宋初極其隆盛，後即逐漸式微，到宋代中葉便法脈斷絕，其間不過百年。

- **文益禪師**

文益 (885—958) 七歲出家，二十歲受戒，後至育王寺從希覺學律。文益通大乘佛教各宗派，且涉儒家經籍，希覺視之為佛門的子游、子夏。時南方興禪，文益便南下福州長慶院向慧棱禪師學習。爾後，文益在地藏院，得桂琛禪師點化覺悟佛法，終成一代宗師，著有《宗門十規論》等。

Hidden Brilliance, Fayan Style

The top of Penetrating Mysteries Peak

Is not a place for mortals.

Outside the mind, there are no dharmas.

All around me, I behold green mountains.

— Chan Master De Shao

The Fayan School developed out of the Dharma lineage of Qingyuan Xingsi and is the last of the Five Houses and Seven Schools of Chinese Chan Buddhism. It was founded by Wen Yi at the end of the Tang dynasty and the beginning of the Song dynasty during the Five Dynasties period (885-958).

One day, Luohan Guichen pointed to a rock lying on the ground by the gate and asked Wen Yi, "Is this rock inside or outside of mind?"

Wen Yi answered, "It is inside the mind."

Gui Chen said, "How can a pilgrim carry such a rock in his mind while on pilgrimage?"

Wen Yi became speechless, and for months he could not understand it. Later, he was enlightened by Gui Chen, who said, "If you want to talk about the Buddhadharma, everything you see embodies it." Hearing these words, Wen Yi became suddenly enlightened.

Thus, Wen Yi founded the Fayan School, its style being "Prajñā is notknowing" and "all things are as they are." He advocated in his works the

tenets of "non-duality of principle and phenomenon, their value being their mutual harmony," and "not seeking outside but creating within." Huiyan Zhizhao of Mount Yue in the Song dynasty said, "The Fayan School practices exchanges of sharp words that correspond with one's capacities. At the beginning it focuses on the practice, and eventually arouses conviction in one's heart. Then it eliminates and cleanses [afflictions], adjusting the mind to go along with surroundings, in the process expelling obstructions and getting rid of ignorance."

The Fayan School originated from the Qingliang Monastery in Nanjing. The Dharma lineage was directly passed down from Wen Yi to De Shao and then to Yan Shou. At the beginning of the Song dynasty, the Fayan School became very popular but gradually declined; by the middle period of the Song dynasty, the Dharma lineage became extinct. It existed for only one hundred years.

Basics of Buddhism:

• Chan Master Wen Yi

Wen Yi (885-958) became a Buddhist monk at the age of seven and received ordination when he was twenty. He went to the Temple of King Ashoka and studied Vinaya from Master Xi Jue. Wen Yi was well educated and erudite in all the Schools of Mahayana Buddhism. He also studied the Confucian classics and was considered by Master Xi Jue as Zi You and Zi Xia of Buddhism. At that time, Chan practice was very popular in the south, so Wen Yi went southward to the Changqing Monastery in Fuzhou to learn from Chan Master Hui Leng. Later, he was enlightened by Master Gui Chen at the Dizang Monastery and finally became a great Chan master. His works include the Treatise of the Chan Schools' Ten Rules (Zongmen Shigui Lun).

念佛是誰

十方同聚會，各個學無為，
此是選佛場，心空及第歸。

—— 古德

參禪在於要明心見性 —— 明悟自心、徹見本性。唐宋以前的禪德，多由一言半句便悟道，以心印心的法門，並沒有甚麼實法，只不過是平日參問酬答，隨方解縛、因病與藥而已。

宋代以後，或因學人的根器問題，講了卻做不到的多，故祖師們惟有教人參公案、看話頭，目的是以一念抵制萬念，讓人緊緊咬死一個念頭，不通不止，這實是不得已的辦法。

古人的公案多得很，後來專講看話頭，而「念佛是誰」跟其他「拜佛是誰」、「吃飯是誰」等等，目的都是一樣，讓人看「話頭」。但萬法皆從心起，話頭亦即是念頭，一念未生之前就是話頭，故看話頭就是觀心，而性即是心，故「反聞聞自性」，亦即反觀觀自心。

所以說，看話頭又或看「念佛是誰」，其實就是觀照自心清淨覺體、自性佛。如此鍥而不捨地看下去，直至漆桶落底，就會猛然省悟自己的「本來面目」。

• 話頭禪

　　一日，學人問禪師，「心性幽微，深奧難明直契心源，祕訣何在？」老禪師慢悠悠地說，「鐘，重叩重鳴，輕叩輕鳴，不叩不鳴。求道如叩鐘，要領在於起疑情：大疑大悟，小疑小悟，不疑不悟。所以參禪時，應把我看成是一口鐘，把心中的疑問當做槌，狠狠地『敲擊』我，必能打破疑團，廓然大徹。」

　　這則公案說出了「起疑情」乃參禪悟道之關鍵。一切眾生，皆具如來智慧德性，與佛無二無別；只因無明不覺，顛倒妄執，認假作真，起惑造業，才在生死苦海中頭出頭沒，永無了期。故《法華經譬喻品》云：「三界無安，猶如火宅，眾苦充滿，甚可怖畏，常有生老病死憂患，如是等火，熾然不息。」儘管「生死事大，無常迅速」，然而，酒不醉人人自醉，色不迷人人自迷。可憐世人誤以「我」為實有，醉心於名利，對世間五欲之樂執迷不覺。若世人能對「我」、「名利」和「世間欲樂」的真實性生起疑情，了知世界一切事物都是無常變化的，因而不是真實的，這才是捨妄歸真的關鍵。

　　禪宗大德，悲憫眾生，應機施教，對症下藥，以參一句「念佛是誰」的話頭，逼令世人生起這種疑情。正如順治皇帝問自己的四句話：「未生我時誰是我？生我之時我是誰？長大成人方是我，合眼矇矓又是誰？」近代禪門泰斗虛雲、來果禪師多年苦參：「我是誰？」「誰是我？」「未生之前我是誰？」「死去之後誰是我？」如此鍥而不捨地層層剝皮、自我反詰，直到漆桶落底，兩位大德終於參透生死，猛然省悟自己的「本來面目」。

Who Is Reciting the Buddha's Name

All sentient beings gather from the ten directions,

Everyone studies the unconditioned.

This is the place for rising up Buddhas,

Empty the mind and return successfully.

— An ancient sage

The key for Chan practice is to understand one's mind and see one's intrinsic nature. The enlightened Chan masters before the Tang and Song dynasties were normally awakened to the Way through a few words. The dharma being transmitted from mind to mind is nothing but only daily questions and answers that expediently untie the knots, just like giving medicine according to one's ailment.

After the Song dynasty, perhaps due to the weakening of practitioners' capacities, many only paid lip service to the Dharma. As a result, the patriarchs could only teach them how to meditate on koans and observe Hua Tou, so that they could stop their flow of thoughts with the one thought. They taught them to keep close watch on the one thought continuously until they became enlightened. They had no alternative but to use this method.

There were many koans taught by an ancient sages, but later on they only focused on the mindful observance of Hua Tou. Whether it was "Who is reciting the Buddha's name," or "Who is bowing to the Buddha," or "Who is taking the meal," their purpose was the same, that is, to guide the practitioners to mindfully watch the Hua Tou. All things arise from the mind, thus to mindfully watch Hua Tou is to observe the mind itself--Huatou and thought is one and the same. That which comes before the arising of a thought is the Huatou, and to observe the Huatou is to observe the mind. One's instrinsic nature is the mind. As such, "to contemplate on one's intrinsic nature" is "to reflect on one's mind."

Therefore, to mindfully watch Hua Tou or "Who is reciting the Buddha's name" is to contemplate on one's inner pure capacity for enlightenment, that is, one's inherent Buddha-nature. If one keeps on watching in this way until the bottom of the barrel falls off, there will be sudden realization of one's original face (his true nature).

Basics of Buddhism:

• Hua Tou Chan

One day, a practitioner asked a Chan master, "Our mind-nature is very subtle, profound, and incomprehensible. It directly tallies with the source of the mind. What is the secret?" The Chan master answered slowly, "For a bell, it rings loud when you knock it hard, low when you knock it lightly, and makes no sound when you don't knock it at all. Seeking the Way is similar to that. The key is to arouse your doubts. You will attain great enlightenment when you have great doubts, little enlightenment when you have few doubts, and no enlightenment when you have no doubts. Therefore, in practicing Chan, you should consider the self as a bell, and the doubts in your heart as a mallet. 'Beat' the self-hard, and you will surely break your doubts and attain perfect enlightenment."

This koan explains the key point of Chan practice for enlightenment, that is, to arouse the spirit of doubt. All sentient beings possess Buddha's wisdom and merits that are perfectly the same. Yet, because of ignorance, lack of knowledge, delusion, attachment

to the false, taking the false as the true, and creating afflictions and unwholesome karmas, they experience samsara in the ocean of suffering through birth and death, forever without an end. As recorded in "A Parable" of the Wonderful Dharma Lotus Flower Sutra, "In the three realms there is no peace; they are like a burning house, filled with many sufferings, and frightening indeed. Ever present are the woes of birth, old age, sickness, death, fires such as these, raging without cease. "Birth and death are great matters, and impermanence comes quickly." However, wine doesn't make men drunk; men get themselves intoxicated. Lust does not overpower men; men surrender themselves to lust. Pitifully, the worldlings mistakenly believe "the self" as substantial and are obsessed with fame and fortune, with the joys of the five desires, but they are not aware of it. If they arouse the spirit of doubt about the reality of "the self," "fame and fortune," and "mundane desire and pleasure," they would realize that everything in the world is impermanent and ever-changing, and therefore they are not real. This is the key to returning to truth from falsehood.

The great Chan masters had great compassion for sentient beings. They taught at the opportune moment and knew the right prescriptions to solve problems. They urged the worldlings to arouse the spirit of doubt by meditating on the Hua Tou "Who is reciting the Buddha's name." The Shunzhi Emperor asked himself the following four lines, "Who was I before I was born? Who am I after I am born? Grown up as an adult, so this is me; With my eyes shut and dozing off to sleep, who again am I?" And the great Chan masters Xu Yun and Lai Guo meditated on "Who was I?" "Who am I?" "Who was I before I was born?" and "Who am I after I die?" To peel off one layer upon another with such perseverance and to counterquestion themselves till the barrel's bottom came off, the two great elders finally penetrated the truth of birth and death and suddenly realized their own original face.

十六觀

四

Part Four:

The Sixteen Visualizations

逆子囚父

　　佛陀時代，頻婆娑羅王晚年得子，叫阿闍世。長大成人後，受提婆達多的煽動，把父王關進了監獄，只等把他餓死，自己就可以做新國君。王后韋提希營救丈夫的行動暴露後，也被囚禁起來。頻婆娑羅王命在旦夕，眼看不孝之子阿闍世即將犯下殺父篡位的彌天大罪，韋提希悲痛萬分，遙向在耆闍崛山的世尊禮拜求救。世尊對發生在宮廷中的這一幕人倫慘劇悉知悉見，即同侍者阿難與弟子目犍連，出現在王宮，為韋提希夫人說法，成為佛陀講述《觀無量壽佛經》的緣起。這部經為未來無量苦惱眾生開啟了殊勝的極樂淨土法門。

※※ [佛教小知識]

• 為甚麼知苦對於求解脫尤為重要？

　　任何一種解脫都是從知苦入手。對苦的了解決定了一個人的發心和修何種法。譬如說，了知地獄苦，便會發積德行善心，修人天乘法；了知輪迴苦，便會發解脫心，修解脫道；了知眾生苦，便會發菩提心，修菩薩乘。知苦是離苦的開始，《觀無量壽佛經》主角韋提希遭到至親骨肉的叛逆、加害，深感人間之苦，成就了佛陀演說這部經的因緣。

An Unfilial Son Imprisons His Father

At the time of Śākyamuni Buddha, King Bimbisāra fathered a son in his old age whom he named Ajātashatru. When Ajātashatru grew up, he was instigated by Devadatta to imprison his father, so that he could ascend the

throne after his father was starved to death. He also imprisoned his mother, Queen Vaidehī. Seeing that the king was seriously ill and her unfilial son was going to commit the heinous sins of killing his father and usurping the throne, the queen was stricken with grief. To help change the destiny of the family, the Buddha, without being requested, taught the method of visualization of the Buddha of Infinite Life for Queen Vaidehī and countless miserable beings of the future to practise, opening up the wonderful dharma-door of rebirth in the Pure Land of Ultimate Bliss. This was the background to the Sutra of Visualization of the Buddha of Infinite Life.

Basics of Buddhism:

• **Why understanding sufferings is important to liberation ?**

To reach liberation of any kind, we need to start with understanding suffering. Knowing suffering will determine one's resolve for liberation and what path to follow. For example, when we understand the sufferings of the hells, we would be motivated to perform virtuous deeds and accumulate merits, following a path that would lead to rebirth in the human and heavenly worlds; when we understand the sufferings of samsara, we would be inspired to follow the path to liberation; when we understand the sufferings of sentient beings, we would develop the Bodhicitta and walk the bodhisattva path. Understanding of suffering marks the beginning of eliminating suffering. Queen Vaidehī, the main character in the Sutra of Visualization of the Buddha of Infinite Life, deeply experienced the suffering of the Saha world after being betrayed and harmed by her own son. Her suffering was what prompted the Buddha to preach the sutra.

哀韋
請提
　希

　　王后得悉逆子阿闍世想餓死親生父親，嘗試把細小的飯團藏於髮
髻之內，帶進囚室；她又曾將自己身體上塗滿了麨蜜，以為這樣可以瞞
過守衛，但最後全都被揭發了，弄得自己也被禁錮起來。

　　在極度哀傷和絕望之下，王后遙對着耆闍崛山向佛行禮，請佛救
度。佛陀應機為韋提希宣說了往生西方極樂世界的「十六觀」法門，其
中涵蓋了淨土法門的定善、散善，并在最後付囑阿難：「汝好持是語，
持是語者，即是持無量壽佛名」。

※ [佛教小知識]

- 一個人痛苦時求助，佛菩薩真的能聽到嗎？

　　有一個古老的哲學問題，「森林中一棵樹倒了下來，那兒不會有人聽
到，那麼能說它發出聲響了嗎？」同樣如此，當一個受苦受難的人向我
們求救時，如果我們不用心去傾聽他的故事，痛苦的求救聲能得到善意
的回應嗎？佛陀深知，幫助身在苦難中人們最好的方法就是傾聽，設身
處地同情和理解王后的苦惱，才能找出最有效的辦法幫助她。

Vaidehī's Prayer

When Queen Vaidehī learned about Ajātashatru's plan to starve his father to death, she hid tiny rice balls inside her hair and went to visit the king in prison. She also secretly covered her body with a mixture of honey and flour trying to get pass the guards and bring more food to the king. But she was caught by the guards and became imprisoned herself.

Full of grief and despair, the queen faced the direction of Gṛdhrakūṭa Mountain and prostrated herself to pay homage to the Buddha and seek his help. The Buddha taught her the Sixteen Visualizations, a method of practice to attain rebirth in the Pure Land of Ultimate Bliss.

Basics of Buddhism:

• Can Buddhas and bodhisattvas truly hear the prayer of a person in pain?

There is an old philosophical question: "If a tree falls in a forest and no one is around to hear it, does it make a sound?" Similarly, if a person in pain asks for our help and we don't listen to what he says, would the request be responded with kindness? The Buddha knows that the best way to help those in distress is to listen to what they say; it is only when he could empathize with Queen Vaidehī's suffering that he would find the most effective way to help her.

日想觀

　　佛陀首先告訴韋提希：看到太陽要落下去的時候，應生起正念，面向西方坐定，做到心無二用地專注夕陽沉落的地方，專心想念這個太陽，不要讓這個顆心有機會移到別處去。

　　此時就能見到太陽要落下去時候的形狀，像懸掛在空中的一面銅鼓。看見日落的形狀後，要做到不管是閉眼或是張眼，也能夠了然於心，就是第一觀的日想觀，又叫初觀。

※※ [佛教小知識] ────────────────────

• 十六觀為何從「日想觀」入手？

　　《佛遺教經》云，「制心一處，無事不辦。」一個人若在同一時間，專心做一件事，定能成功。這種「專注」的精神是《觀無量壽佛經》修觀成敗之關鍵。本經引導人們從專注於一方作為修觀的入手處。西方讓人們聯想到西方極樂世界，落日使人聯想起美好事物，故觀日落西方，自然成為十六觀的第一觀 ──「日想觀」。

────────────────────────────

Visualization of the Setting Sun

The Buddha told Queen Vaidehī: When the Sun is setting, you should develop right mindfulness and sit properly facing the west. Then concentrate your mind on the sunset, and be mindful of the sun without wandering elsewhere.

Then, you will see the setting sun look like a bronze drum hanging on the horizon. After seeing the sun in this shape, you should keep this image vividly in your mind whether your eyes are open or shut. This is the first visualization—visualization of the setting sun.

- **Why does the practice of Sixteen Visualizations start with visualization of the Sun?**

    The Sutra on the Buddha's Bequeathed Teaching states, "When the mind concentrates on one, all can be accomplished." If one concentrates on doing something for long enough, one will surely succeed. This spirit of "concentration" is the key to whether the visualizations taught in the Sutra of Visualization of the Buddha of Infinite Life would succeed or fail. The sutra guides us to begin with fixing our attention upon one object. Sitting while facing the west reminds us of the Western Pure Land of Ultimate Bliss, and the setting sun reminds us of beautiful things. As such, visualizing the sun setting in the west becomes naturally the First Visualization exercise — visualization of the setting sun.

水想觀

　　落日時天水相連，由觀落日自然過渡到「觀水」（第二觀）：因觀落日而看到夕陽消失於天水相連之處，故從落日而觀想到水。集中意念，觀想在西方日落之處，有一望無際的大水，一邊觀想清澈的水，使其心專注在水上面不散亂，然後把水轉成冰。再把照起來透明的冰轉成琉璃，最後把琉璃轉成琉璃地。若觀想成功，就能夠看到西方極樂世界的琉璃大地，內外透明清澈。這就是水想觀，名為第二觀。

※※ ［佛教小知識］ ───────────────────────

• 為何「水想觀」有助於我們的修為？

　　水觀的一個功能是教導人們學習水的隨緣自在、圓融無礙之理。

　　唐代善靜禪師要去參訪，師父問他：「四面是山，你往哪兒去？」

　　善靜禪師答：「竹密豈妨流水過，山高那礙野雲飛？」

　　流水無論遇到任何阻礙，都能順其自然，穿過茂密的竹林，繞過阻擋它的石頭，涓涓不息，終為江河，滔滔不絕，勇往直前，直奔大海。

　　修水想觀，就是要求我們向流水學習，無論面對任何逆境，都能做到不變隨緣，隨緣不變，圓融自在。充分運用已有的條件，謹慎、積極去克服困難。

Visualization of Water

The sun sets on the horizon where the sky merges with water. This leads you naturally to the visualization of water (the second visualization). After you visualize the sun disappearing into the water, you will naturally shift the visualizing object from the setting sun to the water. Concentrate your mind on visualizing a vast expanse of water where the sun sets. Keep the mind concentrated on the water surface, and then turn the water in vision to ice, then to lapis lazuli, and eventually to the ground of lapis lazuli. Were this visualization exercise successful, you will see the ground of lapis lazuli in the Western Pure Land of Ultimate Bliss, sparklingly limpid throughout. This is the Second Visualization exercise—visualization of water.

Basics of Buddhism:

• **How does the visualization of water help with our practice?**

One of the benefits of visualizing water is to guide us to learn to be flexible, free, inclusive, and unobstructed, just as water is.

Chan Master Shan Jing of the Tang dynasty was leaving the temple for Dharma journeys. His master asked him, "There are mountains all around us, where can you go?"

Master Shan Jing replied, "Dense as it is, a bamboo forest can never stop a running creek. High as it is, a mountain can never hinder a flying cloud."

Water runs its own course despite obstacles in its way. It cuts through the dense bamboo forest and bypasses the boulder. Forever running forward, the small creek turns into a great river marching to join the sea.

Visualization of water helps us to learn from water-that is, when facing obstacles, we must adapt to the circumstances while remaining unmoved within, and use wisdom to embrace all life events while staying detached from them. We should be flexible and cautious to use what we already have to actively solve the predicaments we face.

地想觀

　　由日想觀自然過渡到水想觀，轉水成冰，轉冰成琉璃，轉琉璃成琉璃地，令人容易聯想起西方極樂世界的琉璃大地，從而進入第三地觀：琉璃大地由七種寶貝組成的八角形金剛幢支撐，每一面都是百寶雜陳，寶珠顏色繽紛，放出千萬道光芒，璀璨耀目；每一道光芒又有八萬四千種顏色，映照在琉璃大地上，猶如仟億日光照耀，令人無法辨清其中有多少不同的光色。

　　觀想極樂世界七寶莊嚴，下有金剛、上擎寶幢、地面間錯着黃金繩的琉璃地，直至此觀恆不消散，即名第三觀的「地想」。

　　佛陀告訴阿難：你記住我的話，為未來世一切大眾，有想要脫離苦難的人，說此觀地法。若修行的人能觀見極樂國土，即能除去八十億劫生死之罪；而且命終時，一定能往生極樂，心中沒有任何懷疑。

• 為甚麼說「地想觀」成了連接現實世界和極樂世界之橋樑？

　　日、水為現實世界人們所熟知之事物，正常的思維就可以觀想。而西方極樂世界的琉璃大地超越常識，已進入定境，無法想像，只能心觀。所以佛陀以世間常見之物 —— 日、水為觀想之開始，觀落日定方位（西方），由水聯想到冰；再由冰聯想到極樂世界的琉璃大地，這就是第三觀 —— 地想觀。由此可見，地想觀是連接現實世界和極樂世界之橋樑。我們的心通過正確的觀想，就可以通達極樂世界了。

Visualization of the Ground

The visualization of the setting sun leads you naturally to the visualization of water. When the water turns into ice, ice into lapis lazuli, and lapis lazuli into a ground of lapis lazuli, it reminds you naturally of the lapis lazuli ground of the Western Pure Land of Ultimate Bliss. As such, you enter into the Third Visualization: visualization of the ground. The lapis lazuli ground is supported by octagonal diamond banners made of seven kinds of precious materials. Each side of the banners has a hundred jewels, and each multi-colored jewel emits thousands of light rays. Each ray of light has eighty-four thousand colors, reflected on the lapis lazuli ground. It is as if thousands of millions of suns are shining on the ground, making it hard to distinguish how many kinds of lights there actually are.

Visualize that in the World of Ultimate Bliss, the lapis lazuli ground, adorned with the seven treasures, is supported by diamonds below and jeweled banners above, with the surface of the ground crisscrossed with golden cords. Visualize it till the image persists without vanishing. This is the Third Visualization exercise—visualization of the ground.

The Buddha told Ānanda: Remember my words. Share this teaching of visualization of the ground with all future beings—those who wish to be liberated from suffering. If the practitioners can visualize the Pure Land of Ultimate Bliss, their offences created in the past eight billion kalpas can be eradicated. And at the time of death, they will harbor no doubts in mind and surely be reborn in the Pure Land.

☸ Basics of Buddhism:

- **Why do we say that visualization of the ground serves as a bridge to connect our world and the Pure Land?**

  The sun and water are things we are familiar with in our world. We are able to visualize them easily in imagination. However, the lapis lazuli ground is beyond human imagination. It is a kind of Samādhi that cannot be imagined but only contemplated through our mind. For this reason, the Buddha guides us to start from what we are familiar with, that is, the sun and water. The visualization of the setting sun fixes our mind (upon the west), and the visualization of water leads us to think of ice, which in turn reminds us of the lapis lazuli ground of the World of Ultimate Bliss to reach the Third Visualization: the ground. We can thus understand that visualization of the ground serves as a bridge to connect our world with the World of Ultimate Bliss. Through proper visualization, the World of Ultimate Bliss becomes reachable.

寶樹觀

　　由極樂淨土琉璃大地觀想到大地上的樹（第四觀）：極樂國土的琉璃地觀成以後，佛陀教人循序漸進，觀想淨土勝景。首先觀想琉璃大地上佈滿七寶合成的寶樹。修行者觀寶樹時，必須要一棵一棵的逐一觀想，然後觀想每一棵寶樹上的莖、葉、華和果，每一個部位都清楚分明地顯現。此稱為樹想，名為第四觀。

[佛教小知識]

• 如何觀想？

　　樹體由根部和地上部兩大部分組成。根部是指整個根系，包括主根、側根和鬚根，而地上部包括樹幹（莖）、枝、芽、葉、華和果實。佛陀引導人們依次序觀想極樂世界的根、莖、葉、花、果實、種子，感受極樂世界遍地是寶樹。這是第四寶樹觀。

Visualization of the Jeweled Trees

After visualizing the lapis lazuli ground in the Pure Land of Ultimate Bliss, you can further visualize the trees on the ground (the Fourth Visualization). When you successfully visualize the lapis lazuli ground, the Buddha guides you to further meditate on the wonderful scenery of the Pure Land. First, visualize the trees of seven treasures growing from the ground. Practitioners must visualize the trees one by one, and then visualize all the details of the trees in an orderly manner, including the trunks, the branches, the leaves, the blossoms, and the fruits, until each part appears vivid and distinct in vision. This is the Fourth Visualization—visualization of the jeweled trees.

Basics of Buddhism:

- **How do we visualize a tree?**

    A tree includes two parts: the root underneath the ground and the other parts above the ground. The root system is comprised of the main roots, the lateral roots, and the fibrous roots; the part above the ground includes the trunk, the branches, the sprouts, the leaves, the blossoms, and the fruits. The Buddha guides us to visualize the roots, the trunks, the leaves, the blossoms, the fruits, and the seeds successively until we see the jeweled trees everywhere in the World of Ultimate Bliss. This is the visualization of the jeweled trees.

寶池觀

　　觀想極樂世界的寶樹成就後，接着下來觀想池水。極樂國土有無數的八功德水池，每一個水池都由七寶合成。因池水從如意珠王而生，其質柔軟，流落池中，常常盈滿，分作十四支流。每一個分支，都有七寶妙色，黃金為溝渠，渠底是五彩綜合色的金剛沙。這裏的池水聲音微妙，演說着苦、空、無常、無我等度眾生往彼岸之法，又有讚歎諸佛相好莊嚴之音聲。如意珠王湧出金色微妙光明，而此光則化為百寶色鳥，一起在那裏唱和，常讚念佛、念法、念僧。

　　這就是「八功德水想」，名為第五觀。

[佛教小知識]

• 池水說法

　　　　　水聲傳佛號，法界普聞知，
　　　　　四生登九品，三有托蓮池。

　　　　　　　　　　　　　　　　　　　　—— 古德

　　常樅臨終前，老子問他，「老師去世後，我當以誰為師？」常樅意味深長地說，「以水為師」。老子花費了很多年觀察水，終於悟出老師的深意，「上善若水，水善利萬物而不爭」。他從水中領悟到做人的道理。在中國，「上善若水」成為當今很多中國人的座右銘。無獨有偶，印度人也從水中領悟到苦、空、無常的人生哲理。這是第五寶池觀的本意。

Visualization of the Lotus Ponds

When the visualization of the jeweled trees has been completed, visualize the ponds next. There are countless lotus ponds full of water endowed with eight virtues in the Pure Land of Ultimate Bliss. Each lotus pond is made of seven treasures and water flows out of a wish-granting jewel. The soft water that overflows from the pond divides into fourteen streams, and each stream is as colorful as the seven treasures. The water ducts are made of gold the bottom of which is covered with five-colored diamond sands. The exquisite sound of the flowing water preaches the teaching of suffering, emptiness, impermanence, non-self, and more to deliver sentient beings to the other shore (enlightenment). It also praises the distinguishing and sublime marks of the Buddhas. From the wish-granting jewel emit wondrously golden rays of light that become birds colorful as a hundred jewels, singing harmonious songs that praise the mindfulness of the Buddha, Dharma, and Sangha.

This is the Fifth Visualization—visualization of water endowed with eight virtues.

• Preaching Dharma via the sound of water

Buddhas' names sung by the water

Are heard across all Dharma realms.

All life forms can ascend to the Pure Land,

Beings of the Three Realms of Existence can be reborn in the lotus

ponds.

— An ancient sage

When Chang Cong was on his deathbed, Lao Zi asked him, "Teacher, after you go, who can be my teacher?" Chang Cong replied with a meaningful look of deep significance, "You should take water as your teacher." For many years after that, Lao Zi observed water and finally realized the profound meaning of Chang Cong's last words. "Highest good is like water. Because water excels in benefitting the myriad creatures without contending with them." He learned from water how to conduct himself. In today's China, many people take "Highest good is like water" as their motto. Coincidentally, the ancient Indian sages also comprehended the philosophies of life through water, such as suffering, emptiness, and impermanence. This is the fundamental meaning of the Fifth Visualization—visualization of the lotus ponds.

寶樓觀

　　在眾寶所成的國土上有無數八寶池，每一個池岸上有五百億寶樓；在樓閣中，有無數諸天女，演奏着天伎樂；又有樂器，空懸在虛空中，就好像天寶幢，不鼓自鳴，在和中，此眾多的音聲，都會演說念佛、念法、念比丘僧。

　　此觀想成就後，就可稱為略見極樂世界的寶樹、寶地、寶池，此稱為總觀想，名為第六觀。

※※ ［佛教小知識］

• 何謂「依報」？

　　第三地想觀、第四寶樹觀和第五寶池觀成就之後，第六觀重點是觀想極樂國土的樓閣和聲塵，最終將極樂國土的各種依報莊嚴一起觀想，故名為總觀想。

　　由極樂淨土琉璃大地觀想到大地上的樹（第四觀）、池（第五觀）和樓（第六觀），構成極樂世界的國土莊嚴，以上六觀稱為「觀依報」。

Visualization of the Jeweled Palaces

In the land adorned with various kinds of jewels, there are countless lotus ponds full of water endowed with eight virtues. Along the bank of each pond stand fifty billion jeweled palaces. In each palace, there are countless celestial maidens playing heavenly music. And musical instruments suspend in the sky like heavenly jeweled banners, producing sounds without being played. The various sounds are the sharing of the teaching of mindfulness of the Buddha, Dharma, and Sangha.

When this visualization has been completed, you can see the jeweled trees, the jeweled ground, and the jeweled ponds in the World of Ultimate Bliss. This is a unified visualization, which is known as the Sixth Visualization.

Basics of Buddhism:

- **What is "circumstantial reward"?**

  When the visualizations of the jeweled trees, the jeweled ground, and the jeweled ponds have been completed, the Sixth Visualization focuses on the palaces and sounds as well as the various dignified circumstantial rewards in the Pure Land of Ultimate Bliss. Thus, it is called a unified visualization.

  The visualization of the lapis lazuli ground in the Pure Land leads us to the visualization of the jeweled trees (the Fourth Visualization), the visualization of the lotus ponds (the Fifth Visualization), and the visualization of the jeweled palaces (the Sixth Visualization). These embody the adornments of the World of Ultimate Bliss, so the above-mentioned six visualizations are called the visualization of the circumstantial reward.

華座觀

　　佛陀在前六觀中勾勒了極樂世界美妙的勝景（依報觀），接下來引導眾生進一步觀想極樂世界之聖眾（正報觀）。佛陀告訴韋提希，如果想見佛菩薩，首先就要觀佛及二菩薩所坐之蓮華座，觀想蓮花一一葉作百寶色，有八萬四千脈，猶如天畫，一一脈有八萬四千光，了了分明皆令得見。

　　蓮華座上有五百億微妙寶珠，以為映飾。每一顆寶珠散發出八萬四千道光芒，每一道光芒有八萬四千種特殊的金色，各種各樣的金色遍佈寶土之上，變化萬千，各自形成特別的形相，或為金剛台，或作真珠網，或作雜花雲，變化自如，於十方面隨意變現，施作佛事，隨機利物。此稱為蓮花座觀想，名為第七觀。

[佛教小知識]

- 在十六觀中，「華座觀」有何特殊功能？

　　聖眾抽象、微妙難觀，因此佛陀引導眾生從觀佛坐處 —— 華座入手（第七華座觀），然後觀華座上的聖像（第八聖像觀），再由聖像進入正觀佛身（第九佛身觀），觀音和大勢至菩薩侍立左右，相好光明，尊貴無比。四周流水，清風鳥鳴，彼唱此和，演說着無上妙法，使我們的情感得以淨化，心智得以提升，最後心智大開，煩惱頓除。

Visualization of the Lotus Seat

In the previous six visualizations, the Buddha gives a brief account of the beautiful scenes in the World of Ultimate Bliss (the meditation on circumstantial reward). After that, he guides us further to visualize all the sages there (the meditation on direct retribution). The Buddha told Queen Vaidehī: In order to see the Buddha of Infinite Life and the two bodhisattvas, you need to initially visualize their lotus seats. Visualize that each petal of the lotus flower, as colorful as hundreds of jewels, has eighty-four thousand veins that look like heavenly pictures; each vein has eighty-four thousand rays of light that are perfectly clear and visible to all.

The lotus seat is adorned with fifty billion exquisite jewels. Each jewel emits eighty-four thousand rays of light, and each ray of light has eight-four thousand different shades of golden color, shining all over the jeweled land and changing into various forms. Some look like diamond pedestals, some nets of pearls, and some clouds of different flowers. In all the ten directions, they change and manifest according to one's wishes, perform the works of the Buddhas, and benefit sentient beings in accordance with their capacities. This is visualization of the lotus seat and is called the Seventh Visualization.

Basics of Buddhism:

- **What is the special role of the visualization of the lotus seat among all the sixteen visualizations?**

   As the sages' images are abstract and subtle for us to visualize, the Buddha guides us to start from visualizing the lotus seat of the Buddha (the Seventh Visualization). Next is to visualize the sacred images who are seated on the lotus seat (the Eighth Visualization), and then to visualize properly the body of the Buddha (the Ninth Visualization), with Avalokiteśvara Bodhisattva and Mahāsthāmaprāpta Bodhisattva standing in attendance to the left and the right, who are incomparably noble with excellent characteristics. All around them are flowing waters, refreshing breeze, and singing birds, like a chorus that chants the supreme and wondrous Dharma. Our feelings are thus purified, our minds elevated; till finally, we are enlightened and our afflictions instantly cease.

像想觀

　　觀像與想佛是兩個不同層次的修行。第八像想觀要求修觀者先觀想一閻浮檀金色佛像坐蓮花上，左觀音、右勢至二菩薩像侍於其傍，各放金光。這是十六觀中最重要的一觀。

　　由觀像再引導人們觀佛之威德，這是本觀之要點。諸佛如來是法界身，遍入一切眾生心想中，故是心作佛，是心是佛。諸佛正遍知海從心想生，是故應當一心繫念，諦觀佛陀種種威德。觀想成者，近則可以見到淨土之光明，聽到淨土所說之妙法，遠則為僧祇劫後成佛之因。

　　眾生無始以來，無法見佛真容，常見丈六金身佛像。所以觀佛像是觀真佛之前奏。這是開示眾生成佛之要道。由觀佛相，相現心中，此心即具佛之相好，故云是心作佛。

　　《勢至圓通章》亦云，「十方如來憐念眾生，如母憶子」。此明佛常念眾生。「若子逃逝，雖憶何為？」此明眾生不念，有感無應。「若眾生心憶佛念佛，現前當來必定見佛，去佛不遠。」此明眾生念佛，感應道交。此實彌陀世尊同體大慈悲善根力，隨緣赴感，應物垂形，不思議用。若明此理，定能見佛。由第八「像想觀」到第十三「雜想觀」是觀想極樂淨土的正報 —— 淨土聖眾。

● 佛教造像有何功用？

　　佛像為住持三寶之一，象徵佛寶。關於佛像起源，《增一阿含經》記載：釋尊在世時，曾往忉利天為母說法，三月未還，信徒優填王與波斯匿王思佛心切，各以牛頭栴檀與紫磨金塑佛形象，用以供奉，見之如對佛前。

　　佛陀入滅後，佛像更成為神聖的象徵，為信徒所瞻仰、禮拜、供養。

　　佛教造像之首要目的，在於「令十方瞻仰慈容者，皆大歡喜，信受皈依，廣種善根，潛消惡念」。這種寓教於形的親切方式，使佛教得以從精神聖殿走向社會，向民眾傳達慈悲喜捨的內涵，示現彼岸淨土的境界。

　　在所有的佛教寺院中，不論是南傳、漢傳還是藏傳，無不供奉着相好莊嚴的佛菩薩造像。雖然造型各異，體量有別，既有高哉偉哉的巨型塑像，也有不及盈寸的精雕細刻，但都體現了信徒心目中佛菩薩的慈悲形象。

　　那麼，佛像是否等同於佛陀真身呢？關於這個問題，禪宗「丹霞燒佛」的公案能給我們以啟發。丹霞禪師為唐代人，曾至洛東慧林寺掛單，因天寒而燒殿中木佛取暖。住持見之怒曰：因何燒佛？師云：燒取舍利。住持詫異：木佛何來舍利？師對曰：既無舍利，再取兩尊燒之。住持聞言有省。禪師的所行，是為了破除世人執相之弊 —— 僅執土木造像為佛，卻不見自性真佛。當然，對於禪宗祖師為教化愚蒙而採用的特殊方式，我們切不可輕易仿效。因為佛像雖非佛陀真身，卻是我們見賢思齊、憶念佛陀品質的重要增上緣，激勵我們聞佛所言，行佛所行。

Visualization of the Buddha and Bodhisattvas

Visualizing the images and perceiving the Buddha are two different stages of cultivation. In the Eighth Visualization, practitioners should first visualize a golden-colored image of the Buddha sitting upon the lotus seat, with Avalokiteśvara Bodhisattva and Mahāsthāmaprāpta Bodhisattva standing in attendance to the left and the right, each shining with a radiant golden light. This is the most important one among all the Sixteen Visualizations.

The key of this visualization is to guide us to meditate on the Buddha's respect-inspiring virtue through the visualization of his image. All buddha-tathāgatas represent the body of the dharma realm that penetrates into the minds of all sentient beings. Therefore, when the mind creates the Buddha, the mind becomes the Buddha. Since the right omniscience of Buddhas arises from the mind, we should whole-heartedly think of and contemplate various kinds of virtues of the Buddha. When we successfully complete this visualization, we will immediately see the light of the Pure Land and hear the wondrous Dharma, and it will serve as a cause for us to attain Buddhahood after innumerable kalpas.

Since beginningless time, sentient beings seldom see the real appearance of a Buddha; what we often see is a golden image of the Buddha that is sixteen feet high. As such, visualizing the image of the Buddha is a prelude to visualizing the real Buddha. It is an essential way to guide sentient beings towards attaining Buddhahood. Through visualizing the Buddha's image, the image will be reflected in our mind, and then our mind will possess the same primary and secondary marks as that of the Buddha's. Thus, it is said that the mind creates the Buddha.

"Great Strength Bodhisattva's Perfect Penetration Through Mindfulness

of the Buddha" of the Śūraṅgama Sutra also states, "The Thus Come Ones in all the ten directions are mindful of living beings, out of pity for them, in the same way that a mother is mindful of her child." This shows the Buddha recollects sentient beings constantly. "If the child runs away, of what use is the mother's concern?" This means if sentient beings do not remember the Buddha, even there is response from the Buddha, they will not connect with the saving power of the Buddha. "If living beings remember the Buddha, then certainly they will see the Buddha, either now or in the future. They will never be far from the Buddha." This means when sentient beings are mindful of the Buddha, there will be interaction between sentient beings and the Buddha along a common path. This is demonstration of the power of the virtuous roots of Amitābha Buddha's great loving-kindness and compassion, which is responsive to all sentient beings in accordance with the right conditions and adapting to their capacities. It is indeed inconceivable. When we understand this, we will surely see the Buddha. From the eighth visualization of the Buddha's image to the thirteenth composite visualization, we visualize the direct retribution of the Pure Land of Ultimate Bliss, that is, visualization of the Buddha and bodhisattvas of the Pure Land.

Basics of Buddhism:

• **What is the use of making an image of the Buddha?**

A Buddha's image is a symbol of the Buddha, one of the Three Jewels of Buddhism. The Ekottara Āgama recorded the origin of making the image of the Buddha. When Śākyamuni the Honored One was in this world, he had visited his mother in Trāyastriṃśas (Heaven of the Thirty-three devas) for three months to teach her the Dharma. His disciples, King Udāyana and King Prasenajit missed him very much, so they made images of the Buddha, one with ox-head sandalwood and the other with pure gold with a violet tinge, so that they could worship the Buddha's images as if they were seeing the Buddha in person.

After the Buddha's nirvana, the Buddha's image became an even more sacred symbol for Buddhist followers to revere, worship, and make offerings.

The main purpose of making the Buddha's image is to "give joy to those in the ten directions who worship his kind appearance. It gives them confidence to take refuge in the Buddha, cultivate wholesome roots extensively, and eliminate unwholesome thoughts."

This form of teaching through images helps Buddhism to come closer to society, extending Buddhism as the spiritual sanctuary to the social level of disseminating its content of loving kindness, compassion, joy, and equanimity to the common people, thus illustrating the realm of the Pure Land on the other shore.

In all the Buddhist monasteries found either in Therevada tradition, Chinese tradition, or Tibetan tradition, we can see the images of Buddhas and bodhisattvas adorned by excellent characteristics. They may be different in shape and size, with some being huge images that are tall and grand, while others are fine sculptings of less than one inch high. But all of them aim to manifest the compassionate images of Buddhas and bodhisattvas that have always prevailed in the hearts of the followers.

Then, is the Buddha's image equal to the real Buddha? The story of Chan Master Dan Xia's burning of a Buddha image will give us some insight. Dan Xia was a Chan master in the Tang dynasty. Once, he spent a night at Huilin Monastery in Luoyang. It was very cold, so he took a wooden Buddha statue and burned it as firewood to keep himself warm. The abbot of the monastery was angry and scolded him, "Why are you burning the Buddha?" The Chan Master said, "I'm burning it to get relics." The abbot asked in surprise, "How can you get relics from a wooden Buddha statue?" The Master said, "Since there is no relic in this one, go and get two more statues to burn." Hearing these words, the abbot seemed to have understood something. The Chan Master did this to help the worldlings get rid of attachment to marks, that is, they are attached to the wooden image of the Buddha but pay no attention to the real Buddha within their own nature. However, we should not blindly copy the special way Chan patriarchs used to teach and guide the ignorant, because even though the Buddha's image is not the real body of the Buddha, it is an excellent reminder for us to emulate the Buddha and remember the virtuous qualities of the Buddha; it encourages us to study what the Buddha taught and practice what the Buddha practised.

真身觀

　　觀佛像後，接下來便是觀想無量壽佛之真身，如大家每做晚課時
念誦的那樣：

　　　　　阿彌陀佛身金色，相好光明無等倫，

　　　　　白毫宛轉五須彌，紺目澄清似大海，

　　　　　光中化佛無數億，化菩薩眾亦無邊。

　　　　　四十八願度眾生，九品咸令登彼岸。

[佛教小知識]

• 真身觀的加持力

　　　　　一燈能除千年暗，一智能滅萬年愚。

　　　　　　　　　　　　　　　　　　　　　——《六祖壇經》

　　佛家常以黑暗比喻愚昧無知，以光明比喻智慧。無論地宮已黑暗多
少年，光明能立即驅散黑暗；同理，一個人因愚昧無知就會煩惱不斷，
但當智慧生起，便能立即化解煩惱，獲得解脫。本觀講述阿彌陀佛身光
明無量，其意為阿彌陀佛擁有無限的智慧，幫助人們化解煩惱，脫離苦
海。這是第九觀——「真身觀」的核心內容。

Visualization of Amitābha Buddha's Body

When visualization of the Buddha's image completes, next comes visualization of the physical body of the Buddha of Infinite Life, just like what you would chant during the evening recitations:

Amitābha's body is the color of gold;

The splendor of his hallmarks has no peer.

The light of his brow shines round a hundred worlds;

Wide as the sea are his eyes pure and clear.

Shining in his brilliance by transformation

Are countless Bodhisattvas and infinite Buddhas.

His forty-eight vows will be our liberation;

In nine lotus-stages we reach the farthest shore.

❈ Basics of Buddhism:

- **Empowerment gained through visualization of the physical body of Amitābha Buddha**

Just as a single lamp is able to eradicate a thousand years of darkness, so can a single [moment of] wisdom extinguish ten thousand years of stupidity.

— The Platform Sutra

In Buddhism, darkness is often an analogy for ignorance and brightness for wisdom. No matter how long an underground palace

has remained in darkness, once a ray of light enters, darkness is dispersed instantly. Similarly, no matter how afflicted a person may be due to ignorance, once wisdom arises, his afflictions will be immediately dissolved, and liberation will be attained. The ninth visualization, visualizing the immeasurable brightness of the body of Amitābha Buddha, carries the meaning of the infinite wisdom of the Buddha helping to dissolve our afflictions and liberate us from the sea of suffering. This is the essence of the Ninth Visualization—visualization of the body of Amitābha Buddha.

觀音觀

　　觀想無量壽佛了了分明之後，接下來觀想觀世音菩薩。此即觀觀
世音菩薩真實色身想：此菩薩身長八十億那由他恆河沙由旬，身紫金
色，頂有肉髻，項有圓光，面各百千由旬，其圓光中有五百化佛，皆如
釋迦牟尼。一一化佛，有五百菩薩與無量諸天以為侍者。

　　舉身光中，五道眾生，一切色相皆於中現。修行者若要觀見觀世
音菩薩者，應先觀想其頂上的肉髻，其次再觀想其天冠，而其餘各種身
相，也按照順序一一觀想，令其清楚明了，如同觀掌中之物。作如此觀
的，名為正觀；若作他種觀的，名為邪觀。

───────────────────────────────

▓▓ [佛教小知識] ─────────────────────────────

• 觀音菩薩為何與我們特別有緣？他是如何幫助苦難眾生的？

　　　　　瓶中甘露常遍灑，手內楊枝不計秋；

　　　　　千處祈求千處應，苦海常作度人舟。

　　　　　　　　　　　　　　　　　　　　── 古德

　　在觀音觀（第十觀）中，觀音菩薩周身的光明中不僅有化佛和化
菩薩，而且有五道眾生（天、人、畜生、餓鬼、地獄），修羅一道從天
道中分離出來，而成六道，以此表示觀音菩薩與婆婆世界六道眾生特別

有緣，救苦救難。人世間的幫助，大多的愛是有條件的，只有母親對兒女之愛是無私的。因此，在漢地，觀世音菩薩常以女性形象出現，藉母愛之偉大以表其大慈大悲的精神，無條件地幫助苦難眾生。現實生活中需要幫助的人很多，一雙手根本照顧不過來，於是就出現了千手千眼觀音，表達觀音菩薩有求必應的大悲心、大願力。

Visualization of Avalokiteśvara Bodhisattva

When your visualization of Amitābha Buddha remains distinct, next visualize Avalokiteśvara Bodhisattva with regard to his physical body. The bodhisattva's purple-golden body is as high as eight billion nayuta yojanas. There is a protuberance on his frontal crown with a halo surrounding his head, with shining light on each side reaching as far as one hundred thousand yojanas. There are five hundred transformation bodies of the Buddha within the halo, all looking the same as Śākyamuni Buddha. Each transformation Buddha is attended by five hundred bodhisattvas and innumerable devas.

Within the light emanating from Avalokiteśvara Bodhisattva's body, sentient beings of the five realms are seen in all forms. Practitioners who wish to visualize Avalokiteśvara Bodhisattva should first visualize the protuberance on his head and then the frontal crown; after that they should visualize his other physical characteristics in the order described above one by one, till the image becomes vivid and clear, as if they were watching something in their palms. Visualization in this way is called right visualization; or else it will be wrong visualization.

※ Basics of Buddhism:

- **Why does Avalokiteśvara Bodhisattva have a deep connection with us? How does the bodhisattva help sentient beings in distress?**

Sweet dew from his vase constantly sprinkles everywhere,

In his hand, he holds a willow branch through countless autumns.

Prayers depart a thousand hearts; in a thousand hearts he answers.

He constantly sails the sea of suffering, crossing people over.

— An ancient sage

In the tenth visualization, there are not only the transformation Buddhas and bodhisattvas but also living beings of the five realms (Deva realm, Human realm, Animal realm, Hungry Ghost realm, Nāraka realm) within the light emanating from Avalokiteśvara Bodhisattvas's body. Later on, the Asura realm separated from the Deva realm and thus became the sixth realm. This shows Avalokiteśvara Bodhisattva has a unique connection with sentient beings of the six realms in the Saha world and is always there saving us from suffering and difficulties. In the secular world, there are normally conditions set for us when we need help, but a mother's love for her children is unconditional.

Similarly, Avalokiteśvara Bodhisattva is often depicted as a mother, implying that his motherly love as manifested through the bodhisattva's spirit of great loving-kindness and compassion, drives him to help sentient beings in distress unconditionally. There are many people in real life who need help, and it is not easy to do so with only one pair of hands. As such, the image of Avalokiteśvara Bodhisattva with a thousand arms and a thousand eyes symbolizes his great compassion and great reslove to respond to all requests for help.

　　再接下來，修行者應觀想大勢至菩薩：此菩薩身量與觀世音菩薩相同，圓光面各百二十五由旬，照二百五十由旬，舉身光明照十方國，作紫金色，有緣眾生皆悉得見。但見此菩薩一毛孔光，即見十方無量諸佛淨妙光明，是故號此菩薩名無邊光，以智慧光普照一切，令離三塗得無上力，是故號此菩薩名大勢至。

※※ ［佛教小知識］ ⋯⋯⋯⋯⋯⋯⋯⋯⋯⋯⋯⋯⋯⋯⋯⋯⋯⋯⋯⋯⋯⋯⋯⋯⋯⋯⋯⋯⋯

* 大勢至菩薩為甚麼得名「大勢至」？

　　大勢至菩薩走路時，「十方世界，一切震動」。這種震動指眾生心靈的震動，即大勢至菩薩以般若智慧破除眾生心靈深處的煩惱惑，心魔震動。據《大乘寶要義論》記載，大迦葉受佛點化，皈依佛門，發大菩提心度眾生時，「魔宮震動，一切天魔咸生恐慄。」很顯然，菩薩度眾，修行人多一個，魔子魔孫少一個，魔軍自然會震動。故《思益經》云，「我投足一處，震動大千，及魔宮殿，故名得大勢。」《悲華經》說，當阿彌陀佛入滅後，由觀世音菩薩補其位；觀世音菩薩入滅後，則由大勢至菩薩補處成佛，「以智慧光普照一切，令離三塗，得無上力」，因此稱為大勢至菩薩。

Visualization of Mahāsthāmaprāpta Bodhisattva

Next, practitioners should visualize Mahāsthāmaprāpta Bodhisattva. The bodhisattva's body is the same size as that of Avalokiteśvara Bodhisattva's. The halo surrounding his head is as wide as one hundred and twenty-five yojanas, with its shining light reaching as far as two hundred and fifty yojanas. The light emanating from his body illuminates all the lands in the ten directions; these lands shine with a purple golden color, visible to those who have a connection with the bodhisattva. Even seeing only one ray of light from one of the pores of the bodhisattva, practitioners will immediately see the pure and marvelous light of immeasurable Buddhas of the ten directions. That is why he is called "Boundless Light Bodhisattva." With the light of wisdom, he illuminates all beings everywhere so that they can be liberated from the three miserable realms and attain supreme strengths, thus he is also called "Great Strength Bodhisattva."

Basics of Buddhism:

- **Why Mahāsthāmaprāpta Bodhisattva is called Great Strength Bodhisattva?**

When Mahāsthāmaprāpta Bodhisattva walks, "the worlds of the Ten Directions all tremble and quake." It makes the minds of living beings tremble. With his wisdom, Mahāsthāmaprāpta Bodhisattva eradicates afflictions and delusions from the depths of the hearts of all living beings, making the demons in their minds tremble. As the Sūtrasamuccaya recorded, Mahākāśyapa, guided by the Buddha,

decided to take refuge with the Buddhadharma and developed the aspiration for enlightenment in order to liberate all sentient beings. At that very moment, "the demons' palaces shook and all the māras became extremely terrified." Obviously, the more followers of the Dharma, the fewer number of the Mara's troop. That's why the Māra-pāpīyān (the demon king) trembled. The Sutra of the Questions of Viśeṣa-cinti-brahma states, "As I move, a billion worlds and the Māras' palaces shake. That is why I am called the One Who Has Attained Great Strength."

The Compassionate Flower Sutra states, after Amitābha Buddha enters into nirvana, Avalokiteśvara Bodhisattva would fill the position as Buddha; after Avalokiteśvara Bodhisattva enters into nirvana, Mahāsthāmaprāpta Bodhisattva would fill the position as Buddha. " And with this light of wisdom all beings are illuminated, enabling them to be freed from the Three Evil Paths and to attain unsurpassed powers." That is why the bodhisattva is called "Great Strength Bodhisattva."

自往生觀

　　修行者第十一觀成就時，心中應生起自己誠心往生於西方極樂世界之想，於蓮花中結跏趺而坐，作蓮花開、合之想。

　　觀想蓮花開時，有五百種顏色的光照在自己身上。睜開眼時，則見佛菩薩佈滿虛空中，水鳥、樹林以及諸佛菩薩，所發出的音聲，都在開示演說着妙法，這一切都與十二部經相契合。如果在出定的時候，也要牢記受持並保持不忘失。觀想看見此事後，名為見無量壽佛極樂世界。這就是普觀想，名為第十二觀。無量壽佛化身無數，並與觀世音大勢至二菩薩，常常會來到修行者當中度化眾生。

░░ ［佛教小知識］

• 如何修自往生觀？

　　觀想完各種依報和三種正報後，對極樂世界應已了解熟悉。修觀者應依經觀想自身往生在西方極樂世界，於蓮花中結跏趺坐，閉目靜思。此時心中對塵世間住房、財產、名利等不再起任何貪戀，完全放下，一心只想自己的身體在蓮花中化生，清淨無比，就能親身體驗一下極樂風光。如果我們通過修行，完成以上觀想，那麼我們將能親身體驗極樂世界的風光 —— 大家想像一下，那會是多麼的美妙！

Visualization of Oneself Being Reborn in the Pure Land

When the eleventh visualization has completed, practitioners should develop an earnest aspiration to be reborn in the Western Pure Land of Ultimate Bliss. Visualize that you are sitting in the lotus position inside a lotus flower that opens and closes.

Visualize that when the lotus flower blooms, rays of five hundred colors shine upon your body. When you open your eyes, you see Buddhas and bodhisattvas all over the sky. All the sounds you hear, from the water, the birds, the trees, and Buddhas and bodhisattvas, are preaching and expounding the wondrous Dharma, which is in accordance with the twelve divisions of the Buddhist canon. Even after you emerge from meditation, you should remember and uphold it, and retain it constantly. This is called the visualization of the World of Ultimate Bliss of the Buddha of Immeasurable Life Span. This is the Twelfth Visualization, the comprehensive visualization. The Buddha of Immeasurable Life Span has innumerable metamorphosic bodies; together with Avalokiteśvara Bodhisattva and Mahāsthāmaprāpta Bodhisattva, he often comes among practitioners to help and save sentient beings.

Basics of Buddhism:

- **How to practice the visualization of oneself being reborn in the Pure Land?**

  When you have completed the visualizations of various

circumstantial rewards and of the three direct retributions, you have already become familiar with the World of Ultimate Bliss. You should follow the instructions in the sutra and visualize that you have been reborn in the Western Pure Land of Ultimate Bliss, sitting with crossed legs in a lotus flower and meditating with eyes closed. You should have no craving for any secular things such as your properties and possessions, fame and fortune; you should completely let go of them and concentrate your attention on visualizing yourself being reborn in the lotus flower, purified of all defilements. Then you will be able to personally experience the beautiful sceneries in the Land of Ultimate Bliss. Imagine, what a wonderful experience that would be!

雜想觀

　　由第八像想觀到第十三雜想觀，觀想的對象都是極樂世界的聖眾，而現在第十三雜想觀所要觀的佛，正是我們於此世間所熟悉的一丈六尺佛像。佛陀告訴韋提希，若人至誠懇切，希望往生西方淨土的話，首先應當觀想立於水上的一丈六尺佛像，阿彌陀佛於十方國土變現自在，或現大身，滿虛空中；或現一丈六尺或八尺的小身，所現之形都是真金色，並有之前所說的圓光化佛及寶蓮花等。至於觀世音和大勢至二位菩薩，則於一切處現眾生身。而當我們見到菩薩像時，可以觀察其像首之相，便可分辨出是觀世音還是大勢至。以上為雜想，名第十三觀。

[佛教小知識]

• 回到人間

　　在第九觀 ——「真身觀」中，「佛身高六十萬億那由他恆河沙由旬」。這是阿彌陀佛的法身，普通人難以想像。而第十三觀 ——「雜想觀」觀阿彌陀佛丈六八尺的應化身，常人可以理解、接受。「雜想觀」因而成為從西方極樂世界回到人間的轉折點，為以下凡人三輩九品往生作鋪墊。

The Composite Visualization

From the eighth visualization till the thirteenth, you visualize the sacred assembly of the World of Ultimate Bliss. But in the thirteenth visualization, the Buddha you are going to visualize is a sixteen-foot image of the Buddha, with which we are quite familiar. The Buddha told Queen Vaidehī: If you sincerely and earnestly wish to take rebirth in the Western Pure Land, you should, first of all, visualize a sixteen-foot image of the Buddha standing above the water. Amitābha Buddha can freely manifest himself in all the lands of the ten directions, sometimes as big as a body filling the whole sky, sometimes as small as sixteen or eighteen feet. All these manifestations are in pure golden color, endowed with the transformation Buddhas in the halo and the jeweled lotus flowers. Avalokiteśvara Bodhisattva and Mahāsthāmaprāpta Bodhisattva always appear as living beings. When we see their images, we can distinguish between them by observing the features on their heads. This is the composite visualization that is called the Thirteenth Visualization.

✸ Basics of Buddhism:

• Return to the human world

In the Ninth Visualization of the body of Amitābha Buddha that "Buddha's body is as tall as the number of yojanas equaling that of the sands of six sextillions of Ganges Rivers." This is actually the dharmakāya (dharma body) of Amitābha Buddha, which is difficult for ordinary beings to visualize. But the Thirteenth Visualization—

visualizing the transformation body of the Buddha of sixteen feet and eight inches tall—is easier for us to relate to and accept. Therefore, the composite visualization serves as a turning point between the Western Pure Land of Ultimate Bliss and the human world, laying a foundation for the three grades and nine classes of beings who are going to be reborn in the Pure Land.

上輩觀

　　能解第一義諦，即大乘空義，是「上輩往生」之最大特色。換而言之，上輩往生者，都是大乘根機之人。若能領悟到緣起性空的智慧，便知萬法是現象的有，本體空，不生不滅。達本無法，故叫無生；把心安住（忍）在不生不滅的本體上，叫無生法忍。看破、放下之心隨之而生起，瀟灑自在的人生由此而獲得。

Visualization of Superior Rebirth

For those who get the superior rebirth, the most prominent feature is that they have realized the supreme truth, that is, emptiness of the Mahayana vehicle. In other words, they are people with great inclinations for the Mahayana path. When they are enlightened with the wisdom of dependent origination and that all phenomena are known to exist only because of their appearances, they will know that all dharmas are but empty in nature, neither

arising nor ceasing. Realization of no-dharma is called "without being born or produced." Abidance of the mind on suchness that neither arises nor ceases is called "acceptance of the non-arising nature of all phenomena." A penetrative insight to see things as they are develops naturally, and a free life is attained.

Basics of Buddhism:

• Nine classes of rebirth

Death is a horrible and miserable experience for ordinary people. But for those who understand transmigration in samsara, death marks another beginning of a new life, a glorious moment when a life of wisdom of the dharma-body starts. Because of this, they can face death with equanimity and talk about life and death with ease. The causes they plant will bring them the corresponding results; this is the basic rule of the karmic law. According to a person's karma in previous lives, they can experience a rebirth in the Western Pure Land of Ultimate Bliss of the highest grade, the middle grade, or the lowest grade. Within each grade, there are the highest level, the middle level, and the lowest level. Therefore, there are nine kinds of rebirth in the Western Pure Land, that is, rebirth in the highest level of the highest grade, rebirth in the middle level of the highest grade, rebirth in the lowest level of the highest grade, rebirth in the highest level of the middle grade, rebirth in the middle level of the middle grade, rebirth in the lowest level of the middle grade, rebirth in the highest level of the lowest grade, rebirth in the middle level of the lowest grade, and rebirth in the lowest level of the lowest grade. Whatever the rebirth type is, they all share one thing in common, that is, they will all be reborn in a lotus flower. That is why it is called "nine grades of lotus."

第十五中輩觀分三品：

1. 若有人修善積福，受持五戒八戒，不造五逆，離諸過患，得中品上生；

2. 若有人受持沙彌戒、比丘具足戒、八關戒，三業威儀，護持無缺犯，得中品中生；

3. 若有人孝養父母，奉順六親，行世仁慈，博施濟眾，得中品下生。

［佛教小知識］

• 中輩往生

第十五觀是「中輩往生觀」，攝四果聲聞眾，分上、中、下三品。其中，第四品——「中品上生」救度的對象是以持戒、行善的在家眾為主體，第五品——「中品中生」救度的對象是小乘凡夫，第六品——「中品下生」救度的對象是普通善人。

Visualization of the Middle Grade Rebirth

In the Fifteenth Visualization on the middle grade, there are three levels.

For those who have cultivated virtue and accumulated merit, who have taken and upheld the five precepts and the eight precepts, who have not committed the five heinous crimes, and who are free from various faults, they will be reborn in the Pure Land in the highest level of the middle grade.

For those who have taken and upheld the precepts for novices, the full precepts for bhikṣus, or the eight precepts of a one-day vow holder, and who have protected and maintained their dignity in their deeds, words, and thoughts without breaking or offending anything, they will be reborn in the middle level of the middle grade.

For those who have been filial to their parents, who have honored and obeyed the six immediate relations, who have done benevolent deeds for society, and who have practiced generosity to help others, they will be reborn in the lowest level of the middle grade.

꽃 Basics of Buddhism:

• **The middle grade of rebirth**

The Fifteenth Visualization is that of the middle grade of rebirth. It includes the srāvakas with four fruitions and is divided into the highest level, the middle level, and the lowest level. Among them, those who will be reborn in the highest level of the middle grade are mainly lay people who have observed precepts and cultivated wholesome karma; those who are reborn in the middle level of the middle grade are ordinary beings of the Hīnayāna(small vehicle); those who are reborn in the lowest level of the middle grade are the good common people.

下品上生者屬愚昧無知、糊塗之人，下品中生者屬壞人，下品下生者屬惡人。但只要當他們在生命將盡時，若遇到善人開導，一念之間歸向善，臨終時誦念阿彌陀佛名號，他亦能夠因之蓮花化生，往生極樂淨土。

※ ［佛教小知識］

• 下輩往生

　　第十六品「下輩往生」的眾生，因愚昧無知而作惡，且沒有任何慚愧心。又可分為上、中、下三品。其中，第七品——「下品上生」救度的對象是生前偶爾作惡而無反思能力之人，第八品——「下品中生」救度的對象多為貪名利、破淨戒的出家五眾，第九品——「下品下生」救度的對象多為作各種不善之業，五逆十惡之罪。值得注意的是，從第六品——「中品下生」至第九品——「下品下生」的人，都有一個共同的特徵：當他們在生命將盡時，若遇到善知識開導，一念之間向善，臨終時願意往生西方極樂世界，念誦阿彌陀佛名號，才有可能往生極樂淨土。九品往生揭示了佛教解脫的大門對所有人開放。

Visualization of the Low Grade Rebirth

Those who will be reborn in the highest level of the lowest grade are deluded and ignorant beings. Those who will be reborn in the middle level of the lowest grade are morally inferior beings. Those who will be reborn in the lowest level of the lowest grade are evil beings. However, if they meet a virtuous teacher who enlightens them when they are dying and they choose to return to goodness in a moment of thought, chanting the name of Amitābha Buddha at the end of their life, they will be reborn in a lotus flower in the Pure Land of Ultimate Bliss.

- **The lowest grade of rebirth**

In the Sixteenth Visualization, beings who will be reborn in the lowest grade are those who have created unwholesome actions due to delusion and ignorance and without a sense of regret or remorse. They can be further divided into the highest level, the middle level, and the lowest level. Among them, the beings of the seventh class—those who will be reborn in the highest level of the lowest grade—are those who have done evil occasionally but have been unable to reflect upon themselves during their lifetime. The beings of the eighth class—those who will be reborn in the middle level of the lowest grade—are the five groups of monastics who have craved for fame and fortune and have broken the pure precepts. The beings of the ninth class—those who will be reborn in the lowest level of the lowest grade—are those who have created various unwholesome karma, and who have committed the five heinous crimes and ten unwholesome deeds.

Notably, these beings from the lowest level of the middle grade to the lowest level of the lowest grade share one thing in common, that is, if they encounter a virtuous teacher who enlightens them at the end of their life, and if in a single moment of thought they decide to return to goodness, aspire to take rebirth in the Western Pure Land of Ultimate Bliss, and chant the name of Amitābha Buddha, then, and only in this way, can they be reborn in the Pure Land of Ultimate Bliss. The nine classes of rebirth show that the gate of liberation in Buddhism is open to all sentient beings.

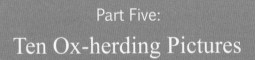

Part Five:

Ten Ox-herding Pictures

茫茫撥草去追尋，水闊山遙路更深；
力盡神疲無處覓，但聞楓樹晚蟬吟。

　　牧童發現自己的牛丟失了，便撥開茫茫荒草，到處去追尋它；他
渡過寬闊的水流，來到綿綿無盡的大山裏，卻只見前路茫茫，越行越
深。到了日落時分，精疲力盡的牧童已近乎絕望，他只好在一棵大楓樹
下面停下來休息，此刻，耳畔忽然響起傍晚的蟬鳴。

［佛教小知識］

• 牧童尋牛，苦惱人覓心

　　「從來不失，何用追尋？由背覺以成疏，在向塵而遂失。家山漸遠，
歧路俄差；得失熾然，是非蜂起」。想要「牧牛」，首先要尋找到「牛」
才行。同樣，想要修行，首要任務是找到自己的「本心」。「我有明珠一
顆，久被塵勞封鎖，今朝塵盡光生，照破山河萬朵。」每一個人都有一
顆清淨的菩提自性，從來不曾失去，為何還要四處去追尋呢？因為眾生
一念無明起，生起貪、嗔、癡之心，污染了我們清淨的心，從此陷入你
爭我奪的紅塵中，痛苦不堪。欲滅苦，先覓心。

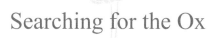

Searching for the Ox

One incessantly pushes the grasses in search,

The rivers are wide, the mountains far away, and the path becomes longer.

Exhausted and dispirited, knowing no where to search,

One hears only the late autumn cicadas chirping in the maple woods.

A ox herder found his ox lost, so he tried to search for it by sweeping away the grasses. He crossed rivers and reached the endless ranges of mountains, only to find that the road ahead was unclear and stretching far beyond. At sunset, feeling exhausted and hopeless, the cowherd rested against a big maple tree. At that very moment, he suddenly heard the cicadas chirping around.

Basics of Buddhism:

- **The cowherd is looking for his ox, while people in distress are looking for their original minds**

    "Because the ox has intrinsically never been lost, what need is there to go in pursuit? Since the herd boy has turned his back on his true-nature, he is far away from it; with the dust before his eyes, he loses sight of the ox. Having left his ancestral home far behind, he gradually becomes lost on crisscrossing paths. Thoughts of loss and gain rise up like flames, ideas of right and wrong spring up like sword points." To herd an ox, you need to find the ox first. Likewise, to practice the Dharma, you need to find your original mind first. "There is a bright pearl within me, buried for a long time under dust. Today, the dust is gone and the light radiates, shining through all the mountains and rivers." Everyone is endowed with his or her intrinsic nature of enlightenment, which has never been lost. Why bother to go everywhere to find it? Because of ignorance, we are entangled in craving, hatred, and delusion, which have polluted the originally pure mind. Since then, we have been caught in a world with fierce rivalry. To eliminate sufferings, we must find our original mind first.

見跡

水邊林下跡偏多，芳草離披見也麼，

縱是深山更深處，遼天鼻孔怎藏他。

　　牧童不怕疲勞艱辛，堅持「尋牛」，終於，他發現了牛的腳印，而且越來越多，水邊林下到處都是；只要分開草叢，隨時都可以看到「牛跡」，可為啥還沒見到「牛」呢？雖然牛還沒見到，但是，牧童很清楚，自己離牛已經很近了，縱然它有可能藏在深山的最深之處；「牛跡」的顯露，使牧童感受到了牛的氣息，他似乎已經體會到，「牛」正仰着它那通天鼻孔呼氣呢，哪裏藏得住它呢？

✼ ［佛教小知識］ ────────────────────────────────

• 依經解義，閱教知蹤

　　「依經解義，閱教知蹤；明眾器為一金，體萬物為自己。正邪不辭，真偽奚分？未入斯門，權為見跡」。修行人通過學習經論，理解了關於「心性」的法義，也就知道了該如何觀察，才能夠找到「心性」。他已明白，萬法不離此心，萬物無非自性。倘若沒有如此之正知見的話，就會

正邪不分，又如何能夠辨別「真悟」和「假悟」呢？他只是明白了教義，還沒有契入當下的「心性」之門，所以暫時只能叫做「見跡」，還不能叫做「見牛」。

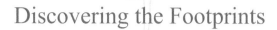

Discovering the Footprints

By the water, and under the trees,

There are numerous traces.

Fragrant grasses grow thickly,

Did you see the ox?

Even in the depths of the distant mountain forest,

How could the upturned nostrils of the ox be concealed?

The cowherd spared no effort to "look for his ox" and found its footprints at last. More and more footprints appeared, spreading everywhere at the waters' edge and under the trees. Whenever he brushed aside grasses, the ox's footprints were there. But where was the "ox"? Though he did not see it, he was clear that the ox was somewhere near him, even though it might have hidden itself in the deepest mountain. The exposure of the ox's footprints made the cowherd feel its breath. It seemed that the ox was breathing with its huge nostrils. Where could it hide itself?

Basics of Buddhism:

- **Relying on scriptures to understand the Dharma; Learning the Buddha's teaching to know the ox's track**

  "He has understood the meaning of the sutras and knows about the tracks through the teachings. It is clear to him that all vessels are made of gold, and he knows that the myriad things are himself. But if he cannot distinguish between right and wrong, how can he separate the true from the false? As he has not yet entered this gate, he can be said to have merely seen the tracks." A practitioner understands the meaning of "mind-nature" through studying the sutras and sastras and then knows how to contemplate in order to find the "mind-nature." He has already realized that all dharmas are inseparable from the mind and everything is nothing but manifestations of the intrinsic nature. Without such right knowledge and right view, one will not be able to distinguish between right and wrong, let alone real and false enlightenment. At this stage, he only understands what the teachings mean but has yet to enter the gate of the "mind-nature." That is why he is only "seeing the tracks" rather than the real "ox."

見牛

黃鸝枝上一聲聲，日暖風和岸柳青。
只此更無回避處，森森頭角畫難成。

　　牧童歷盡千辛萬苦，終於望見了自己的「牛」，只這一眼，頓時心
花怒放，如沐春風。耳邊喜聽黃鶯聲聲歌唱，眼前乍現兩岸楊柳青青。
到如今，再也不會懷疑自己，再也不需要四處追尋了；只是還無法見到
牛的全貌。

［佛教小知識］

- 牧童因腳印得見牛，求道人因聞法而自性顯露

　　「從聲入得；見處逢源；六根門著著無差，動用中頭頭顯露。水中鹽
味，色裏膠青；眨上眉毛，非是他物」。修行人在「閱教知蹤」的基礎
上，或者從耳根反聞而契入「聞性」，或者從眼根反觀而明達「見性」，
等等，終於有了個入處。從此，不論它六根門頭如何顯現，自己很清
楚，無非都是自性；乃至於一切生活動用當中，處處都是自性的顯露。
自性就好比水中的鹽味，以及顏料裏面的明膠一樣，雖然絲毫也看不
見，但確實存在。就在一抬手，一眨眼之處，即是自性，並非其他。

Seeing the Ox

The bush warbler sings on the branch.

The sun is warm, the breeze gentle, and the willows on the riverbank are green.

There is no place you can escape from him.

That majestic head and horns could never be painted in a picture.

The young cowherd saw his ox at last despite twists and turns. The mere sight of the ox made him so elated and delighted. The bush warbler was heard singing happily; the willows on the riverbank were seen so green. He needed no longer to doubt himself or search it everywhere. But he just could not see the whole body of the ox yet.

☷ Basics of Buddhism:

- **By following the hoofmarks, a cowherd sees the ox. By hearing the teaching, the seeker of the Way has his intrinsic nature revealed**

    "If you attain by way of sounds, you will encounter the source of all seeing. The six sense organs are each no different from this; in all actions, the head is revealed. It is like the salty taste of the water, the binder in the paint. Raise your eyebrows, and this is nothing other than THAT itself." Based on "knowing about the tracks through the teachings," the practitioner has got an entrance either related to "hearing" through listening with the faulty of hearing or related to "seeing" through watching with the faculty of seeing. From then on, no matter what the six sense faculties experience, it is very clear that all are from one's intrinsic nature. And even all actions are manifestations of the intrinsic nature. It is like salt in water and color in dyestuff, invisible but always there. Every move and every blink we make is the intrinsic nature, not anything else.

竭盡精神獲得渠，心強力壯卒難除。

有時纔到高原上，又入煙雲深處居。

　　牧童費了九牛二虎之力，終於握住了牛的韁繩；但是，這頭牛野慣了，哪裏肯聽主人的話呢？它野心極強，體力又壯，一時難以改變，還需要牧童耐心調教。最開始的時候啊，牧童幾乎是被牛拽着跑，一會兒跑上了高原，一會兒又下到了煙霞深處，象徵着修道人道業之起伏。

❀ ［佛教小知識］ ────────────────────────

• 牧童得牛，求道者見性

　　「久埋郊外，今日逢渠；由境勝以難追，戀芳叢而不已。頑心尚勇，野性猶存；欲得純和，必加鞭撻。」修行人無始以來遺忘了自家寶藏，任由它被埋在荒郊野外；直到今天，終於與它歡喜重逢了。由於心性勝境不可思議，稍不留神，就會習慣性地生起分別念頭而迷失；一旦迷失，仍會和以往一樣貪戀於種種美妙境界。這愚頑的分別心還很勇猛，它四處攀緣的野性依然存在。因此，修行人要想到達自然純和之心境的話，就必須隨時鞭策自己。

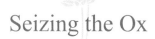

Seizing the Ox

With all my energy, I seize the ox.

His will is strong, and his power inexhaustible,

He cannot be tamed easily.

Sometimes he charges to the high plateau.

And there he stays, deep in the mist.

The cowherd made tremendous efforts to get hold of the ox's bridle. But the ox was used to being wild and wouldn't obey its owner. Ambitious and strong, it could not be changed within a short while but needed patient guidance from the cowherd. At the beginning, the cowherd was pulled to run after the ox, up to the high plain or deep down in clouds and smoke. It is a metaphor for the ups and downs experienced by practitioners in cultivation.

Basics of Buddhism:

- **The cowherd 'seized his ox,' and the seeker of the Way 'sees the nature'**

     "For a long time he has been living in obscurity in the countryside; today you have met him. Because he enjoys his former situation so much, it is difficult to drive him out. He cannot stop loving the fragrant grasses; his stubborn will is still strong and a wild spirit remains. If you wish to make him pure and obedient, you must apply the whip." The practitioner has left his own treasure in the wild since beginningless time. It is not until now that he reunites with it joyfully. But the former wonderful situation was so incredible that out of occasional mindlessness, his discriminating thoughts arise habitually and the treasure gets lost again easily. Then, he would be obsessed with all fantastic situations as before. The discriminating thought is still stubborn and strong with its wildness of always trying to cling onto something. Thus, if the practitioner wants to achieve a pure and natural mind, he must keep reminding himself about this every now and then.

鞭索時時不離身，恐伊縱步入埃塵；

相將牧得純和也，羈鎖無拘自逐人。

　　牧童「得牛」之後，一手把着韁繩，一手拿着鞭子，不敢有絲毫
鬆懈；恐怕一放縱它的牛脾氣，就會再次被牛拽入迷途。到後來，牧童
終於把牛調教好了，「牧牛」成功，相處得一團和氣；甚至，已經不用
牽得太牢，也不用怎麼管教，牛自然就跟着牧童往回走。

- - -

❈ [佛教小知識]

- **牧童調伏牛脾氣，修行人調伏分別、執着之心**

　　「前思才起，後念相隨；由覺故以成真，在迷故而為妄。不由境有，
惟自心生；鼻索牢牽，不容擬議」。修行人「見性」之後，還需要調順
自己的心念，如何調順呢？就在前念才起，後念相隨之際，及時覺察，
就不會流連其中，則念念清澈，念念不離真如；否則的話，一旦隨念而
迷惑，就會陷入虛妄執着。要知道，一切感受與分別，並非因外境而
有，都是自己內心發生的；雖然已經「見性」，還是要把心念牢牢盯住，
不容它討價還價。

Taming the Ox

Whipping does not depart from the body at any moment.

Lest he follow his own whim, entering the dust and dirt.

If you devotedly tame him, he will be pure and gentle.

Without bridle and chains, he will follow you of his own accord.

After getting back his ox, the cowherd held the bridle on one hand and whip on the other, daring not to relax. He was afraid that he would get back to the deluded path by the ox if its wild temper was let loose. Finally, the cowherd tamed the ox and got along well with it. Moreover, without necessity of a tight grip or control, it followed the cowherd willingly.

▨ Basics of Buddhism:

- **The cowherd subdues the temper of the ox; the practitioner subdues his discriminating thoughts and attachments**

    "Illusive thoughts arise one after another immediately. Through mindfulness of them, the truth is realized; but in heedlessness, one gets lost in illusions. Illusions derive from the mind, not the environment. So hold tight to the bridle, and leave no room for the ox to wabble." After the practitioner sees his nature, he needs to tame his mind and thoughts. How? Should one be aware of the moment when a previous thought arises and just before another one follows, one will not be attached to it, and each thought will be clear and inseparable from Tathatā. On the contrary, once led by deluded thoughts, one will be attached to what is delusional. We must know that all feelings and discriminations happen within our own mind. Although one has already seen their nature, one still needs to guard his mind closely and should not give it any room for negotiation.

騎牛迤邐欲還家，羌笛聲聲送晚霞；
一拍一歌無限意，知音何必鼓唇牙。

　　牧童騎着已經調順的牛，沿着曲折連綿的山路回家；只見他一路吹起羌笛聲聲，迎來了朝陽，送走了晚霞，好不自在呀。那每一個節拍，每一聲曲調，都蘊含着無限深意；您要是知音的話，儘管如此受用，又何必開口呢？

Riding the Ox Home

You mount the ox and want to make your way slowly home.

A barbarian plays the flute in the red glow of sunset.

Each measure, each tune is filled with ineffable tones.

Among true intimates, what need is there for words?

The cowherd already tamed the ox and went home along the winding and stretching hill path; he was playing the flute all his way from dawn till night. What a great state of freedom! Deep meaning is implicated in each tempo and tune. If you are a friend who understands, then just enjoy without saying a word.

Basics of Buddhism:

- **Riding the ox to return home; the practitioner feels peace of mind**

    "The battle is already over, gain and loss are also empty. He sings a woodcutter's rustic song and whistles a child's tune. Straddled on the ox's back, he gazes at the clouds. Though you call him he will not return; though you try to catch and hold him, he will not stay." Now the practitioner has tamed his mind, his thoughts are no longer apart from the intrinsic nature, and his actions synchronize with non-interference. Now, his inner contradictions and conflicts have ended. His attention towards gains and losses has disappeared. Staring at the sky and singing country melodies as the cowherd does, the

practitioner is returning home. He will not be entangled again by
worldly temptations, nor stop for any beautiful scenery.

忘牛存人

騎牛已得到家山，牛也空兮人也閒。
紅日三竿猶作夢，鞭繩空頓草堂間。

　　牧童騎牛回到了家，在自家廣大的山谷裏，再也不擔心牛會丟失了；於是，他甚至把牛的存在忘得一乾二淨，自己呢，也變得無比閒適安然。每天，都日上三竿了，他還在那兒呼呼大睡，在夢境裏面，一路牧牛的習氣還在顯現，所以，他還在重溫舊夢呢。而實際上，牧牛早已結束，鞭子和韁繩已經閒置在了草堂裏。

░░ [佛教小知識]

• 牧童忘牛，修行人心平

　　「法無二法，牛且為宗。喻蹄兔之異名，顯筌魚之差別。如金出礦，似月高雲，一道寒光，威音劫外」。修行人超越了兩邊對立，能修的人和所修的法同歸於真如一心，這叫做「能所一如」；本來無法可立，也不妨特開方便，以「心性之牛」為修行宗旨。打個比方呢，就好比順着野兔的蹄子印，就能找到野兔；善用筌（漁具），就可以捕到魚，得魚則可以忘筌矣。到這裏，修行人的「心性法身」已經完全顯露，就好比礦石裏面提煉出了純金，皎潔的月光遠離了烏雲一般；那一道清涼的心光，透徹今古，一直超出那無量劫前的初始佛 —— 威音王佛之外呀。

Ox Forgotten, the Person Remaining

You have mounted the ox and already reached your home in the mountains.

The ox is gone and the person has nothing more to do.

Though the morning sun has already risen three bamboo lengths, he dreams on.

The whip and the halter, no longer of use, are hung up in the stall.

The cowherd returned to his own home; in the vast valley, he was no longer worried about losing his ox. He even forgot about the existence of his ox. Thus, he enjoyed the leisure and woke up late after sunrise every day, dreaming about taming the ox. In reality, herding is already ended, with the whip and bridle laying aside in the thatched hall.

※ Basics of Buddhism: ─────────────────────────────

- **The cowherd forgets the ox; the practitioner's mind is at rest**

   "In the dharma there is no duality; the Ox is the foundation. It may be compared to the rabbit and the snare; it is expressed in the difference between fish and weir. Like gold coming from ore, like the moon emerging from behind the clouds. A single ray of cold light has been shining ever since the time of Ion beyond the kalpas." The practitioner transcends clinging to dualistic points of view; his discrimination between the cultivator and the cultivated ceases, both becoming the one true mind. In reality, there is no substantial dharma, hence the freedom to employ expedient means (to lead all beings to realization of truth). The analogy of the ox serves just this purpose.

For example, you can find rabbits by following their footprints, or catch fishes with proper tools. Once the fish is caught, you can leave the tools aside. At this stage, the practitioner's "intrinsic nature and dharma body" is completely disclosed, like pure gold refined from ore or the bright moon emerging from behind the clouds. The clear cool light of enlightenment transcends the present and the past, till far beyond the Bhīṣma-garjita-svara-rāja, the initial Buddha who appeared innumerable kalpas ago.

人牛俱忘

鞭索人牛盡屬空，碧天寥廓信難通。
紅爐焰上爭容雪，到此方能合祖宗。

　　就好比牧童在家鄉自在逍遙，完全忘懷了鞭子、韁繩，更忘懷了自己和牛一樣；此時，菩薩已到無修無證之地，縱目所及，猶如水天一色，心法皆空，更無絲毫資訊可通。只是啊，法性紅爐的熊熊火焰之上，怎會容得一丁點兒煩惱之雪的存留呢？到這裏，就完全契合了佛陀與祖師們的功德。

──── [佛教小知識] ────────────────────────────

• 牧童人牛俱忘，修行人物我雙忘

　　「見情脫落，聖意皆空。有佛處不用激遊，無佛處急須走過。兩頭不著，千眼難窺；百鳥銜花，一場懡㦬！」此時的修行人，凡夫之情見徹底脫落，聖者之清淨心也不存留。在大覺而不流連，處無明而信步走過。就這樣兩邊不住，任它佛眼也難窺見；即便如牛頭法融禪師一樣，感應來百鳥銜花之瑞相，也不過是一場鬧劇罷了。

──

Person and Ox Both Forgotten

Whip, tether, person and ox - all are empty.

The blue sky spreads out far and wide, it cannot be communicated.

On a red-hot oven, how can there be any place for snow?

Having come this far, you understand the intention of the patriarchs.

Just as the cowherd, who is free and unfettered at home, forgets about the whip and bridle, and himself and the ox, a bodhisattva has reached the stage of nothing to practice and nothing to realize. Whatever he sees, water and sky are as one, both mind and dharma are empty, and no message is to be conveyed. However, above the raging fire of dharma-nature, how can the tiniest snowflake of affliction be tolerated? This is the point when one is completely integrated with the merit and virtue of the Buddhas and the patriarchs.

Basics of Buddhism:

- **The cowherd forgets both the person and the ox; the practitioner forgets both the object and the self**

    "Ordinary feelings have fallen away, thoughts of holiness are all empty. We should not linger where there is Buddha; we should pass quickly by where there is no Buddha. If we do not stick to either, it will be difficult for a thousand eyes to perceive us. For myriad birds to carry flowers is a shame all around." Now, the practitioner has transcended both the feelings and views of an ordinary being and the pure mind of a sage. He will not linger in great enlightenment, nor be stopped by ignorance. He abides in neither; even the Buddha's eyes cannot find his track. Amazing as it is that Master Fa Rong of Oxhead Mountain attracted hundreds of birds to offer him flowers, but no more than a mere play it remains.

返本還源已費功，爭如直下若盲聾。
庵中不見庵前物，水自茫茫花自紅。

　　菩薩夢中修行，一路返本還源，難免歷經了幾多造作折騰；如今
已是心包太虛，見聞覺知之當下，實無可見可聞，更何妨如聾似啞？端
坐茅庵之中，不見庵前有一物實存；雖如此，也不妨礙那煙水茫茫，柳
綠花紅。

❀❀❀ [佛教小知識]

- **識心達本，解無為法**

　　「本來清淨，不受一塵；觀有相之榮枯，處無為之凝寂。不同幻化，
豈假修治？水綠山青，坐觀成敗」。修行人到此，處處是本來清淨，不
曾有一毫煩惱塵勞；雖明照幻有萬相之榮枯變化，而安處無為之天然寂
滅。本來不同於幻化之相，哪裏需要藉助於修行和對治呢？任它水綠山
青，因緣變幻，菩薩不妨坐觀成敗，本自如如。

Returning Home

Having come back to the origin and returned to the source, you see that you have expended efforts in vain.

What could be superior to becoming blind and deaf in this very moment?

Inside the hermitage, you do not see what is in front of the hermitage.

The water flows of itself and the flowers are naturally red.

Cultivating in dreams, the bodhisattva returns home after inevitable twists and turns. Now that his mind holds the unlimited space, there is nothing to see or hear at the moment of seeing, hearing, sensing, or cognizing, why not act as if a deaf or a mute? Sitting in the abode, he does not see any substantial existence in front. However, the water is still misty, willows still green, and flowers red.

❀ Basics of Buddhism: ────────────────────

- **With consciousness of mind reaching its source, unconditioned phenomena are understood**

    "It is originally pure and clean without a speck of dust clinging. He observes the flourishing and dying of form while remaining in the silence of no-action. This is not the same as illusion; what need is there for striving or planning? The water is blue and the mountains green; he sits and watches phenomena take form and decay." At this

stage, the practitioner sees all things as originally pure and clear and is freed from the slightest defilement of afflictions. Although he knows clearly the flourishing and withering of illusory phenomena, he abides in the natural silence of no-action. Suchness differs from illusive phenomena, so what is there to cultivate or battle against? The water is blue, the mountains green, and the causal conditions keep changing, but the bodhisattva could just sit and watch phenomena rise and fall in silent stillness.

入塵垂手

露胸跣足入塵來，抹土塗灰笑滿腮。
不用神仙真祕訣，直教枯木放花開。

　　菩薩自度已經圓滿，名為「等覺」，覺同諸佛故。於是便興大慈
悲，坦胸裸足地化現在塵世間，無比自在；縱然混得一身灰頭土臉，也
還是一團和氣，笑意滿懷。他不需要甚麼神仙的真傳祕訣，直下就能夠
讓法性無為之枯木，綻放出自在解脫之花朵。

※※ ［佛教小知識］ --

• 隨緣度眾

　　「柴門獨掩，千聖不知；埋自己之風光，負前賢之途轍。提瓢入市，
策杖還家；酒肆魚行，化令成佛！」菩薩安處無為法性，則縱然千佛出
世，也不知他所在。不過，如此埋沒自己之本地風光，實有負於先佛眾
聖之弘化大道。因此呢，菩薩拎著家當，懸壺濟世來也，只見他揮動手
杖，威武地回入三界老家；能夠在那酒館、魚鋪，甚至妓院、屠場裏
面，教化一切眾生，皆令成佛。

Entering the World with
Arms Hanging Loose

Shoeless and bare-chested he enters the World;

He is daubed with earth and ashes, and a smile fills his face.

Making no use of the secrets of gods and wizards,

He causes withered trees to bloom.

The bodhisattva has already perfected self-deliverance, that is, "perfect enlightenment," the enlightenment that is equal to that of all Buddhas. Out of great compassion, he then manifests himself in the world at ease with bare chest. Even daubed with earth and ashes, he is still smiling. He does not need any secret from an Immortal; he can immediately cause the withered trees of the Dharma nature of no-action to blossom into the flower of ease and liberation.

Basics of Buddhism:

- **Saving sentient beings according to conditions**

   "He closes the thatched gate to his hermitage so that even the thousand sages do not know of him. He buries the light of his own knowing and goes against the tracks left by former sages. Carrying a gourd, he enters the World; holding his staff, he returns home, Bestowing Buddhahood on barkeeps and fishmongers." When a bodhisattva dwells in the unconditioned Dharma nature, even thousands of Buddhas are unaware of his whereabouts. However, considering it is a waste of his achievements and a disappointment to the past Buddhas and sages who pursued the promotion of the teachings, he then comes to the world with everything he has to save sentient beings. He waves his staff and mightily returns to the old home, that is, the Three Realms. He can teach all sentient beings to be enlightened and achieve Buddhahood, whether in bars, fish markets, or even brothels and slaughterhouses.

參透因果

Part Six:

Understanding Cause and Effect

水懺法會緣起

> 修善如春日之草，未見其長而有所增；
> 行惡如磨刀之石，未見其減而有所損。

—— 古德

　　悟達禪師因受封為國師而自命不凡，其時，膝蓋上陡然冒出一個人面瘡，醫治無方。後在迦諾迦伐蹉尊者的指導下，以三昧法水清洗，豈知人面瘡竟開口說話：「十世前，我是被冤殺的晁錯，你是袁盎。一直想找你報仇。無奈你一直是持戒嚴謹的高僧，使我無機可趁，近日終得機緣。」禪師聽後慚愧萬分，康復後撰寫了《慈悲三昧水懺》的懺悔法門，長傳後世，廣利眾生。此乃水懺法會之起源。

※※ ［佛教小知識］

* **懺悔得清淨**

　　改惡修善是佛教根本教義。特別是大乘佛教，認為人生是由久遠生死相繼而來，今後還須經無數生的修行，以至於成佛。其間主要的是要消除以往無量劫中所造的罪惡，發願今後精進修行，永不退轉。因此，修習懺法便成為大乘修行的不可缺少的行儀。每逢清明節，寶蓮禪寺都要啟建清明水懺法會，由大德高僧主法，禮拜《慈悲三昧水懺》，令眾生至誠懺罪，以消釋宿世冤業，消災免難，以此功德迴向世界和平、國泰民安。

The Background of Compassionate Samadhi Water Repentance Assembly

Origin of the Compassionate Samadhi Water Repentance Dharma Assembly

Cultivating wholesomeness is like spring grass, it grows without being noticed.

Cultivating unwholesomeness is like a grindstone, it diminishes but its damage remains undetected.

— An ancient sage

Chan Master Wu Da was once pretentious having been granted the title of an Emperor's Teacher. One day, a human-faced sore suddenly appeared on his knee, and no doctor was able to cure it. Later, under the right guidance of Arhat Kanakavatsa, Wu Da used the samadhi-water to clean the sore, and the human-faced sore started to speak, "You were Yuan Ang and I was Chao Cuo ten lifetimes ago. I have been looking for revenge life after life, but I could not get any chance since you have been an eminent monk and observed precepts rigorously. Finally, I have got this favorable chance to take revenge." After hearing the story, Wu Da felt ashamed and repented for his pompous behavior. After recovery, he wrote the Compassionate Samadhi Water Repentance, a method for people to repent with. His contribution was passed down through generations and benefited innumerable sentient beings. This is the origin of the Water Repentance Dharma Assembly.

- **Repentance brings purity**

    Eradicating the unwholesome and nurturing the wholesome is the fundamental teaching of Buddhism. Especially in Mahayana Buddhism, it is believed that we have experienced life and death in succession since beginningless time, and we must practice diligently this life onward until Buddhahood is realized. The most important element of the practice is to eliminate the unwholesomeness created in past countless kalpas and make a vow to practice until one never again regresses from the path.

    Therefore, practicing Repentance becomes an indispensable sadhana for Mahayana practitioners. On each Qingming Festival, Po Lin Monastery holds the Qingming Water Repentance Dharma Assembly, presided over by the noble and virtuous Sangha members. All participants bow down while chanting the Compassionate Samadhi Water Repentance and confess their wrong-doings sincerely to purify the unwholesome karma of the past, be sheltered from calamities, and dedicate the merits and virtues to world peace, national prosperity, and well-being of all beings.

盂蘭盆
法會緣起

若問前生事，今生受者是；
若問後世果，今生做者是。

—— 佛說三世因果經

　　大目犍連證得六通後，看到亡母生於惡鬼道中。目連盛飯奉母，但食物尚未入母口中便化成火炭，其母不能得食。目連哀痛，於是乞求佛陀。佛陀告訴目連，其母罪根深結，非一人之力所能拯救，應仗十方眾僧之力方能救度。於是教他在七月十五僧自恣日，為父母供養十方大德眾僧，以此大功德濟度其母。目連依佛意行事，其母終得解脫。

　　這一事跡後來演變成盂蘭盆法會的傳統。盂蘭盆法會表達了人們對現世及累劫父母的感恩與追思，更能濟度三途眾生，令其離苦得樂，不僅契合中國人提倡的慎終追遠的孝道精神，更是將無量功德惠及七世父母、五種親屬，其大悲精神亦具有深遠的社會意義。

［佛教小知識］

• 人生在「感恩」中昇華

　　受人恩惠，若不知恩，怎懂報恩？在現實生活中，有不少人把別人的幫助視為理所當然，無慚無愧，不知反思，只知外求。其必然結果是：得到的幫助愈多，生起的貪心愈大。人與動物最根本的區別是：人有反思能力而知慚愧，而動物則無。正如《佛遺教經》云：「若無愧者，與諸禽獸無相異也」。生起慚愧心的關鍵是感恩、反思。不知恩者，無慚愧心，與禽獸何異？

知恩報恩，是人生昇華的基石。學會用一顆感恩的心去生活，生命之舟便進入一片嶄新的天地：感恩傷害你的人，他磨煉了你的心智；感恩折磨你的人，他強化了你的意志；感激欺騙你的人，他增強了你的智慧；感激蔑視你的人，他覺醒了你的自尊；感恩出賣你的人，他教你如何看清這個世界；感恩競爭對手，他令你拼搏奮進；感恩敵人，他令你有危機意識，鞭策你自強不息，不斷進取⋯⋯學會感恩，便能笑對人生的種種煩惱，生命就在心中充滿感恩中不斷昇華、完善！

Origin of the Ullambana Dharma Assembly

Were you to inquire what your past life was like,

Look no further but what you experience Now for an answer;

Were you to inquire what your next life will be like,

Look no further but what you do Now for an answer.

— The Buddha Speaks of the Cause and Effect Sutra

After attaining the six supernatural powers, Venerable Maudgalyāyana saw that his deceased mother was reborn in the realm of hungry ghosts. Maudgalyāyana fed rice to his mother, but she could not eat because the food

turned into burning coals in her mouth before she could swallow it. Venerable Maudgalyāyana felt sad and begged the Buddha for help. The Buddha told Maudgalyāyana that due to his mother's grave unwholesome karma, he alone could not save her; he would need help from the Sangha of all ten directions. The Buddha instructed Maudgalyāyana to make offerings to the virtuous Sangha on the fifteenth day of the seventh lunar month (on this day all monks perform pravarana, or mutual confession and reflection) for the sake of his mother. Maudgalyāyana followed the Buddha's instruction, and his mother was eventually liberated.

This event in the Buddhist history started the tradition of Ullambana Dharma Assembly. The Ullambana Dharma Assembly is to express gratitude and remembrance for one's parents of this lifetime and the past. Moreover, the ceremony also benefits beings of the three lower realms by relieving them from sufferings. Considerable virtues and merits will be generated in the ceremony to benefit one's parents of seven lifetimes and five kinds of relatives. The spirit of the Ullamana Dharma Assembly accords with the filial piety tradition in Chinese culture, and the spirit of compassion the ceremony embodies contributes profoundly to social harmony.

✿ Basics of Buddhism:

- **Gratitude elevates our life**

   How would you gratefully repay kindness if you have taken it for granted? In daily life, many people take others' help for granted without any sense of shame and even ask for more without any self-reflection. Naturally, the more help they get, the greedier they become. The fundamental distinction between human beings and animals is that humans have the ability to introspect and know shame, while animals do not have. As the Sutra on the Buddha's Bequeathed Teaching states, "Those who never feel ashamed are not different from animals." And the key to generating shame is gratitude and self-reflection. What difference is there between an ungrateful, shameless human being and an animal?

Being grateful and repaying the debt of gratitude lay the cornerstone of an elevated life. Learn to live with a grateful heart, then the boat of life will enter a brand-new world. Be grateful to those who hurt you, because they toughen your mind. Be grateful to those who torment you, because they strengthen your will. Be grateful to those who deceive you, because they improve your wisdom. Be grateful to those who despise you, because they awaken your self-esteem. Be grateful to those who betray you, because they teach you how to see the world clearly. Be grateful to your competitors, because they make you work harder. Be grateful to your enemies, because they keep you always on alert for danger and motivate you to be better and go further. Learning to be grateful enables you to face miseries in life with a smile. With gratitude in heart, your life is graciously enriched and elevated.

水陸法會緣起

苦極則修，樂極則流。

禍福無窮，糾纏相求。

遂超欲色，至非非想。

不如一念，真發無上。

—— 水陸法像贊

　　相傳梁武帝夜夢神僧，告知六道四生受苦無量，何不作水陸普濟群生？這是所有功德之冠。醒後，梁武帝在寶志禪師指點下，研讀佛教經論三年，撰成水陸儀文。於金山寺舉辦首次水陸法會，追薦祖先，超度水中、陸上和空中的一切亡魂，普濟六道眾生離苦得樂，並以此功德祝願齋主增福延壽，祈求風調雨順，國泰民安。

[佛教小知識]

• 報四恩

　　水陸法會是佛教寺廟中所舉行的大型佛事活動，它的全稱是「法界聖凡水陸普度大齋盛會」。有的叫水陸道場、水陸齋，以供飲食為主，為超度水陸一切亡魂而設。在天壇大佛開光周年紀念期間（農曆十一月十二日至十九日），自 1993 年起，寶蓮禪寺每年舉辦消災水陸梁皇寶

懺大法會，救濟六道眾生，將此功德回施主自身及其眷屬，得以延壽增
福，融戾氣為祥和，化干戈為玉帛，祈求眾生安樂、香港繁榮、祖國富
強，世界和平，以此報四恩：父母恩、眾生恩、國土恩、三寶恩。

Origin of the Water and Land Dharma Assembly

After extraordinary pain, one turns to cultivation.

After extraordinary pleasure, one carries on transmigration.

Misfortune and fortune are endlessly entwined,

One chasing after another.

So you resolve to go beyond the Desire and the Form Realms,

To reach as high as the Neither-Perception-Nor-Non-Perception in the Formless Sphere.

What's better yet above them all,

Is that sincere thought to seek for Supreme Enlightenment.

— Encomia for the Dharma Images of the Water-Land Assembly

According to legend, Emperor Wu of Liang had a dream one night, in which a Buddhist monk told him about the immense sufferings of sentient beings in the Six Realms of Existence and advised him to host a Water and Land Dharma assembly to give merits to all beings, as the merits thus generated is the greatest of all. After waking up from the dream, under the guidance of Chan Master Bao Zhi, the emperor spent three years studying Buddhist scriptures and wrote the ritual scripts for the Water and Land Dharma Assembly. He hosted the first Water and Land Dharma Assembly in Jinshan Temple to commemorate ancestors, cultivate merit and virtue for the deceased dwelling in water, on land, and in the air, and to liberate all beings of the Six Realms from suffering. The inconceivable merits were also dedicated to benefactors of the Assembly for them to have a long and blessed life as well as to the nation and all the people for peace and prosperity.

Basics of Buddhism:

• Repaying four kinds of kindness

The Water and Land Dharma Assembly is a major function in Buddhist monasteries and temples. The full name is the "Great Assembly to Liberate All Beings of Water and Land." Some people call it "Water and Land Bodhimanda" or "Water and Land Festival," where drinks and food are offered for all the beings dwelling in water and on land who need to be released from suffering. Since 1993, during the anniversary of Tian Tan Big Buddha's consecration in Po Lin Monastery (from the twelfth to the nineteenth day of the eleventh lunar month in the Chinese calendar), a Water and Land Dharma Assembly based on the confessional manual of Emperor Wu of Liang has been held every year to protect all beings from calamities, to benefit sentient beings in the six destinies, and dedicate merits to the benefactors and their dependents for a long, happy, and harmonious life away from enemies and hostility. In the ceremony, invocations are made for the happiness of all sentient beings, the prosperity of Hong Kong, a developed and mighty country, and a peaceful world. This is a way to repay the four kinds of gratitude to our parents, to all sentient beings, to the state leader, and to the Three Jewels.

地獄不空，誓不成佛；
眾生度盡，方證菩提。

—— 地藏菩薩

地藏菩薩於過去無量劫中曾為「光目」孝女，其母在世時，最愛吃魚、蝦、烏龜等，尤其愛吃魚子。其母死後以殺生之惡罪，墮大地獄受苦。光目女由羅漢處得知其母墮地獄之事，為救度亡母而廣作功德善事，以誠孝的力量，拔救母親脫離地獄之苦。

地藏王菩薩的本願已為我們所熟知 ——「地獄不空，誓不成佛；眾生度盡，方證菩提。」孝女光目的因緣說明，地藏的法門乃是以孝親為基礎開始的，也就是將救度自己親人的心願擴展到救度一切苦難眾生，這種果報極為殊勝。光目女亦是一切學佛人的榜樣！

〔 佛教小知識 〕

• **地獄救度法門**

地藏菩薩示現出家相，以建立清淨僧團為佛法中心。依此基本精神，地藏菩薩發願，在惡世中以方便將眾生從墮落的邊緣救出來。這並非一定要顯神通，把要墮落地獄的眾生拉出來，而是開示正理，令其了解，令其不作墮落地獄的重罪，不作破壞三寶的重罪。以《地藏十輪經》為主的法門開示，能使五濁惡世眾生不入地獄。

Guangmu Rescuing Her Mother

I vow not to accomplish Buddhahood before the hells are emptied;
I will only realize Bodhi when all living beings have been saved.

— Ksitigarbha Bodhisattva

Innumerable kalpas ago, Kṣitigarbha Bodhisattva was once a filial daughter named Guangmu. Her mother liked eating fish, shrimp, turtles, and so on, especially caviar. After passing away, her mother suffered greatly in hell for her grave karma of killing. After hearing from an arhat that her mother had fallen into hell, Guangmu, out of immense filial piety and sincerity, performed many meritorious deeds to accumulate merits for her mother. Her mother was then delivered from the horrors of hell.

We are all familiar with the original vows of Kṣitigarbha Bodhisattva: "I vow not to accomplish Buddhahood before the hells are emptied; I will only realize Bodhi when all living beings have been saved." Guangmu's experience shows that Kṣitigarbha Bodhisattva's way of cultivation is to start with filial piety, not only towards one's own family, but all living beings that are in suffering. This practice will bring extraordinary karmic rewards. Guangmu sets a good example for all Buddhists.

- **Dharma-door of delivering beings from the hells**

Kṣitigarbha Bodhisattva appears as a monk and fosters his teaching around the goal of building a pure Sangha. Based on this, Kṣitigarbha Bodhisattva vowed to save all sentient beings in the world from the edge of degeneration with his skillful means. However, this does not mean that he must use supernatural powers. Instead, Kṣitigarbha Bodhisattva protects beings from falling to the hells by teaching them the Dharma, so that they could learn to refrain from committing the grave wrongdoings that would lead them to hells or the wrongdoings of harming the Three Jewels. These teachings mainly expounded in the Ten Cakras of Kṣitigarbha can help sentient beings keep away from the hells.

福田七法

修福不修慧，大象披瓔珞；
修慧不修福，羅漢托空缽。

—— 古德

　　有一天，帝釋天帶着三萬二千天子來拜訪佛陀，他禮拜佛陀並啟請問佛陀說：「世尊，人們修功德就如同種田，都希望收穫果報。那麼，有沒有甚麼法門，只要種髮絲那麼點的功德種子，就能收穫無量的福德果報呢？」

　　佛陀回答說：「帝釋天，你問得很好！我將為你講福田之法，所謂福田，就是能通過播種供養而收穫福報，乃至最終成佛。對出家人而言，有五種福田的功德，包括發出離心；毀其形好；永割親愛；捨身犧牲；志求大乘。出家弘聖道，願度一切人，如是修行，其中的福德不可稱量！對於在家人而言，則有福田七法：第一，興建寺廟佛塔、僧堂精舍；第二，佈施清涼瓜果、建設沖涼浴池、提供樹蔭給人納涼；第三，經常佈施醫藥，扶危濟困、救死扶傷；第四，製造牢固大船，方便人民渡江過河；第五，鋪設橋樑，方便弱者跨越小溪；第六，在道路旁側打井，方便口渴困乏的旅人飲水；第七，建造圍欄廁所，方便衛生。通過修行這七法，能獲梵天福報，生作梵天。」

- **種善因，得善果**

　　福田七法揭示了善果因緣的關鍵是起心動念：為功德而行善，以私利為動機，施得越多，私心越大，自然無法得到善果；反之，若用一顆無私、真誠、隨喜的心，去做對大眾有益之事，可獲無限善果。

Seven Practices to Cultivate Merits

Cultivating only merit but not wisdom,

Is like an elephant adorned with jewels;

Cultivating only wisdom but not merit,

Is like an arhat holding an empty alms-bowl.

— An ancient sage

　　One day, Śakradevānām visited the Buddha with 32,000 devas. He prostrated in front of the Buddha and asked, "World-honored One, like farming a piece of land, humans cultivate merits hoping to reap rewards one day. Is there such a Dharma door by which people will harvest immeasurable fruition of merits through sowing a hair-like seed?"

　　The Buddha replied, "Śakradevānām, you raised a good question! I will teach you the practice of the Field of Merit. Field of Merit is where you can sew seeds of merits and reap great blessings and even attainment of Buddhahood.

For Buddhist monastics, there are five kinds of merits, including the resolve for renunciation, disfiguring one's form, forever severing from intimate ones, sacrificing one's life, and pursuing the Mahayana (the Great Vehicle). Renouncing the secular life to promote the noble path and vowing to save all living beings will bring forth immeasurable merits! For lay practitioners, there are seven practices to cultivate merits: 1) building monasteries, stupas, Sangha halls, and viharas; 2) offering fresh fruits, building shower pools, and planting trees as shelters for people; 3) frequent donation of medicines, rescuing the endangered, succoring the poor, saving the dying, and looking after the sick; 4) building sturdy ships for people to cross the rivers; 5) building bridges for the elderly and fragile to cross the brooks; 6) drilling wells on the side of the roads to facilitate water supply for thirsty and exhausted travellers; 7) building fenced toilets for bringing people convenience and hygiene. Through practicing the seven practices, one will be reborn in the Brahma Heaven and receive the blessings of Brahma."

﷽ Basics of Buddhism:

• **A good cause brings a good effect**

The seven practices to cultivate merits reveal the truth that the key to generating wholesome karma is one's intention. If the purpose of doing good deeds is for gaining merits and fulfilling one's selfish motivation, then the more one gives, the greater one's selfishness grows, and surely one cannot obtain any good result. On the contrary, if one works for the benefits of all human beings with a selfless, sincere, and joyful heart, one will reap immeasurable wholesome fruits.

知恩報恩

善惡之報，如影隨形，三世因果，
循環不失。此生空過，後悔無追。

——《涅槃經》

佛陀在前世做菩薩時，曾身為九色鹿王，身披九色茸毛，鹿角如雪一般潔白，時常在恆河邊飲食水草，與鳥為友。會說人話的九色鹿，救了即將溺水的人，不求回報。被救者卻貪圖錢財，企圖將九色鹿獻給國王，說出了它的藏身之處。國王尋得九色鹿，聞知此人忘恩負義的行為，便放走了善良的九色鹿，並嚴懲此忘恩負義之徒。

這則本生故事說明，知恩應當圖報，向他人許下的諾言應當信守，這才是行善的開始。

❋❋❋ [佛教小知識]

• 報恩

佛教徒的報恩觀念就是：得到了恩，先回報給對我們有恩的人，要念念不忘地想着他、懷念他；在適當的時候要表揚他、讚歎他，這是念恩。念了恩之後，更要好好地努力修行來幫助眾生，利益人群。人家如何幫助我，我也要如此助人，而且要付出更多來幫助他人、回饋社會、影響世人，這就是報恩。

Being Grateful and Repaying Kindness

Wholesome and unwholesome karmic retribution,

Follow a person like a shadow.

Karmic law prevails in past, present, and future lives,

Never for once fails its paw.

Waste this life in vain,

There are only regrets that remain.

— The Mahaparinirvana Sutra

During one lifetime as a bodhisattva, the Buddha was a nine-colored king deer. He had beautiful hair and skin of nine-colors and his antlers were white as snow. He often drank and ate plants by the Ganges River and made friends with birds. Speaking human language, the nine-colored deer saved a man from drowning without expecting anything in return. However, the man who was rescued was greedy, and he plotted to offer the nine-colored deer to the king for bounty rewards. He then came to the king and revealed the deer's hiding place. When the king found the nine-colored deer and heard the story about the ungrateful man, he ordered to release the deer and punished that treacherous person.

The story tells us that one should repay the debt of gratitude and fulfill one's promises. This is the beginning of cultivating wholesomeness.

✥ Basics of Buddhism:

• Repaying kindness

For Buddhists, repaying kindness means we should first repay kindness to those who have helped us. We should always bear them in mind and remember them, and extol their kindness at the proper time. This is called the recollection of kindness. Furthermore, we should cultivate diligently for the benefits of all sentient beings just as we have been benefitted by others before. We should offer to help individuals, make contributions to society, and inspire others in the world to do the same. This is what repaying kindness means.

鳴　謝

　　感謝心默法師、楊玨對整個項目的管理和程夢涵對英文翻譯的統籌。本書英文翻譯由程夢涵、Anna、陳心果、孫徐培、王雪、張國瑩、靜遠、陳智、蓮馨、梁士影、葉辛、王峰、關翠玲、了悅協助完成；郭啓新、張純、程夢涵、方海博、陳興、陳心果、傅麗娜、梁士影、洪燁等人參與了一校、二校工作。王寧的插圖，實現了本書圖文並茂、中英對照的心願。

Contributors

Thanks to Xinmo and Jue Yang for managing the entire project and Cheng Menghan for coordinating the English translation.

The English translation was done by Cheng Menghan, Anna, Chen Xinguo, Sun Xupei, Wang Xue, Zhang Guoying, Jingyuan, Chen Zhi, Fu Lina, Liang Shiying, Ye Xin, Wang Feng, Guan Cuiling, and Liao Yue; Guo Qixin, Zhang Chun, Cheng Menghan, Fang Haibo, Chen Xing, Chen Xinguo, Fu Lina, Liang Shiying, Sophie and others participated in the first and second rounds of proofreading.

Wang Ning's illustrations make it a reality that both pictures and text of the book are excellent, shown in both Chinese and English.

佛教兩千六百年入門
INTRODUCTION:
2600 YEARS OF BUDDHISM

淨因 著
Jing Yin

責任編輯	許　穎
裝幀設計	高　林
排　　版	楊舜君
印　　務	劉漢舉

出　版	中華書局（香港）有限公司 香港北角英皇道 499 號北角工業大廈一樓 B 電話：(852) 2137 2338　傳真：(852) 2713 8202 電子郵件：info@chunghwabook.com.hk 網址：http://www.chunghwabook.com.hk
發　行	香港聯合書刊物流有限公司 香港新界荃灣德士古道 220-248 號 荃灣工業中心 16 樓 電話：(852) 2150 2100　傳真：(852) 2407 3062 電子郵件：info@suplogistics.com.hk
印　刷	美雅印刷製本有限公司 香港觀塘榮業街六號海濱工業大廈四樓 A 室
版　次	2021 年 12 月初版 2022 年 9 月第二次印刷 © 2021 2022 中華書局（香港）有限公司
規　格	16 開（240mm×160mm）
ISBN	978-988-8760-02-2